GOD AND THE PROFITS

A STUDY OF CHRISTIANITY AND BUSINESS

The Cuerdale Hoard

This photograph, courtesy of The British Museum, shows a hoard of precious metals buried in Cuerdale, Lancashire c. 905 AD, featuring Islamic coins which had travelled along the early Viking trade routes through the Russian river systems and Scandinavia, the Vikings being content to use foreign money to finance their trading operations.

GOD
and the PROFITS

A STUDY OF
CHRISTIANITY AND BUSINESS

Derrick Hanson

The Pentland Press Ltd
Edinburgh · Cambridge · Durham · USA

© Derrick Hanson 1998

First published in 1998 by
The Pentland Press Ltd.
1 Hutton Close
South Church
Bishop Auckland
Durham

British Library Cataloguing in Publication Data.
A catalogue record for this book is available
from the British Library.

ISBN 1 85821 608 7

Typeset by George Wishart & Associates, Whitley Bay.
Printed and bound by Bookcraft Ltd., Bath.

By the same author:

Moneyguide: the Handbook of Personal Finance	Kluwer, 1981-1989
	Longman Group
	UK Ltd 1989-1997
	Sweet & Maxwell
	1998-
Dictionary of Banking and Finance	Pitman, 1985
Service Banking: the All-Purpose Bank	Bankers Books, 1987
	Third Edition

In June 1998, the University of Lancaster awarded the author the degree of Master of Philosophy, the title of his thesis being 'Christianity and Business: Historical Perspectives and the Contemporary Attitudes amongst British Businessmen'. The text which follows is based on that thesis.

For Jennifer

a Christian in a business world

Contents

God, who givest to every man his work and through his labours dost accomplish Thy purposes upon earth: grant Thy blessing, we beseech Thee, to those who are engaged in the industries and commerce of this land.

Inspire them with the knowledge that, in ministering to the needs of others, they are serving Thee; defend them from injustice and oppression, and give them the due reward of their labours...

An Anonymous Prayer

Illustrations

Preface

During a long career in finance, commerce and, to a lesser extent, in industry I have seen little to condemn in business life. Was I naïve or in some way isolated from the real world around me? I think not. I have tended to be at the centre of things and in my early years, in particular, I was impressed with the absolute integrity of my seniors and indeed of all my colleagues. During my years in 'the City' I and others took for granted the high ethical standards which were observed on all sides. Indeed, I gave the occasional lecture to those on the outside of the square mile who seemed to take it for granted that business life there was dirty, dishonest and even fraudulent. The City was, and of course still is, a village. If anyone was about to step out of line it would soon be quite well known and some senior city figure would step in with a word of caution. I am not sure that it is the same today. There is much greater statutory regulation of business life and sadly, as is often the case, the more regulation the more deviation.

It would be over-credulous to suggest that the apparent integrity of business life stemmed from any great depth of Christian belief among business people. Among the giants of those days there were undoubtedly some of great Christian conviction who would not have allowed the slightest departure from the Christian ethic. More particularly, the quality of business life had its origin in the Christian teaching and traditions of the western world and particularly in the United Kingdom, which found expression in a deep-seated sense of right and wrong coupled with a disinclination to tarnish one's own reputation.

There is a general belief that the younger generations have grown up without the constraints of that Christian teaching which was taken for granted by former generations. This is less so in America where church attendance has increased and where 82 per cent of respondents in a recent survey considered themselves to be 'religious' compared with a comparable figure of 55 per cent in Britain (*The Economist*, 8 July 1995).

It may be that the Church has been slow to relate the essentials of New Testament teaching to present-day economic and business life. For example, Michael Novak has said (*The Spirit of Democratic Capitalism*) that: 'There exists no serious, disciplined body of

theological reflection on the history and foundations of economics,'
and

> ... there is a great gap between the word of God and systems of economic,
> political, social and cultural thought in modern societies.

This is something to be addressed in Part III.

Acknowledgements

I am greatly indebted to all those who have assisted me in the preparation of this work. In particular, my thanks are due to Stephen Watson, Dean of the Management Centre and Linda Woodhead of the Department of Religious Studies at Lancaster University. They have pointed me in the direction of the vast range of published and unpublished works and guided me in the content and presentation of this text.

I am greatly obliged to Andrew Buxton, Chairman of Barclays Bank Plc, for permission to draw on the content of his Presidential Address to the Chartered Institute of Bankers.

My thanks are due also to those Church and business leaders, whose names appear on pages xvi to xviii, who gave me so much of their time and friendly encouragement in the interviews outlined in Chapter XII. In similar vein, I am indebted to all those senior executives of some of our largest and medium-sized companies, who responded to the survey discussed in Chapter XIII, but whose names must remain confidential.

In particular, I am indebted to my friend, the Rt. Rev. Ian Griggs, former Bishop of Ludlow, who very kindly arranged introductions to a number of the leading names mentioned in these pages and who very generously read the entire text and made a number of suggestions, which I have of course incorporated. My thanks are due to my wife who very kindly read the proofs and, as always, I am immensely grateful to my secretary, Jennifer Ray who transposed seemingly miles of tape talk into immaculate print.

D.G. Hanson

Some Participants in the Discussions

The following very kindly gave their time and consideration to many of the issues in these pages and the resulting discussions are summarized in Chapter XII and, to a degree, in Chapters XIV and XV.

Michael Blackburn
Director and Chief Executive, Halifax Plc.

The Rt. Rev. Ronald Oliver Bowlby
Bishop of Newcastle (1973-80) and of Southwark (1980-91); Member, Church of England General Synod Board for Social Responsibility (1986-90); President, National Federation of Housing Associations (1987-93).

The Rt. Rev. John Brewer
Roman Catholic Bishop of Lancaster; Auxiliary Bishop of Shrewsbury (1971-83); Agent of Roman Catholic Bishops of England and Wales in Rome (1964-71).

Sir Leslie Fielding, KCMG
Vice-Chancellor, University of Sussex (1987-92); former Diplomat and Director General for External Relations at the European Commission in Brussels; currently adviser to a number of organizations; Church of England Reader and Member, General Synod (1990-92).

The Rt. Rev. Dr Alec Graham
Bishop of Newcastle (1981-97); formerly Warden of Lincoln Theological College (1970-77); Bishop Suffragan of Bedford (1977-81); Chairman, Doctrine Commission (1987-95).

The Rev. Dr Leslie John Griffiths
Superintendent Minister, Wesley's Chapel, London; former President of the Methodist Conference (1994-95).

The Rt. Rev. Richard Douglas Harries
Bishop of Oxford (1987-); Dean, King's College, London (1981-87); Chairman, Church of England General Synod Board for Social Responsibility (1996-); author of numerous publications on theology and Christian ethics.

The Rt. Rev. Dr David Edward Jenkins
Bishop of Durham (1984-94); Chaplain, Queen's College, Oxford (1954-69); Director – Humanum Studies, World Council of Churches (1969-73); Professor of Theology, University of Leeds (1979-84); Hon. Professor of Divinity, University of Durham (1994-); numerous theological publications.

The Rt. Rev. Dr Hugh William Montefiore
Bishop of Birmingham (1978-87); Dean of Gonville and Caius College, Cambridge (1954-63); Suffragan Bishop of Kingston-upon-Thames (1970-78); Chairman, Church of England General Synod Board for Social Responsibility (1983-87); Chairman, Friends of the Earth Trust (1992-97); numerous theological publications.

Sir Richard O'Brien, DSO, MC
Chairman, Manpower Services Commission (1976-82); Director of a number of leading industrial companies (1948-76); Chairman, CBI Employment Policy Committee (1971-76); Chairman, The Archbishop of Canterbury's Commission on Urban Priority Areas – *Faith in the City* (1985).

The Rev. Dr Michael Quicke
Principal, Spurgeon's College, London (1993-); Minister, St Andrew's Street Baptist Church, Cambridge (1980-93) and Baptist Chaplain to the University; Member of Council, Baptist Union of Great Britain; Member, Baptist Worldwide Alliance.

Roger Sawtell, MA
Director, Spear & Jackson Ltd. (1950-66); Adviser to co-operative businesses; Founder of two ongoing co-operatives, Trylon Ltd. (1968) and Daily Bread Co-operative Ltd. (1980); Chairman, Industrial Common Ownership Movement (1974-77); Adviser to Government, Industrial Common Ownership Act (1976).

The Rt. Rev. Dr Peter Selby
Bishop of Worcester (1997-); Suffragan Bishop of Kingston-upon-Thames (1984-92); former William Leech professorial Fellow in Applied Christian Theology, University of Durham (1992-97); author, *Grace and Mortgage: the Language of Faith and the Debt of the World* (1997).

Lord Thomas of Macclesfield, CBE
Immediate past Managing Director, The Co-operative Bank; former Visiting Professor, Sterling University; Member, the Corporate Governance Committee of Kleinwort Benson's Tomorrow's Company Fund.

K.D. Temple
Chief Registrar, the John Lewis Partnership (1995-); Personnel Director, Waitrose Limited (1989-95).

Sir Philip Wilkinson
Deputy Chairman (1987-90) and formerly Group Chief Executive, National Westminster Bank; former Member, Board of Banking Supervision, Bank of England.

Synopsis

Introduction

Business defined – the profit motive – wealth creation – business motivation and Christian attitudes – what is meant by 'Christian ethics' – the problem of relating Christian ethics to social ethics and business ethics – are Christian love and business compatible? – can business succeed in an exclusively Christian environment? – what is the role of the Church and Christian people in the business world of today and tomorrow?

<u>Part I</u>
<u>The Past</u>

Chapter I: The Old Testament

Wealth as the blessing of God – the preservation of resources – the egalitarian structure of the Israelite clans – the nature of trade (an agrarian society existing on the principal trade routes of the then known world) – wealth creation ('The slack hand brings poverty, the diligent hand brings wealth.') – acquisitiveness and love of money condemned – work and employment (the emphasis on honest labour and the worthiness of all legitimate occupations) – payment for work (hired servants not to be exploited but debtors might suffer temporary 'slavery') – money and the means of exchange (the usury laws; coins unknown but precious metals measured and valued by weight served as a means of exchange and a store of wealth) – the stewardship of wealth (tithes, the gleanings laws, concern for the poor, the widowed and the orphaned) – the family – inalienable land, the role of a 'redeemer' or 'kinsman', land as an inheritance from Yahweh.

Chapter II: The New Testament

Little reference to trade and business – no code of conduct, no catalogue of rules in contrast with the Old Testament – some reference

to the evils, dangers and responsibilities of wealth, particularly in the
Synoptic Gospels – some apparent acceptance by Jesus of money and
wealth as a fact of life – the responsibilities of wealth (St Luke) and
community of ownership – the Acts and the Epistles – comment on the
dangers and responsibilities of wealth – respect for the state and
taxation, and an emphasis on honest labour – concern for the poor –
the stewardship of wealth – difficulties of interpretation for our own
time.

Chapter III: The Early Church

The Acts as a historical source – some historical delineation of the
'early Church' – the Christian message followed the main trade routes
– the urbanization of society – a growing concern about money – the
socio-economic make-up of the early Church – the relevance or
otherwise of the early Church to modern business life.

Chapter IV: Rome

Urbanization and the explosion of economic growth – the Church as a
centre of charity – the beginning of conflict between faith and money –
Christians and trade – the Church and 'the world' – private property
and the renunciation of possessions.

Chapter V: Monasticism

The renunciation of possessions and the development of Christian
monasticism – the 'rich young man' – a protest against worldliness –
Benedictine monasteries and the work ethic – monasticism in Britain –
the dissolution – the significance of monasticism – Martin Luther and
Dietrich Bonhoeffer.

Chapter VI: The Middle Years

The changing environment – the increased centralization of the Roman
Church – the rise of European states and the decline of the Roman
Empire – the Middle Ages and the importance of land ownership and
primo geniture – Thomism and Natural Law – Lutheranism and
private property – Calvinism and the importance of one's calling – the
beginning of modern Christian stewardship.

Chapter VII: The Quest for Wealth

Major events in the two centuries prior to the Industrial Revolution –

emigration, colonization and 'temporal profit and glory' – the emergence of a middle class – the preoccupation of the Church with its own concerns – little, if any, concern for 'Christian economics' – the approach of the Industrial Revolution.

Chapter VIII: Industrialization

The mechanical age – the availability of natural resources at home and abroad and of capital – Britain, the 'workshop of the world' – demographic changes – the development of capitalism – the early development of trade unions – the attitude of the Church – non-conformist movements – the decline of owner employers and the spread of shareholdings.

Chapter IX: The Church and Business

Historical resumé – Catholicism and 'Law' – Protestantism and 'Grace' – Luther and dualism – Calvinism – profit as a blessing of God – rich and poor, the Church's failure – William Temple and his influence – some Christian entrepreneurs – dualism again.

Part II
The Present

Chapter X: Capitalism ... or What?

The impact of Christianity on modern business – capitalism defined – the separation of ownership from management – Michael Novak and *The Spirit of Democratic Capitalism* – alternatives to capitalism – modern socialism – common ownership in the early Church – non-profit organizations, e.g. building societies, mutual life offices, friendly societies, credit unions and co-operative societies – communitarianism.

Chapter XI: Contemporary Concerns

Business ethics as a live contemporary issue – contemporary writings – distinguish 'Christian' ethics – some typical subjects of concern (advertising, charitable giving, competition, corrupt practices, the environment, health and safety, human rights, insider dealing, 'perks', pollution, remuneration levels, tax evasion and 'whistle-blowing') – codes of practice – the most respected companies – bribery and corruption – some 'pros' and 'cons' of codes – ethical investment – faith and ethics – consumer debt.

Chapter XII: Selected Interviews

A digest of contemporary discussions with leaders in business and in the Church, giving a cross-section of opinions on some fundamental issues.

Chapter XIII: A Survey of Attitudes

A personal and confidential survey among the senior executives of a number of major British companies and some medium-sized and smaller companies, seeking to establish the relationship, if any, between personal Christian conviction and contemporary business decisions – statistical summary and analysis.

<u>Part III</u>
<u>The Hope</u>

Chapter XIV: Some Practicalities and Proposals

The Companies Acts – companies and conscience – stakeholder capitalism – mission statements – possible legislative changes – alternative structures – the Industrial Common Ownership Movement (ICOM) – The Co-operative Bank – the John Lewis Partnership – the Scott-Bader Commonwealth.

Chapter XV: The Kingdom and the World

The basic questions restated – some answers attempted in the light of the interviews and the survey – some views of leading theologians – church attitudes – the basic conflict – faith and 'the world' – true discipleship – the kingdom – eschatological hope.

A Postscript

Introduction

In a work which has its origins in the University of Lancaster it seems appropriate to begin with the words of John Ruskin.

> *The first of all English games is making money. That is an all-absorbing game; and we knock each other down oftener in playing at that than at football, or any other roughest sport: and it is absolutely without purpose; no-one who engages heartily in that game ever knows why. Ask a great money-maker what he wants to do with his money – he never knows. He doesn't make it to do anything with it. He gets it only that he may get it.*
> *'What will you make of what you have got?' you ask.*
> *'Well, I'll get more,' he says.*
> *Just as, at cricket, you get more runs. There's no use in the runs but to get more of them than any other people is the game. And there's no use in the money but to have more of it than other people in the game.*[1]

It may be that Ruskin's strictures are too severe and, in any case, ought not to be confined to the English. Here, however, we are not primarily concerned with money as such but with 'business'. The boundaries of business and money are not coterminous. It may be, as we shall suggest, that the making of money is a principal ingredient of business, but clearly money can exist without a business motive, for example, by inheritance, gifts or even the National Lottery.

So to 'business'. It seems desirable to define the word, not least to set the parameters for what follows. We lean to the view that business is the deployment of resources, whether human, financial or physical, for the purpose of monetary gain. We recall from student days the quaint wording of the Partnership Act of 1890 that a partnership is the relationship between persons carrying on a business in common 'with a view of profit'. Perhaps we can adopt that requirement for a far wider field than partnership law – let us say, therefore, that there is no *business* without a profit motive even though the sought-after profit may be no more than sufficient for everyday subsistence. Thus, the profit motive is the thread which runs through that which we call industry, or commerce, or trade, or the professions. They are all aspects of 'business'. Charities and certain non-profit-making concerns are not businesses for the purpose of this discourse. We may say that the Church or the National Health Service should be run on 'business

---

1 John Ruskin, *The Crown of Wild Olives*, 1866.

lines', but such institutions are outside our definition (and, in any case, such exhortations are probably invalid).

For our purposes here the large international corporations, the banks, the building societies (despite their mutual status), the co-operative societies, the village greengrocer, the solicitor, the farmer, the doctor (with private patients) and arguably the National Trust, a charity, in its Enterprises role, are all businesses. It follows that 'business' is often synonymous with 'wealth creation' and thus historical attitudes to wealth creation are explored in the following pages. One may have wealth creation without business activity, e.g. by a purely altruistic development of the earth's resources, but monetary gain in business necessitates wealth creation (at least for the business person).

Before closing the boundaries of business, we ought to look at the world of art, whether in literature, music, the performing arts or the visual arts. There is little doubt that some very distinguished authors, for example Charles Dickens and Anthony Trollope, churned out manuscripts in order to make money. Byron tells us:

> ... an author's time above all men's is money. A manuscript once completed, he will as soon lock it in a box as a financier hoards gold pieces in a vault.[2]

On the other hand, many a great composer has lived, however modestly, on patronage and his manuscripts in some cases have come to light two hundred years later. In our own time, a handful of authors and composers are among the richest of the rich. Many an artist strives only for perfection and makes money only if he or she has a bent for business. It is not always *ars gratia artis* – it is all very subjective and depends on motivation. It helps to remind us, therefore, that an essential ingredient of business is 'motivation'. Unless there is a conscious desire to make money, it is probably not business. Thus, we must look to the motivation. And this leads us naturally to the defining of Christian attitudes because the Christian faith, like most of the world's leading religions, is a personal matter calling for personal belief and dedication. If we accept that the Christian life is not primarily a matter of doctrine nor a set of rules, but more a question of attitude (which embraces faith and belief), we have the slightly easier task of relating two intangibles, viz. business motivation and Christian attitudes. In other words, I am not required, fortunately, to say in my business life that I should not do this or that because it does not conform to some Christian rulebook, but I may be encouraged to measure my motivation in business against the requirements of Christian love, the teachings of Christ Himself and the eschatological hope of the coming of His Kingdom.

2 Robert Byron, *The Byzantine Achievement*, 1929.

All of which brings us to the difficult subject of Christian ethics.

'Christian ethics' must surely mean that standard of behaviour which accords with the teaching of Jesus Christ, but this invites two very basic questions: first, what is the teaching of Jesus Christ and second, how has that teaching been interpreted and applied?

Christianity is essentially a religion of love. Christians are enjoined to love God 'with all your heart, with all your soul and with all your mind'[3] and 'to love your neighbour as yourself'.[4] In fact, these two great commandments, in answer to a question from the Pharisees, were no more than a restatement of ancient Hebraic Law.[5] If we were to stop there, Christian teaching would be more closely identified with Judaism but more particularly, we must look to the teaching of Jesus as portrayed in the Sermon on the Mount,[6] the parables of the Kingdom, the doctrine of forgiveness and the love of God exemplified by Christ's own life and death. Thus, it adds up to a prophetic, growing, eschatological religion based on redeeming love, the hope of Heaven and calls for personal faith and sacrifice.

Perhaps it is not surprising, therefore, that interpretations of Christ's teaching have varied over the centuries and between differing cultures and institutions. Thus, the excesses of the Crusades, the Inquisition and Apartheid (all claiming to a degree a Christian heritage) seem to bear little relation to the Christian doctrine of redeeming love, and even the severity of the Puritans and Pilgrim Fathers can look strange in this more liberal age. We must, therefore, amend our attempt at a definition and say that Christian Ethics is that standard of behaviour which accords with the teaching of Jesus Christ as interpreted by the exponents of those teachings, whether they be the individual or the State, or the Church or other institutions, and varying from age to age and from place to place. It follows, we think, that there is no universal or timeless concept of Christian Ethics and insofar as the Church is the proponent of Christian conduct, we may draw on the words of Stanley Hauerwas:

> The kind of alternative the church provides will differ from society to society, system of belief to system of belief, from culture to culture, state to state. Indeed, the church will often learn from different cultures what is, and is not, essential to its own life. Too often the church becomes but a mirror of one cultural option rather than a mirror to which each culture should compare itself.[7]

---

3 *Matthew* 22:37.
4 Ibid. 22:39.
5 *Deuteronomy* 6:5 and *Leviticus* 19:28.
6 *Matthew* 5, 6 and 7.
7 Stanley Hauerwas, *A Community of Character*, Notre Dame, University of Notre Dame Press, 1981, p. 105.

Perhaps the greatest difficulty in relating Christian teaching to a legal structure is that Christ did not lay down a code of ethics. Thus, Niebuhr wrote:

> The ethic of Jesus does not deal at all with the immediate moral problem of every human life – the problem of arranging some kind of armistice between various contending factions and forces. It has nothing to say about the relativities of politics and economics, nor of the necessary balances of power which exist and must exist in even the most intimate social relationships.[8]

and again: 'No social ethic can be directly derived from a purely religious ethic.'[9]

As we have said, Christianity is a matter of faith. It is said that faith can only be caught not taught. In any case, there are two essential ingredients of any religion, viz. faith and conduct. Faith cannot be commanded nor legislated for: conduct can.

To return to the underlying theme of business, our concern here is first to examine the extent to which Christian ethics have influenced the world of business throughout the Christian era and second, to consider the impact of Christian thinking and Christian standards on contemporary business life in the United Kingdom. Accordingly, in Part I the aim is to trace the development of Christian attitudes to what we now call 'business' over the entire Christian era and to draw as far as possible on contemporary theological and philosophical sources. Although, as we have said, business and money are not by any means synonymous, such a study encompasses a wide range of social and moral attitudes towards, for example, work and employed labour, poverty, greed, communal sharing, taxes, usury, inherited wealth, property in its various forms and the role of the State.

Are we correct that the purpose of business is 'wealth creation'? In other words, is money the motivation? Indeed, if we accept, from the Sermon on the Mount,[10] that one 'cannot serve God and money', we must ask whether wealth creation is compatible with Christian love.

Is business not concerned primarily with 'winning', that is to say the making of a gain or profit? If so, are there not reciprocal 'losers'? In a so-called free market there can be many losers. In a monopolistic situation there are arguably vast numbers who remain 'at the bottom of the pile'. Is it a case of love my neighbour or 'beggar my neighbour'?

In business life can the end justify the means? Does philanthropy justify exploitation? After all, the Industrial Revolution brought about great exploitation in terms of low wages and poor working conditions which enabled great fortunes to be made and some memorable charitable works undertaken.

8 Reinhold Niebuhr, *An Interpretation of Christian Ethics*, 1936, p. 49.
9 Ibid. p. 61.
10 *Matthew* 6:24.

Is it not possible that Christian love and business motivation are incompatible and that one should be satisfied with that return on one's labour which takes care of one's own subsistence, but those needs are themselves vastly different between 'the rich man in his castle and the poor man at his gate'.[11]

The individual, whether Christian or pagan, is gifted with varying talents – imagination, energy, creative skills, organizing ability, qualities of leadership and so on – and living as one must in the modern world is it not inevitable and entirely acceptable that those talents should be converted into money, provided it is done with honesty, fairness and complete integrity? Does the ultimate test lie, therefore, in personal attitudes and priorities and most of all in the stewardship of the resulting gain?

Part II addresses some of those subjects in the present-day world, together with such live issues as wages and prices, the environment, marketing and advertising, problems of the under class, the elderly and the Third World, equal opportunities and wealth redistribution. Through interviews and surveys among business leaders, we shall seek to establish whether there is a common acceptance of Christian ethics in business in this country today. Failing that, is there a residual belief that Christian teaching and Christian standards underlie some sort of moral code in business. Indeed, is it possible for business to thrive or even survive in an exclusively Christian environment? In these days when most business is conducted in an incorporated form, is it possible for a corporation to have a 'conscience' or to pursue a Christian policy other than one which happens to coincide with the best interests of the shareholders?

Lastly, in Part III we look at some practicalities and possible future developments, and then attempt to reconcile the conflicting claims of the Kingdom and the world. At the present time there is growing concern over ethical behaviour in public life, business life and indeed in private life. This is expressed in different ways by such phrases as 'back to basics' or 'return to true values' or 'standards in public life', but often these become no more than political clichés and owe nothing overtly to Christian teaching. What then is the role of the Church and Christian people in the business world of tomorrow? Should Christians withdraw from the world or seek to change the world? On the whole, Christians have not been noted for their unanimity in tackling the realities of the world around them. And yet if Christianity be nothing else it is a religion of hope and it could be that Christians have a very special part to play in the more enlightened business world of today.

---

11 *All Things Bright and Beautiful*, Cecil Frances Alexander (1818-95).

Thus, we have entitled Part III 'The Hope'. Meanwhile, back to Ruskin:

> There is no wealth but life, including all its powers, of love, of joy and of admiration ... that man is richest who, having perfected the functions of his own life to the utmost, has also the widest helpful influence, both personal and by means of his possessions, over the lives of others.[12]

---

12 John Ruskin, *Unto This Last*, 1860.

PART I

The Past

CHAPTER I

The Old Testament

When will New Moon be over
so that we can sell our corn,
and Sabbath, so that we can market our wheat?
Then by lowering the bushel, raising the shekel,
by swindling and tampering with the scales,
we can buy up the poor for money,
and the needy for a pair of sandals,
and get a price even for the sweeping of the wheat.[1]

In those terms, Amos in the eighth century BC condemned the corrupt business practices of his day; and yet it would be wrong to categorize the trading history of the Jews in such strident terms. For a thousand years or so before Christ, the Old Testament tribes seem to have had what one might call a religious respect for the care of the earth's resources, the creation of wealth, the care of the family, the gleanings and usury laws, the concern for the poor and the widows and orphans. Theologians would probably agree that no study of Christianity is complete without a due appreciation of Hebrew history. Certainly the ingredients of Christian ethics are there to be found in the writings of the Old Testament.

According to Lord Griffiths: 'The starting point for any Christian view of economic life is our view of the physical world.' He argues that as man is made in the image of God, his very *raison d'être* like that of the Creator is to work and that:

> If we accept that man is created with a desire to work, subject to a charge to control and harness the earth, it follows that the process of wealth creation is something intrinsic to a Christian view of the world.[2]

In the Old Testament, wealth is seen as the blessing of God.

> Thou shalt remember the Lord thy God: for it is He that giveth thee power to get wealth, that He may establish His covenant which He sware unto thy fathers.[3]

It seems that the Hebrews developed a fairly sophisticated system of taxation and income distribution and control of what we would call

---

1 *Amos* 8:4-6.
2 Lord Griffiths, *Morality and the Marketplace*, Hodder & Stoughton, 1982, p. 28.
3 *Deuteronomy* 8:18.

today the capital market. The usury laws were strictly enforced as a means of protecting those of the Hebrews' own race who fell on hard times.

> Do not demand interest on loans you make to a brother Israelite, whether it is in the form of money, food or anything else. You may take interest from a foreigner but not from a fellow Jew.[4]

It was this Biblical facility for lending money 'upon usury' to strangers that contributed to the Jewish business of moneylending throughout Europe and in our own country the lending of money was monopolized by the Jews until their expulsion by Edward I in 1290.

Generally, it was part of the Jewish tradition that wealth was a gift, especially when not sought[5] and idleness was not encouraged.

> He becometh poor that dealeth with a slack hand: but the hand of the diligent maketh rich ... He that sleepeth in harvest is a son that causeth shame.[6]

The love of money was emphatically condemned as in the Tenth Commandment[7] and in Isaiah: 'Woe unto them that join house to house ...'[8]

There are of course many other Old Testament references describing the degree of economic management of the Jews. It seems that it was not a growth economy – rather they would be more concerned with preserving resources, dividing them equally among the family (with no doubt the occasional prodigal son) and coping with years of famine. They were capitalists in that they owned and sought to preserve their private assets (the word 'capital' apparently had its origin in '*capitalis*' or 'head' of cattle), but their laws were predominantly of a caring nature. It is not surprising that Christ did not overtly condemn wealth as such because this would have been contrary to Old Testament teaching.

In any study of business ethics, whether Christian or not, there are certain recurring themes. These include (i) the nature of trade, (ii) wealth creation, (iii) work and employment, (iv) money and the means of exchange and (v) concepts of stewardship. Here then is an attempt to develop those themes in the light of Hebrew traditions and history and Old Testament teaching.

---

4 Ibid. 23:9.
5 *1 Kings* 3:13.
6 *Proverbs* 10:4.
7 *Exodus* 20:17.
8 *Isaiah* 5:8.

The Nature of Trade

Trade, in economic terms, involves the exchange of goods or services, or the payment for those goods or services, between parties. It normally involves a profit motive, but can be altruistic. Our main theme of 'business' is something wider than trade. It is, as we have said, the deployment of resources with a view of gain.

An observer of economic life in Old Testament times might reflect on two almost contradictory characteristics. On the one hand, the Hebrew tribes enjoyed a predominantly agrarian and, by modern standards, a comparatively simple existence (although many of their laws and customs were remarkable for their sophistication and common sense). Until the urbanization of later centuries they were either, figuratively speaking, sons of Cain tilling the soil or of Abel pursuing a more pastoral and, to some extent, nomadic existence. Life was uncluttered by international corporations, third-world starvation, economic sanctions or many of the problems of modern business ethics, e.g. industrial relations, manipulative advertising and unfair competition.

The second, perhaps contradictory feature, is that for most of their long history the Hebrew tribes dwelt on or near the principal trade routes of the then known world. Palestine was the bridge between Europe and Asia and the main corridor of trade between North Africa and Southern Europe. The King's Highway linked Damascus with the Gulf of Aqaba and the Way of the Sea ran through Philistia (from which Palestine is derived) and the coastal plain of Sharon. The Israelites themselves, for want of owning any natural harbours on the Mediterranean coast, apparently relied on Phoenicia for maritime trade so that Ezekiel was able to refer to 'Tyre, that city standing at the edge of the sea, doing business with the nations in innumerable islands'. And 'All the ships of the sea and the sailors in them visited you to trade with you.'[9] I think we may assume that the 'trade' was quite big business.

In fact, we are told that, during the time of Israelite kings, the population grew immensely and reached a density of about 250 inhabitants per square mile and

> the alliance between the Phoenician city of Tyre with its maritime resources and Solomon, master of the gateway to the Red Sea, opened to Phoenician and Israelite merchant adventurers a safe route to Yemen, East Africa and India. It made Israel's king a partner in the world's greatest commercial organisation of the day.[10]

---

9 *Ezekiel* 27:3 and 9.
10 Salo Wittmayer Baron, *A Social and Religious History of the Jews*, New York, Columbia University Press, 1937 (2nd Edition, 1952), p. 64.

Wealth Creation

In the words of Lord Griffiths, quoted above, ' the process of wealth creation is something intrinsic to a Christian view of the world'. In fact, it is arguable that this Christian view of the world owes more to Old Testament scripture than to New Testament teaching. The virtue of wealth creation is something of a recurring theme in the Old Testament. Thus, from Deuteronomy as quoted above (in the Authorized Version), 'Thou shalt remember the Lord thy God: for it is He that hath given thee power to get wealth ...' and from Proverbs 'The slack hand brings poverty, but the diligent hand brings wealth,'[11] and from the poem on the perfect wife:

> She is always busy with wool and with flax
> she does her work with eager hands.
>
> She is like a merchant vessel
> bringing her food from far away.
>
> She sets her mind on a field, then she buys it;
> with what her hands have earned she plants a vineyard.[12]

And, more particularly from Solomon himself, who of all people knew the pleasures and responsibilities of wealth, 'Treasures wickedly come by give no benefit.'[13]

Thus it would seem that there was approval throughout ancient Hebrew tradition for what we might call today 'value added'. It was concerned with the development and preservation of the earth's resources and the protection of wealth for future generations. Nevertheless, acquisitiveness, covetousness and the love of money are condemned throughout the Jewish tradition. For example, 'Thou shalt not covet ...' from the Decalogue and from Isaiah:

> Woe to those who add house to house
> and join field to field
> until everywhere belongs to them
> and they are the sole inhabitants of the land.[14]

and from the Psalms:

> Why should I be afraid in evil times,
> when malice dogs my steps and hems me in,
> of men who trust in their wealth
> and boast of the profusion of their riches?[15]

To all of which we may add the strictures of Amos with which this chapter began.

11 *Proverbs* 10:4.
12 Ibid. 31:10.
13 Ibid. 10:1.
14 *Isaiah* 5:8.
15 *Psalm* 49:5 and 6.

Work and Employment

The Greeks, we are told, had a somewhat fastidious view of work, regarding it as degrading for free men, work being the responsibility and burden of slaves. In contrast, there is throughout Old Testament history an awareness of, and indeed an emphasis on, all honest labour – man, made in God's image, was expected to display something of God's creativeness. Indeed, the Hebrew *melakhah*, which corresponds to the English word 'calling', combines with the idea of vocation or mission that of an economic occupation.[16] Man was given dominion over the earth[17] and thus work became the responsibility of mankind. Cain (the word itself means 'smith' in Aramaic and Arabic) built a town,[18] Tubal-Cain became the ancestor of all metalworkers[19] and 'Noah, a tiller of the soil, was the first to plant the vine.'[20]

The Old Testament emphasizes the worthiness of all legitimate occupations, whether of an intellectual or manual nature. Even so, work itself was not necessarily glamorized because there was always the memory that man had become alienated from God in the Garden of Eden and ...

> Accursed be the soil because of you.
> With suffering shall you get your food from it
> every day of your life.
> It shall yield you brambles and thistles,
> and you shall eat wild plants.
> With sweat on your brow
> shall you eat your bread,
> until you return to the soil,
> as you were taken from it.
> For dust you are
> and to dust you shall return.[21]

... words which must echo in the ears of many a farmer and gardener!

However, despite the curse of work, human labour continued to have a certain redemptive quality. Thus in the second Isaiah 'They will build houses and inhabit them, plant vineyards and eat their fruit.'[22] and according to Micah, there will still be a need for ploughshares and pruning hooks.[23]

Payment for work, i.e. wages, receives scant attention in the Old Testament, partly because in a predominantly agrarian society the unit is the family, who are fed but not paid, and other work was done by

16 Baron, *A Social and Religious History of the Jews*, p. 9.
17 *Genesis* 1:26 and 28.
18 Ibid. 4:17.
19 Ibid. 4:22.
20 Ibid. 9:20.
21 Ibid. 3:17-19.
22 *Isaiah* 65:21.
23 *Micah* 4:3.

slaves who equally were not paid. The 'hired servants' who were paid
were not to be exploited. Thus,

> You are not to exploit the hired servant who is poor and destitute, whether
> he is one of your brothers or a stranger who lives in your towns. You must
> pay him his wage each day, not allowing the sun to set before you do, for he
> is poor and is anxious for it; otherwise he may appeal to Yahweh against
> you, and it would be a sin for you.[24]

The absence of wages was seen as something of an injustice
subsequently condemned in Jeremiah:

> Doom for the man who founds his palace on anything
> but integrity,
> his upstairs rooms on anything but honesty,
> who makes his fellow man work for nothing
> without paying him his wages ...[25]

and by Zechariah:

> For before the present day men were not paid their wages and nothing was
> paid for the animals either and because of the enemy there was no security
> for a man to go about his business.[26]

As for 'industrial relations', this was something for a much later age.
Nevertheless, the Old Testament prophets, as suggested above, were
not slow to inveigh against oppressive employers and 'I am going to be
a ready witness against ... those who oppress the wage earner.'[27]

It was left to later Christian generations to deal with the ethical
problems of industrial relations.

Money and the Means of Exchange

The earliest Biblical reference to money appears to be in the Book of
Genesis with the reference 'He that is born in thy house, and he that is
bought with thy money ...'[28] However, money in coined form was
unknown at the time and thus most early references to payment are
expressed in silver or gold, e.g. 'And unto Sarah he said, Behold I have
given thy brother a thousand pieces of silver ...'[29] and, at a somewhat
later date, Joseph was sold to the Ishmeelites 'for twenty pieces of
silver'.[30]

It is generally accepted that the earliest exchanges of goods and
services were by means of barter, but this had its limitations where, for

24 Deuteronomy 24:14-15.
25 Jeremiah 22:13.
26 Zechariah 8:10.
27 Malachi 3:5.
28 Genesis 17:13.
29 Ibid. 20:16.
30 Ibid. 37:28.

An Egyptian Hoard

These pieces of silver are part of a hoard of gold and silver discovered in the excavation of the ancient city of el-Amarana, apparently originating from the period of King Akhenaten's reign (1352-1336 BC), and illustrate how assorted fragments of precious metal were weighed and used for payment purposes before the introduction of coinage (see page 15). Photograph, courtesy of The British Museum.

example, third parties were involved or where, as between two parties, there was some over-production of a commodity or where it became necessary to have a more universal means of exchange and store of value. Accordingly, from about 2000 BC silver, and sometimes gold, were being used to make purchases and also to pay wages.[31] The precious metals were not coined but were valued by weight. Thus the earliest forms of 'money' were gold or silver bars, rings and fragments measured by weight in shekels, minas and talents. We are told that Abraham purchased the burial site for his wife, Sarah, with a payment of 400 shekels' weight of silver, viz.

> Abraham agreed to Ephron's terms and Abraham weighed out for Ephron the silver he had stipulated ... namely 400 shekels of silver, according to the current commercial rate.[32]

The first issue of coins in the Western world is believed to have been in the reign of King Ardys of Lydia in Asia Minor in the seventh century BC and it was in the reign of Croesus, last King of Lydia, in the sixth century BC, that a bi-metallic system of coinage was first introduced, i.e. gold and silver, and this led in time to a system of exchange throughout the Persian Empire and later the Greek world. Coins were of course easier to handle, to measure out and to identify than irregular pieces of gold and silver.

Apparently, Aristotle regarded money as an alternative to the inconvenience of bartering, viz.

> All the things which we exchange need to be comparable. This led to the invention of money to serve as a medium giving value to everything ... For example, how many shoes are equal to so much food. Without a medium there can be no exchange.[33]

This, however, was only part of the story. Money took on an importance other than a 'medium of exchange'. It became a store of value and, like cattle in earlier days, a measure of individual wealth. It was to become the normal medium of taxation and of punitive fines. Thus, although the theme of these pages is that of commerce, there is every indication that money, whether as coins, cattle or cowrie shells (as in China), met various social needs which had little to do with trade. Thus money, in whatever form, would be used as tribute money, personal gifts, dowries and perhaps above all a measure of social standing. Even to this day it is discourteous to ask a farmer how many head of cattle or sheep he may have – it is like asking how much money he has in the bank.

Returning to Old Testament times, the earliest coins found in

---

31 Joe Cribb (ed.), *Money*, British Museum Publications Limited, 1986, p. 22.
32 *Genesis* 23:16.
33 *Nicomachean Ethics Book 5.*

Palestine were Macedonian in origin from Shechem which, together with Athenian coins from Jerusalem, dated from the sixth century BC. The first Jewish coins appear to be those produced during the Persian occupation of Judah in the fourth century BC. As mentioned above, the shekel was the basic unit of weight in Hebrew and its monetary value was one stater. The denarius or penny was a silver coin and was approximately in New Testament times a day's pay for an unskilled labourer.[34]

To the modern mind, the lending of money is associated with trade or industry, the purchase of houses or consumer credit. We shall seek to examine the ethical aspects of these matters in later chapters. Generally, however, the lending of money for business purposes was unknown in both Old Testament and New Testament times. The Hebrew concept of a loan was either for *use*, e.g.

> When a man borrows an animal from another and it is injured or dies in the owner's absence, the borrower must make full restitution.[35]

and 'Go outside and borrow jars from all your neighbours,'[36] or ... for *consumption*, e.g.

> I too, my kinsmen, and my servants have lent them money and corn. Let us cancel this debt. Return them their fields, their vineyards, their olive groves and their houses forthwith and remit the debt on the money, corn, wine and oil which you have lent them.[37]

We have referred above to the instruction in Deuteronomy[38] not to lend money at interest, i.e. usury, to a fellow Jew although this was permitted in the case of loans to foreigners, thus reiterating the moral law from Exodus:

> If you lend money to any of my people, to any poor man among you, you must not play the usurer with him: you must not demand interest from him.[39]

If it seems strange that a foreigner could be charged interest, but not a fellow Jew, it should be borne in mind that the 'foreigner' was quite often a businessman who borrowed money for profitable, commercial transactions whereas the Israelite farmer was borrowing to satisfy personal needs. There was no law to prevent foreigners from lending money to Jews at interest. Thus, it would have been unreasonable to let a foreign businessman obtain a cheap loan from one Jew in order to lend it at a profit to another.

34 Michael D. Coogan, *Oxford Companion to the Bible*, Oxford University Press, 1993, p. 523.
35 *Exodus* 22:14-15.
36 *2 Kings* 4:3.
37 *Nehemiah* 5:10-11.
38 *Deuteronomy* 23:9.
39 *Exodus* 22:25.

Perhaps it is particularly significant that in Old Testament times money did not seem to have a time value, something which would seem strange to an accountant of our present day. The passing of time did not affect the value of the loan and hence no more than the repayment of the original amount was expected.

It has been suggested that the Exile led indirectly to one of the most notable transformations in economic history. Those who were deported had belonged, almost exclusively, to the urban population of Palestine and many of them poured into the larger cities and entered the active industrial and commercial life of Babylon. The Jewish exiles 'must have been doubly attracted to commerce in that "city of merchants" and "land of traffic" which their prophet was soon to denounce with such vehemence' (Ezekiel 16:29; 17:4).[40]

> The fact that the founder of the House of Egibi, the greatest of the private banking firms, bore the unmistakably Hebrew name Jacob and that most of the early loans are recorded to have been granted without interest may indeed reflect one of the earliest Jewish contributions to mankind's material civilisation.[41]

Later generations of Jews were to become the principal moneylenders of mediaeval Europe and ultimately, founders of some of the greatest European banks.

We come later in these pages to the changing attitudes towards usury from mediaeval times to the present day (see Chapter XI).

To return, however, to the pre-Christian days in the Middle East, Diaspora Jewry in the first century outnumbered by three to one the number of Jews in Palestine and throughout the early days of the Roman Empire 'every tenth Roman was a Jew'. The annual pilgrimage to Palestine brought the Jews there into contact with the Jews of the Diaspora, which in itself created a whole class of Palestinian bankers and moneychangers to attend to the needs of the pilgrims. When Jesus overthrew the tables of the moneychangers he 'merely revolted against certain conveniences that had become attached to the institutionalised "house of prayer"'.[42]

Stewardship

It is extremely unlikely that the word stewardship appears in any English translation of the Old Testament. Yet in Hebrew law and tradition we have outstanding examples of the stewardship of wealth – the dedication of one's resources in this life towards some moral, or indeed spiritual, objective. We may look at some examples going back

---

40 Baron, *A Social and Religious History of the Jews*, p. 108.
41 Ibid.
42 Ibid, p. 258.

to the early days of Hebrew teaching, e.g. tithes, the gleanings laws, compassion for the poor, the widowed and orphaned, and concern for the family.

Tithes

The first use of the word 'tithe', or tenth, as a proportion of one's total wealth appears to be in Genesis 14 where Abram returning victorious through the Valley of the King was blessed by Melchizedek, to whom Abram gave 'a tithe of everything'.[43] The first offering of a tithe to God appears to be that of Jacob at Bethel on what appears to be somewhat conditional terms, viz.

> If God goes with me and keeps me safe on this journey I am making, if he gives me bread to eat and clothes to wear, and if I return home safely to my father, then Yahweh shall be my God. This stone I have set up as a monument shall be a house of God and I will surely pay you a tenth part of all you give me.[44]

In time, the giving of tithes became part of Hebrew law, viz.

> All tithes of the land, levied on the produce of the earth or the fruits of trees, belong to Yahweh: they are consecrated to Yahweh. If a man wishes to redeem part of his tithe he must add one-fifth to its value.

> In all tithes of flock or herd the tenth animal of all that pass under the herdsman's staff shall be a thing consecrated to Yahweh; there must be no picking out of good and bad, no substitution. If substitution takes place both the animal and its substitute shall be things consecrated without possibility of redemption.

> These are the commandments that Yahweh laid down for Moses on Mount Sinai for the sons of Israel.[45]

One may be excused for wondering to whom, in human terms, the tithes were to be paid. Perhaps not surprisingly they were collected in due course by the priesthood, that is to say the Levites, of whom Aaron was, at least in some traditions, the first High Priest of Israel. Thus, in the Book of Numbers

> Yahweh said to Aaron:

> You shall have no inheritance in their land, no portion of it among them shall be yours ... This is a perpetual law for all your descendants: the Levites are to have no inheritance among the sons of Israel. The tithe that the sons of Israel set aside for Yahweh, I give the Levites for their inheritance. For this reason I have told them that they are to have no inheritance among the sons of Israel.[46]

43 *Genesis* 14:20.
44 Ibid. 28:20.
45 *Leviticus* 27:30-34.
46 *Numbers* 18:20-24.

So it was that the Levites became the recipients of the tithes in exchange for not having a share of the land of Israel.

Subsequently, the so-called 'second tithe' (see below) was to be distributed for the benefit of the poor and needy.

It is a little strange that the predominantly, but not exclusively, Hebrew custom of giving tithes is still regarded by some in our contemporary world as a golden rule – a minimum to which one should aspire but beyond which one need not unduly strain!

The concept of the tithe was followed for a while in some of the early Christian churches for the maintenance of the priesthood, but nowhere in the New Testament is it advanced as a Christian duty. Indeed, it would fall short of the Christian view of stewardship as being for all aspects of life.

The Gleanings Laws

Provision for the poor and a degree of redistribution of resources was achieved by the gleanings laws.

> When you reap the harvest on your land you shall
> not reap your field to its very border, neither shall
> you gather the gleanings after your harvest. And
> you shall not strip your vineyard bare, neither shall
> you gather the fallen grapes of your vineyard; you
> shall leave them for the poor and for the sojourner.[47]

and again from Deuteronomy:

> When you harvest your vineyard you must not pick
> it over a second time. Let anything left be for the
> stranger, the orphan and the widow. Remember that
> you were a slave in the land of Egypt. That is why
> I lay this charge on you.[48]

Compassion for the Poor, the Widowed and the Orphaned

The memory of slavery in Egypt is a recurring theme which may well have contributed to the compassion shown in some of the early laws, viz.

> Remember that you were a slave in Egypt, and carefully observe these laws.
> You must celebrate the Feast of Tabernacles for seven days at the time when
> you gather in the produce of your threshing-floor and winepress. You must
> rejoice at your feasts, you and your son and daughter, your serving men and
> women, the Levite, the stranger, the orphan and the widow who live in your
> towns.[49]

---

47 *Leviticus* 19:9.
48 *Deuteronomy* 24:21-22.
49 Ibid. 16:12-14.

And from the Psalms: 'Happy the man who cares for the poor and the weak.'[50]

A prescription of how a rich man should behave in his community is contained in Job:

> My praises echoed in every ear
> and never an eye but smiled on me
> because I freed the poor man when he called,
> and the orphan who had no-one to help him.
> When men were dying, I it was who had their blessing;
> if widows' hearts rejoiced that was my doing.
> I had dressed myself in righteousness like a garment;
> justice, for me, was cloak and turban.
> I was eyes for the blind, and feet for the lame.
> Who but I was father of the poor?
> The stranger's case had a hearing from me.
> I used to break the fangs of wicked men,
> and snatch their prey from between their jaws.[51]

If Hebrew generosity stemmed at times from memories of slavery, it could also be for some a source of merit, e.g.

> I have walked in paths of truth and in good
> works all the days of my life. I have given much
> in alms to my brothers and fellow countrymen,
> exiled like me to Nineveh in the country of Assyria[52]

and

> Better to practise alms-giving than to hoard up gold. Alms-giving saves from
> death and purges every kind of sin[53]

and always there was the belief that benevolence brought happiness, viz. 'Happy the man who cares for the poor and the weak: if disaster strikes, Yahweh will come to his help.'[54] and 'Blessed is he who takes pity on the poor.'[55]

Moral behaviour had its origins in religious faith as expressed in the Law. Ethics and religion were one. Virtually every aspect of Hebrew life had its origin in one or other of the seven hundred or so commandments. Thus, for example, the so-called second tithe, referred to above, first appeared in Deuteronomy:

> At the end of every three years you must take all the tithes of your harvests
> for that year and deposit them at your doors. Then the Levite (since he
> has no share or inheritance with you), the stranger, the orphan and the
> widow who live in your towns may come and eat and have all they want. So

50 *Psalm* 41:1.
51 *Job* 29:11-17.
52 *Tobit* 1:1.
53 Ibid. 12:8-9.
54 *Psalm* 41:1.
55 *Proverbs* 14:21.

shall Yahweh your God bless you in all the work that your hands undertake.[56]

There was a law for everything, but always there seems to have been a greater concern for people than for property and arguably the greatest emphasis was on the family.

The Family

It seems that the family was the economic unit of Old Testament days, based no doubt to some extent on the fifth commandment to honour father and mother.[57] Nevertheless, the family was seen as part of a larger unit, whether it be an extended family (including grandparents, grandchildren, slaves, servants and resident foreigners), or the tribe and at times the nation. We are concerned here not with family life as such, but with its economic importance. The land of Israel was divided among the tribes, who in turn divided it among the family units. In theory, at least, it was inalienable and thus would remain in the family in perpetuity. If a family fell on hard times, there were laws to ensure that, in due time and probably in the Jubilee year, the land returned to the true owners. If property was lost through debt, a 'redeemer' or 'kinsman' was expected to come to the rescue and redeem the property for the family, or to retrieve the owner himself if he was sold into slavery through debt.[58]

On the death of an owner, his property would normally pass to his sons with the firstborn son receiving a double portion.[59] Daughters could nevertheless inherit if a man died without sons, viz.

If a man dies without sons, his inheritance is to pass to his daughter. If he has no daughter the inheritance is to go to his brothers. If he has no brothers it is to go to his father's brothers. If his father has no brothers it is to go to the member of his clan who is most nearly related: he is to take possession. This shall be a statutory ordinance for the sons of Israel as Yahweh has ordered Moses.[60]

Generally, however, there is little in the Old Testament on the subject of financial inheritance – succession is more a matter of theology. For example, Moses refers to 'the prosperous land which Yahweh your God is giving you as your heritage',[61] and

You must not displace your neighbour's boundary mark, set by your forbears, in the inheritance you receive in the land Yahweh is giving into your possession.[62]

56 *Deuteronomy* 14:28-29.
57 *Exodus* 20:12.
58 *Leviticus* 25:25 and *Joshua* 20.
59 *Deuteronomy* 21:17.
60 *Numbers* 27:8-11.
61 *Deuteronomy* 4:21.
62 Ibid. 19:14.

Thus, inheritance is seen as a kind of covenant with Yahweh as the true owner of the land – not far, one might think, from modern concepts of stewardship.

We conclude these thoughts on Old Testament traditions with voices from the past and the present. From Deuteronomy:

> You must not act as we do here today: every man does what seems right to him, for as yet you have not come to the resting place and the inheritance that Yahweh your God is giving you.[63]

In our own times, Chief Rabbi Dr Jonathan Sacks has spoken of the importance of relationships in Hebrew traditions, viz.

> The Hebrew Bible portrays God as One concerned above all with how we behave towards others. God is to be found in relationships, and relationships take place within the framework of society and its institutions and rules. Faith is thus linked with morality, and morality is an essentially shared, collaborative endeavour. Its smallest unit is the family, its largest unit is humanity, and between them lies a variety of communities from the neighbourhood to the nation state. What morality is not, and cannot be, is a private enterprise, a form of self-expression. What liberal individualism takes as the highest virtue – each person doing that which is right in his own eyes – is for the Bible the absence or abdication of virtue, and indeed a way of describing the disintegration of society.[64]

These comments are compatible with those of Wittmayer Baron:

> *The egalitarian structure of the Israelite clans long prevented excessive accumulation of wealth and, without necessarily lowering the average standard of life, militated against any form of conspicuous consumption ... the extremely favourable attitude of the rabbis to labour and to earning a living may have been the effect rather than the cause of economic developments, but there were inherent in the religion as such many impulses to Jewish economic endeavour.*[65]

---

63 Ibid. 12:8-9.
64 Dr Jonathan Sacks, *The Warburton Lecture*, Lincoln's Inn, 16 June 1993.
65 Baron, *A Social and Religious History of the Jews*, p. 54.

CHAPTER II

The New Testament

The Revelation of St John the Divine offers what is arguably the most substantial reference to trade and business among all the New Testament writings. For, as the world mourns for Babylon,

There will be weeping and distress over her among all the traders of the earth when there is nobody left to buy their cargoes of goods; their stocks of gold and silver, jewels and pearls, linen and purple and silks and scarlet; all the sandalwood, every piece in ivory or marble, the cinnamon and spices, the myrrh and ointment and incense; wine, oil, flour and corn; their stocks of cattle, sheep, horses and chariots, their slaves, their human cargo ... all the fruits you had set your hearts on have failed you. Gone forever, never to return, is your life of magnificence and ease.[1]

and St John continues:

The merchants of these things which were made rich by her shall stand afar off for the fear of her torment, weeping and wailing ...[2]

As we have seen, the trade of merchants was an integral part of Old Testament life – the sanctity of work, the harnessing of the earth's resources, usury laws, the gleanings laws, family inheritance and a degree of wealth redistribution all depended on wealth creation. The caravans crossing the desert laden with merchandise were as much an indication of a growth economy as the container ports and freight transport of today. At first sight, therefore, it may seem strange that there is so little mention of trade and business generally in the New Testament. The appearance of particular words naturally depends on the translator. In the Jerusalem Bible there is the rare mention of 'business' in St Paul's Letter to the Thessalonians, viz. 'Make a point of living quietly, attending to your own business and earning your living ...'[3]

In any appraisal of the role of Christianity in business life we must inevitably look to the New Testament as the primary source – and yet there is little or no mention by Jesus Christ himself of trade or business as such. There are possibly two reasons for this. First, the Christian message is essentially concerned with love, forgiveness, personal

---

1 *Revelation* 18:10.
2 Ibid. 18:15.
3 *1 Thessalonians* 4:11.

salvation and the coming of the Kingdom or, in the old words, the means of grace and the hope of glory. Here, there is no code of conduct, no catalogue of rules so beloved by the Hebrews for virtually every aspect of life.

Second, New Testament teaching, insofar as it is concerned at all with the subject of money or wealth, tends to concentrate on its evils, its dangers and its responsibilities. If we keep in mind our thesis that business is the creation of wealth (regardless for the moment of its motivation), we find that there is little enough on the subject in St John's Gospel. Indeed, not much more than 'You have the poor with you always ...'[4] The three Synoptic Gospels are more forthcoming on the subject, particularly on the renunciation and the dangers of wealth. In the first category, viz. the renunciation of wealth, we have:

How happy are the poor ...[5]

Go and sell all you own and give the money to the poor.[6]

Take nothing for the journey ... (the Mission of the Twelve)[7]

Alas for you who are rich ...[8]
Sell your possessions and give alms ...[9]

None of you can be my disciple unless he gives up all his possessions.[10]

And as for the dangers of wealth:

Where your treasure is there will be your heart also.[11]

You cannot be the slave both of God and of money.[12]

It is easier for a camel to go through the eye of a needle than for a rich man to enter into the Kingdom of God.[13]

Watch and be on your guard against avarice of any kind for a man's life is not made secure by what he owns even when he has more than he needs.[14]

Despite these warnings and constraints, there are instances throughout the Gospels where money and other forms of wealth are apparently accepted by Jesus as a fact of life. For example:

4 John 12:8.
5 Matthew 5:3, Luke 6:20.
6 Matthew 19:21, Mark 10:17, Luke 18:22.
7 Mark 6:8.
8 Luke 6:24.
9 Ibid. 12:33.
10 Ibid. 14:33.
11 Matthew 6:21.
12 Matthew 6:24, Luke 6:9.
13 Matthew 19:24, Mark 10:23, Luke 18:24.
14 Luke 12:15.

The Kingdom of Heaven is like treasure hidden in the field.[15]

Does your master not pay the half shekel? (to the Temple)[16]

Give back to Caesar what belongs to Caesar.[17]

The parable of the talents[18] and of the labourers in the vineyard[19] speak of money being put to work and of the integrity of honest labour. Equally, the extremes of wealth seem to be accepted in the Gospel stories, e.g. the widow's mite[20] and, as mentioned above, 'You have the poor with you always.'[21]

Although the Gospel writers, except John, stress the dangers of wealth, it is St Luke who seems to emphasize the responsibilities of wealth. For example:

Give to everyone who asks you and do not ask for your
property back.[22]

Take nothing for your journey.[23]

Sell your possessions and give alms.[24]

Use money, tainted as it is, to win you friends and thus make
sure that when it fails you they will welcome you into the
tents of eternity ... [25]

More particularly, it is in the Acts of the Apostles that Luke describes a community of ownership practised by the early church, e.g.

No-one claimed for his own use anything that he had as everything they
owned was held in common.[26]

We shall return to this theme in the next chapter.

The Acts and the Epistles

The Acts and the Epistles are rich in exhortations to the Disciples and to the early Church on the subject of money. The recurring theme is that of the responsibility of wealth and the worthiness of honest labour.

It would seem from this re-examination of New Testament teaching that there is little condemnation of riches as such, the emphasis being

---

15 *Matthew* 13:44.
16 Ibid. 17:24.
17 *Matthew* 21:21, *Mark* 12:17, *Luke* 20:25.
18 *Matthew* 25:14, *Luke* 19:11.
19 *Matthew* 20:1.
20 *Luke* 21:1.
21 *Matthew* 26:11, *Mark* 14:7, *John* 12:8.
22 *Luke* 6:30.
23 Ibid. 9:3.
24 Ibid. 12:33.
25 Ibid. 16:9.
26 *Acts* 4:32.

almost entirely on the dangers and responsibilities of wealth. This is no doubt the usual (if somewhat comfortable) interpretation of the New Testament ethic.

What then do the New Testament writers, other than the Gospel writers, tell us about business? In contrast to the apparent silence of Christ on the subject of trade and business, the writers of the Epistles are remarkably forthcoming. St James, from a position of some authority as head of the Jerusalem Church, tells us:

> It is right for the poor brother to be proud of his high rank and the rich one to be thankful that he has been humbled because riches last no longer than the flowers in the grass ... It is the same with the rich man: his business goes on; he himself perishes.[27]

And again:

> Here is the answer for those of you who talk like this: 'Today or tomorrow we are off to this or that town; we are going to spend a year there trading and make some money.' You never know what will happen tomorrow: you are no more than a mist that is here for a little while and then disappears.[28]

In the Letters of St Paul we observe an equally catholic, if at times a somewhat ambivalent, view of money and business. There comes through very clearly the respect for authority, the caring for those in need and the emphasis on honest work.

Certainly St Paul would have had no time for tax-dodgers. Thus, from the Letter to the Romans:

> The state is there to serve God for your benefit ... the authorities are there to serve God: they carry out God's revenge by punishing wrongdoers. You must obey, therefore, not only because you are afraid of being punished, but also for conscience sake. This is also the reason why you must pay taxes since all government officials are God's officers. They serve God by collecting taxes. Pay every government official what he has a right to ask – whether it be direct tax or indirect.[29]

and always the concern for the under-privileged, viz.

> The only thing they (James, Peter and John) insisted on was that we should remember to help the poor as indeed I was anxious to do.[30]

The worthiness, indeed sanctity, of all legitimate labour comes through to us time and again – for example, to the Thessalonians:

> We urge you, brothers to keep away from any of the brothers who refuses to work ...[31]

27 *James* 1:9.
28 Ibid. 4:13.
29 *Romans* 13:4.
30 *Galations* 2:10.
31 2 *Thessalonians* 3:6.

and

> We gave you a rule when we were with you not to let anyone have any food
> if he refused to do any work. Now we hear that there are some of you who
> are living in idleness, doing no work themselves but interfering with
> everyone else's.[32]

And to the Colossians:

> Whatever your work is put your heart into it as if it were for the Lord and
> not for men ...[33]

In the language of our own day, we may say that the recurring theme
in St Paul's writings is that of Christian stewardship and the
requirement of charity. Money and business are subordinated to the
need to build up the 'body of Christ', the *ecclesia*. Riches are not
condemned, but they bring their own responsibilities, paid labour is
not only worthy but highly desirable, the state is to be paid its due and
saving and investment is to be commended, but

> warn those who are rich in this world's goods that they are not to look
> down on other people and not to set their hopes on money which is
> untrustworthy, but on God who out of his riches gives us all that we need
> for our happiness. Tell them that they are to do good and be rich in good
> works, to be generous and willing to share – this is the way they can save up
> a good capital sum[34] for the future if they want to make sure of the only life
> that is real.[35]

In the meantime, we are left with a paradox. How can we arrive at a
Christian ethic for business life when Christianity's founder apparently
said so little on the subject and his first followers appeared to have
been drawn almost entirely from the non-commercial world? They had
their occupations, whether as fisherman, farmer, tax collector or even
tent-maker, but there was little sign of the cut and thrust of business.
Was this partly because, in this predominantly Hebrew culture,
everything which needed to be said had already been said in the Old
Testament scriptures? To the extent that Christ claimed to fulfil the law
and not destroy it, is the Christian expected to adopt Old Testament
standards or to be selective – and if the early Christians were to be
selective, cannot the modern man of business choose also to be selective
and adapt his creed to his trade?

The answer must surely be that Christianity is concerned not with
rules and regulations but with relationships – a person's relationship
with God and relationships between people – a recurring theme in
these pages.

---

32 Ibid. 3:10.
33 *Colossians* 3:23.
34 'Lay up for themselves a good foundation against the time to come'.
35 *1 Timothy* 6:17.

CHAPTER III

The Early Church

Religion does bring large profits, but only to those who are content with what they have. We brought nothing into the world, and we can take nothing out of it; but as long as we have food and clothing, let us be content with that. People who long to be rich are a prey to temptation; they get trapped into all sorts of foolish and dangerous ambitions which eventually plunge them into ruin and destruction. The love of money is the root of all evils and there are some who, pursuing it, have wandered away from the faith, and so given their souls any number of fatal wounds.[1]

These words from the first Letter to Timothy typify the attitude adjured upon the early Church, in the Epistles, on matters of worldliness and earthly possessions. It was to be the concern of the Church to proclaim the Kingdom of God and although, as we have said, the recurring theme in the Acts of the Apostles and the Epistles is that of the responsibility of wealth and the worthiness of honest labour, these matters were peripheral to the abiding task of proclaiming Christ's Kingdom.

We need not concern ourselves too precisely with the historical limits to the 'early Church'. Some may argue that it began with the first Pentecost, but there is a case for suggesting that it began with the early authenticated Letters of St Paul, probably around the year AD 50. Similarly, we are not called upon to put any sort of closing date on that first Christian era. Some may see a high water mark in Paul's declaration to the Roman Jews in the closing chapter of Acts.[2] Others might look to the development of the episcopacy and the concept of the apostolic succession listed first of all by Irenaeus in or about AD 190.[3] Lastly, it may be argued that the formative period of the Church ended with the conversion of the Emperor Constantine and the Edict of Milan in AD 313, giving civil rights to Christians throughout the Empire, and the acceptance of Christianity as the state religion in AD 324.

The physical boundaries of the early Church are more clearly delineated, being more or less coterminous with the Roman colonization of the Eastern Mediterranean. The Christian message spread upwards and outwards from Jerusalem through Damascus,

---

1 *1 Timothy* 6:6-10.
2 *Acts* 28:23-31.
3 John Lawson, *The Biblical Theology of St Irenaeus*, Epworth Press, 1948.

Antioch (which became the centre of Paul's activities for many years)[4] and from there to Tarsus, Iconium, Laodicea, Ephesus and Troas. From the west the route lay from Antioch through Zeugma, Megalopolis, across Bithynia to Byzantium, then across to Philippi, Thessalonica and ultimately across the sea from Dyrrhachium through Brindisium to Rome. These were the main trade routes of the then known world. It is not without interest, at least in the context of these pages, that the Christian Gospel followed the paths of business.

There is little doubt that the rapid spread of Christianity was made possible by the infrastructure of the early Roman Empire. There were two principal factors which made mobility possible – the construction of roads throughout the entire region and the Pax Romana which made for the safety of travel, whether by land or sea. It has been suggested that Paul travelled nearly 10,000 miles on routes busy with 'government officials, traders, pilgrims, the sick, letter-carriers, sightseers, runaway slaves, fugitives, prisoners, athletes, artisans, teachers and students'.[5]

There was, however, another major factor in the development of the early Christian Church, the urbanization of society, something which was made possible by the comparative ease of travel. Professor Wayne Meeks has written:

> Pauline Christianity ... is entirely urban. It stood on the growing edge of the Christian movement for it was in the cities of the Roman Empire that Christianity, though born in the village culture of Palestine, had its greatest successes until well after the time of Constantine.[6]

And again:

> In those early years ... within a decade of the crucifixion of Jesus, the village culture of Palestine had been left behind and the Greco-Roman city became the dominant environment of the Christian movement.[7]

It has also been noted that:

> The people of the Roman Empire travelled more extensively and more easily than had anyone before them – or would again until the nineteenth century.[8]

Movement between town and country tended to be one way and was probably irreversible. Relationships were not friendly. We are told that:

> The two worlds regarded each other as on the one side clumsy, brutish, ignorant, uncivilised; on the other side, as baffling, extortionate, arrogant. Peasants who move to a town feel overwhelmed by its manners and dangers

---

4 *Galations* 2:21, 2:1-14, *Acts* 11:25 and 13:1.
5 Ronald F. Hock, *Paul's Tent-making and the Problems of his Social Class*, Journal of Biblical Literature, 1978.
6 Wayne A. Meeks, *The First Urban Christians*, Yale University Press, 1983, p. 10.
7 Ibid, p. 11.
8 Ludwig Friedlander, 1901, Leipzig: Hirzel.

and seek out relatives or previous emigrants from the same village to settle among. Rent or tax-collectors who come out to the country face a hostile reception and can expect attempts to cheat and resist them even by force. They respond with their own brutality.[9]

It is possible that this exodus to the cities brought about the beginning of what we might call 'Christian economics'. Possibly an over-weaning concern about money was less common in pastoral and agricultural societies where climate or disease could destroy a crop or a herd almost overnight with little that the countryman could do about it.

Wayne Meeks tells us how St Paul sometimes used commercial language to describe the relationship between himself and the local congregation and to describe certain theological truths. For example, St Paul uses the language of partnership to reinforce the epistolary form of recommendation – 'If you hold me as your partner, receive him as myself' (Philemon 18:17). In his Letter to Philippi, Paul uses the language of commercial partnerships and refers to the 'receipt' that he gives for the gifts the Philippian Christians have sent him in prison (4:15-19). In the same Letter, Paul speaks of his conversion in terms of gain and loss (3:7). And His disciple writing to Colossae spoke of Christ's sacrifice as 'cancelling the note that was against us' (Col. 2:14).[10]

Although, as we have said, the Christian Gospels make little comment on the subjects of wealth, trade and business, the Epistles show an increasing awareness of the language of business and the responsibilities of wealth not least, we suspect, because of the urbanization of the early Church.

Opinions seem to be divided on what we would call today the socio-economic make-up of the early Church. Celsus, described by Wayne Meeks as the first pagan author we know of who took Christianity seriously enough to write a book against it, alleged that the Church deliberately excluded educated people because the religion was attractive only to 'the foolish, dishonourable and stupid, and only slaves, women and little children'. The Christian evangelists, he said, were

> ... woolworkers, cobblers, laundry-workers and the most illiterate and bucolic yokels who entice children and stupid women to come along to the wool-dresser's shop or to the cobbler's or the washerwoman's shop that they may learn perfection.[11]

That extreme view would not have been shared by Ernst Troeltsch in *The Social Teaching of the Christian Churches*, viz.

9 Ramsay MacMullen, *Roman Social Relations*, Yale University Press, 1974.
10 Meeks, *The First Urban Christians*, p. 66.
11 Chadwick (trans.), *Origen Contra Celsum*, Cambridge University Press, 1965.

It is true that for a long time the church membership was mainly composed of slaves, freedmen and manual labourers. From the very outset, some of the members came from the upper classes; indeed it was they who were chiefly responsible for providing the necessary financial support and the places where the Christians could gather for fellowship and worship.[12]

And again:

The central problem is always purely religious – dealing with such questions as the salvation of the soul, monotheism, life after death, purity of worship, the right kind of congregational organisation, the application of Christian ideals to daily life and the need for severe self-discipline in the interests of personal holiness ... from the beginning no class distinctions were recognised, rather they were lost sight of in the supreme question of eternal salvation and the appropriation of a spiritual inheritance.[13]

We can see, therefore, that urbanization brought a new dimension to the otherwise simple life of the Galilean Christians. This conflict, if conflict it be, runs as a thread through the whole of Christian history. Is it easier in the countryside to achieve the 'eternal salvation' and 'spiritual inheritance' of which Troeltsch wrote? Apparently so, because:

It is clear that Christianity has a distinct leaning towards comparatively simple conditions of living, in which immediate contact with God's gifts in nature determine the way of earning a living and thus, a possibility of maintaining life and keeps vivid the feelings of dependence and gratitude towards the gifts of God in nature.[14]

But:

Jesus does not preach asceticism; in his teaching there is no trace of contempt for the life of the senses for its own sake. He teaches quite plainly that food and work are only of value insofar as they are necessary to life; otherwise they have no ethical value.[15]

Before leaving the early Church we should try to assess its relevance in relation to the business and economic life of future generations. That which we have called the 'early Church' was in fact a collection of like-minded communities drawn, as we have seen, from various walks of life and existing in differing environments. Is there here a blueprint for the future? Probably not. Whilst Christian truths made known to us in the Gospels are immutable, Christians live in a changing world. The early Christians were no doubt aware of unethical business practices. They were familiar with greed, extortion, unfair competition, poverty and inequality. But they knew nothing of some of the major ethical

12 Ernst Troeltsch, *The Social Teaching of the Christian Churches*, 1909, p. 42.
13 Ibid, p. 39.
14 Ibid, p. 86.
15 Ibid, p. 59.

problems confronting business today. There may be little point, therefore, in saying to a modern captain of industry that the early Church would not have approved of this or that mode of conduct. Nevertheless, that Church was the platform from which the more structured Church of later years was launched. Its early growth and influence was quite miraculous and it represented the first attempts to apply Christian teaching to life in society.

Not surprisingly, therefore, Troeltsch was to write:

> *Nowhere does there exist an absolute Christian ethic which only awaits discovery; all that we can do is to learn to control the world situation in its successive phases just as the earlier Christian ethic did in its own way.*[16]

---

16 Ibid, at p. 1,013.

CHAPTER IV

Rome

If the Tiber reaches the walls,
If the Nile does not rise to the fields,
If the sky does not move (drought)
Or the earth does (earthquake),
If there is famine,
If there is plague,
The cry is at once 'the Christians to the lion!'
(Tertullian, Apologeticus 40.2)

We have seen that the urbanization of society led, both for Christians and Jews, to a concentration in larger units in the towns, this in turn resulting in new urban lifestyles, greater social problems and arguably a greater awareness of the evils and responsibilities of wealth and property. Stuart Hall, formerly Professor of Ecclesiastical History at King's College, London reminds us that the city was the focus of civilized living.[1] It was there that the economic resources of the countryside were served by the technical skills of craftsmen. It was the place for the social and political business of law, commerce, education, religion, theatre, sports and that 'indefinable human intercourse which made the central square or forum of an ancient city its vital heart'. Emperors could call upon cities for financial support for the court and the army, particularly when they were passing through or were faced with grave emergencies. This led to the extraction of taxes from city householders, a liability which was passed down the social chain to cause severe hardship for the poor. 'During the early Christian period the rich got richer and the poor poorer most of the time.'[2] Nevertheless, it was a city, that of Rome itself, which gave the next great impetus to the historical development of the Christian Church.

The Christians in Rome saw some momentous developments in the second half of the first century AD. Jerusalem had been destroyed in AD 70 and with it the mother Church. Peter and Paul had died and Nero had embarked on the first of the series of Christian persecutions.

During these early years it seems unlikely that the thoughts of Christians were directed towards the problems of trade and business and the economic realities of city life. Around them, nevertheless, there

---

1 Stuart G. Hall, *Doctrine and Practice in the Early Church*, SPCK, 1991, p. 8, etc.
2 Ibid, p. 8.

was an explosion of economic growth. By the early part of the second century, the population of Rome exceeded a million and it was by far the largest city of the ancient world. A modern writer, Desmond O'Grady tells that

> Not only all roads led to Rome, but also all sea routes bringing the world's riches: grain from Egypt, venison and timber from Gaul; dates from African oases, silk from China, cotton from India; silver, copper and lead from the Iberian Peninsula; ivory from Mauritania, glass from Syria; incense from Arabia, and philosophers from Greece.[3]

Despite, or perhaps because of, the persecutions, the Church continued to grow and apparently flourish. Tertullian tells us that the courage of the Christian martyrs caused the conversion of spectators[4] and St Justin, writing about AD 150, claims that the 'constancy, patience and business integrity of Christians persuaded others to change their ways and join them'.[5] The catechumen, i.e. those undergoing instruction before baptism, were required to provide a tenth of all their produce to the clergy to sustain them and provide opportunity for corporate charity and 'integrity with money and the giving of alms were essential and probably commended the faith in a world full of bribery'.[6] It seems that the Church became not only a centre of charity but was also a source of financial security for its members. We are told that charity meals ('agape') were held (without the formality of the sacrificial bread and wine) and the Church took upon itself the task of protecting widows and orphans, surplus babies and elderly slaves. In the year 251 a Bishop of Rome could claim that his Church included

> above fifteen hundred widows and persons in distress all of whom are supported by the grace and loving kindness of the Master.[7]

Thus, in that age of increasing disparity of riches, membership of the Church offered a number of material advantages. This in turn gave increasing power to those who controlled church membership and 'set a high premium on financial integrity as a qualification for office'.[8]

It was, it seems, in the second and third centuries that for Christians the conflict between faith and money, God and mammon, became more real. For the most part, as we have seen, the Christians were not drawn from the trading classes and, in any case, they were debarred from certain offices of state or local government. They could not serve as judges or as officers in the army. Rather more confining was the

3 Desmond O'Grady, *The Victory of the Cross*, London, Harper Collins, 1991, p. 70.
4 *Apologeticus*, 50, 12-16.
5 *Apologeticus*, 1, 16.
6 Hall, *Doctrine and Practice in the Early Church*, p. 17.
7 Eusebius, HE6.43.
8 Hall, *Doctrine and Practice in the Early Church*, p. 24.

Church's own prohibition on drama or on arts and crafts which had any connection with idolatrous emblems or with pagan worship. For example, in the middle of the third century, Cyprian of Carthage, who was elected to the bishopric within two years or so of his conversion to Christianity, required that an actor converted to the faith could not be allowed to continue in his profession, but should in fact be found other employment or be provided with a pension from the Church.

Nevertheless, Troeltsch tells us that from the third century onwards Christians became more numerous in the higher ranks of society and in the more eminent professions, in the army and in government office, taking the view that these occupations were necessary for the social system. Troeltsch wrote:

> One particularly difficult question was that of trade. Since most Christians lived in cities, that is in conditions which assumed the existence and the use of money, they could not dream of doing away with trade. They therefore accepted it entirely. Even the monasteries sold the products of their labour and right into the fourth century the clergy lived on the proceeds of trade and business. Later on, church property was administered on these lines and it even enjoyed immunity from taxation.

And in words which go to the very heart of the problem confronting Christians in business:

> From the point of view of the principle of love, it [trade] was suspect because it meant taking from one to give to another and enriching oneself at the expense of others... In theological theory, therefore, trade was considered the most reactionary form of earning a living, ethically lower in the scale than agriculture and manual labour and it was safeguarded by the precautionary regulation that in fixing the price all that might be asked was the cost of production plus the additional amount necessary for a moderate profit. All that theologians cared about was to prevent profits exceeding the sum that was necessary for a man to gain a living.[9]

Troeltsch tells us that the development of early Catholicism was, after Pauline Christianity, the second great development of the Christian faith. Although the office and role of bishop (*episkopos*) was known from Apostolic times, it was not until the second century AD that the Church became institutionalized with the tradition of episcopal authority. The concept of sacramental worship, which had been, and remained, central to the life of the Church, was only valid within a properly constituted Christian community through the legally appointed bishops. Outside the Sacrament there was no salvation and there was no Sacrament without a priest, so there was no salvation outside the Church. Thus, the Church became an independent body, gradually founded on its own system of law. The more the Church became an organized and unified body, the more it regarded itself as

---

9 Troeltsch, *The Social Teaching of the Christian Churches*, p. 127.

separate from 'the world'. Troeltsch tells us that the first social problem
with which the Church had to deal was the problem of property.

> ... there was no idea of doing away with private property. Also, the
> frequent exhortations to regard property as nothing and all the talk about
> community of possessions, which are gifts of God like light and air, were
> equally only a challenge to energetic charitable activity.[10]

Thus, he argued, the problem was not that of private property in itself
and the economic order which was based upon it, but the measure and
the range of the duty of love. Therefore:

> The renunciation of possessions now becomes the main demand, whether it
> be from obedience to the commandment of Love, which urges that no-one
> ought to possess anything for himself so long as others are in want, or
> whether the ascetic idea is pre-eminent, that every joy in possession is self-
> love and love of the world and a hindrance to the love of God.[11]

Early Catholicism encouraged the concept of work. It was prized as
an education in sobriety and industry and a means of protection
against certain dangers, including those of the flesh. Labour was
regarded as useful for the purposes of asceticism and the discipline of
the body – the monastic ethic in particular stressed this aspect. On the
other hand, work was also regarded as the consequence of the Fall and
as the punishment for sin. Thus, Christians emphasized the duty of
labour – 'If a man will not work neither shall he eat,'[12] was a precept
strictly enforced. The Catholic Church may have been naïve, or indeed
ignorant, about political and social economics in the language of today,
but they were very practical in economic management. Troeltsch tells
us that the Church, which acquired great wealth in capital, slaves and
land, whose bishops finally played a great part as landowners, whose
assistance was enlisted by the State which was no longer equal to its
responsibilities for police work, the care of the poor and the control of
the population, possessed on the practical side an extraordinary
intelligence in economic matters.

But Rome was to crumble and was eventually sacked by the Goths in
AD 411. It fell to Augustine to rebuild the new Rome with his vision of
the City of God. He was to write:

> *Regarding the authority of the New Testament, by which we are*
> *commanded to love nothing of this world, especially in that passage wherein*
> *it is stated: 'be not conformed to this world': for at the same time, it must be*
> *shown that one is conformed to whatever one loves. If we attend to all of*
> *these words ... we find many things altogether necessary for those who long*
> *to flee this world and to find refuge in God.*[13]

10 Ibid, p. 115.
11 Ibid, p. 116.
12 2 *Thessalonians* 3:10.
13 Augustine, *De moribus ecclesiae catholicae (On the Ways of the Catholic Church)*.

CHAPTER V

Monasticism

We are not really publicity people. We do not
speak at all for the first four hours of the day.
However, we have to live in the modern world.
(Brother Robert, Abbot of Caldey)

These words refer to the decision of the Cistercian Monks of Caldey Abbey in May 1996 to advertise the Abbey and its wares on television, thus demonstrating in our own day the conflict between asceticism and 'the world'.

It was perhaps the story of the rich young man[1] more than any other Christian teaching which emphasized the renunciation of possessions and gave particular impetus to the development of Christian monasticism. Indeed, the story has troubled pulpit and pew for nearly 2,000 years.

Troeltsch could not accept the literal interpretation of the words. He said:

> It is a mistake to found the economic doctrine of the Gospel upon the story of the Rich Young Ruler and certain familiar words which are connected with it concerning rich people. The words about the spiritual danger of riches are quite clear when we understand the fundamental point of view of Jesus and they contain no negation of property, nor indeed any asceticism at all. Jesus' attitude towards the question of possessions is clear enough, namely to seek first the Kingdom of God and not to be anxious for the morrow, but the young man wants to do something special so Jesus invites him to take part in His missionary work and to sell all and give to the poor. (The story is not the key to the economic teaching of the Gospel, but only the key to that of the later Church which, owing to the fact that it had to fight with much more highly developed conditions, felt the difficulty and the contrast far more strongly).[2]

Monasticism existed to a degree in pre-Christian times, particularly in Egypt and Syria. Christian monasticism developed partly because of the reduction in persecution, which left Christians more freedom of movement, but mostly because of the institutionalization of the Church, to which we have already referred. As the Church became, as it seemed, more worldly, Christians sought the solitariness of monastic

---

1 *Luke* 18:18-23.
2 Troeltsch, *The Social Teaching of the Christian Churches*, p. 174(n).

life (the Greek *monachos* meaning 'solitary'). It was largely the life of St Antony (251-356) which set the pattern of fasting, praying and mortification of the flesh. It has been suggested that in or about the year 357 the *Life of Antony*, attributed to Athanasius, played a significant part in the conversion of Augustine in 386.[3] It was apparently those same disturbing words 'sell all you have and give it to the poor ... ' which inspired Antony to take up a solitary life in his Egyptian cell, to be followed after twenty years by a life of travel and Christian work.

It has been said that the great (religious) force in the fourth century was the movement in the direction of a monastic life.[4] We are told that 'The monastic movement was the great protest against the increasing worldliness of the Church of the fourth century,' and 'the deserts of Egypt became peopled with colonies of hermits'.

In those early years the monks were laymen, subsequently to be joined by priests from the Catholic Church. Ultimately, it was to be expected of all monks that they would join the priesthood. It was impossible for St Antony and other solitary monks to live alone and gradually they moved into organized communities, principally under the influence of St Basil, Bishop of Caesarea and

> ... by the close of the century monasteries were everywhere, from remote Britain to the lands beyond the eastern frontiers of the Empire and for over a thousand years Christianity found its strongest arm in the cloisters of the monks.[5]

In the eighth and ninth centuries most of the independent monasteries in the Western world were gradually merged under the leadership of Benedict (c. 480-547). In Benedictine monasteries personal possessions were denied and obedience was required to Christ, the Abbot and, in some cases, to the Pope. A particular characteristic of Benedict's rule was a strong work ethic. Manual labour was assigned to each monk each day, but in later years this was delegated to lay brothers and replaced by the *opus Dei*. Thus, the work of God became exclusively spiritual.

In England by the time of Edgar (959-975) there had been a significant increase in the number of monasteries and by the end of that century England had thirty Benedictine monasteries and six nunneries.[6]

By the time of Chaucer there were something in excess of five thousand monks described by G.M. Trevelyan as

> worldly and well-to-do, living lives of sauntering comfort in the monasteries, or roaming the land dressed like laymen, to hunt game or look after their

3 Hall, *Doctrine and Practice in the Early Church*, p. 175.
4 F.J. Foakes-Jackson, *History of the Christian Church*, George Allen & Unwin, p. 585.
5 Ibid, p. 587.
6 Asa Briggs, *A Social History of England*, Weidenfeld & Nicholson, 1983, p. 47.

estates. Having themselves abandoned the manual labour practised by their predecessors, they maintained armies of servants to carry on the daily routine of their great establishments which often covered many acres of ground. They gave daily alms in money and broken meats to the poor and showed a lavish hospitality to travellers, many of whom were wealthy and exacting guests.[7]

Nevertheless, the monks for the most part were not idle. The building of cathedrals and monasteries flourished in the twelfth century and the monks were instrumental in inventing building techniques, including lifting machinery. Durham Cathedral took a mere forty years to build although the reconstruction of Glastonbury took nearly a century.

We are told that monastic records, including account rolls, are packed with information of every kind and cover far more topics than the monastic chroniclers selected. At their best they reveal much about rents and yields of crops, labour, services and wages. At Canterbury, for example, Archbishop Peckham's archives might suggest that he was as interested in the rent rolls as in the spiritual welfare of priests.[8]

During the fourteenth century the number of monks in Britain fell, but their standard of living rose and by the turn of the sixteenth century the Cistercians at Whalley Abbey in Lancashire, for example, were apparently spending two-thirds of their income on food and drink.

By the year 1450, important monasteries or abbeys had been established throughout the length and breadth of England and in 'The Supplication of the Beggars' to King Henry VIII it was claimed that this 'idle, ruinous sort, which (setting all labour aside) have begged so importunately that they have gotten into their hands more than the third part of all your Realm. Besides this they have the tenth part of all corn, meadow, pasture, grass, wool, colts, calves, lambs, pigs, geese and chickens ... '

Thus, it seems that the ascetic ideal which had been the motivation of the monasteries in earlier centuries was no longer admired by the world or practised by the monks. Perhaps, therefore, the dissolution of the monasteries from 1536-1540 was a natural outcome of the changing scene. It was a two-stage operation beginning with 374 lesser houses with an annual income of less than £200,000 in 1536 and continuing in the second stage with 186 'great and solemn monasteries'. Although the primary intention was to enrich the crown, part of the land was given away to peers and knights and by the end of Henry VIII's reign, two-thirds of the new wealth had been alienated in land-market operations, mostly through and into the hands of existing landowners, the peerage and gentry.

7 G.M. Trevelyan, *English Social History*, London & New York, Longmans Green & Co., 1942, p. 48.
8 Briggs, *A Social History of England*.

MONASTERIES IN ENGLAND c1450
with diocesan boundaries and
approximate dates of foundation

▲ Monastery or Abbey

Holy Isle
Lindisfarne

DURHAM
995
(to York)

CARLISLE
1133

Whitby

YORK
625

Rievaulx
Hyland

Bolton Fountains

Selby
Pontefract

Bardney

BANGOR (to Bangor)
c.550

LICHFIELD
669

ST ASAPH
c.550

Holme

Crowland Thorney
Ramsey **ELY**
1109

NORWICH
1094

HEREFORD
676 Kenilworth

(to Bangor)

LINCOLN
1067

Bury St.
Edmunds

ST DAVID'S
c.550

WORCESTER
c.680 Gloucester

Woburn Cambridge

Oxford

Colchester

Tintern

LONDON
605

LLANDAFF
c.550

Abingdon
Malmesbury

Westminster Waltham

**BATH &
WELLS**
1139 Glastonbury

SALISBURY
1075

Leeds
CANTERBURY
597

Dover

Sherborne

WINCHESTER
c.650

Romsey **CHICHESTER**
1075 Battle

Southampton

EXETER
1050

Launceston

We are not concerned here with the extravagances, excesses and sometimes brutality of the early monks, nor with the accumulation of wealth and corporate power of the later monasteries up to the time of their dissolution. Our principal concern here is that monasticism represents the most significant attempt to separate the Christian life from the world.

In our own time, Dietrich Bonhoeffer was to praise and, to some extent, condemn monasticism. For example,

> it is highly significant that the Church was astute enough to find room for the monastic movement and to prevent it from lapsing into schism. Here, on the outer fringe of the Church was a place where the older vision was kept alive. Here, men still remembered that grace costs, that grace means following Christ. Here, they left all they had for Christ's sake and endeavoured daily to practise his rigorous commands. Thus, monasticism became a living protest against the secularisation of Christianity and the cheapening of grace.

On the other hand,

> monasticism ... was represented as an individual achievement which the mass of the laity could not be expected to emulate. By thus limiting the application of the commandments of Jesus to a restricted group of specialists, the Church evolved the fatal conception of the double standard – a maximum and a minimum standard of Christian obedience ... By and large, the fatal error of monasticism lay not so much in its rigorism ... as in the extent to which it departed from genuine Christianity by setting up itself as an individual achievement of a select few and so claiming a special merit of its own.

Bonhoeffer goes on to relate how Martin Luther 'renounced the world' in order to live the Christian life as a monk, but God 'shattered all his hopes' by showing him, through the Scriptures, that the following of Christ is not the achievement or merit of the select few but the divine command to all Christians without distinction. Thus, 'the monks' attempt to flee from the world turned out to be a subtle form of love for the world.'

Bonhoeffer concludes:

> *Luther's return from the cloister to the world was the worst blow the world had suffered since the days of early Christianity. The renunciation he made when he became a monk was child's play compared with that which he had to make when he returned to the world ... The only way to follow Jesus was by living in the world ... The conflict between the life of the Christian and the life of the world was thus thrown into the sharpest possible relief. It was a hand-to-hand conflict between the Christian and the world.*[9]

---

9 Dietrich Bonhoeffer, *The Cost of Discipleship*, 1937.

CHAPTER VI

The Middle Years

*Love not the world, neither the things that
are in the world. If any man love the world,
the love of the Father is not in him.*

These words from the first Epistle of St John[1] go to the very heart of
the conflict facing Christian believers over almost 2,000 years. The
early Christians saw themselves as new people, a third 'race' among the
Jews and the Gentiles. They saw themselves, and were seen to be, a
race apart.

For our purposes here, 'the world' may be taken to include attitudes
to wealth, trade and business generally, in addition of course to the
wider aspects of worldliness. Thus, we shall return to the Johannine
edict from time to time.

We come then to 'the middle years' – a conveniently elastic title
covering a very long period in western civilization. It begins somewhere
around the mid-fourth century AD following the acceptance of
Christianity as the state religion of Rome and continues through the
centuries down to the Calvinistic era and the beginnings of Christian
socialism.

Here, we are concerned almost exclusively with Europe. Viewed
against the developments of the nineteenth and twentieth centuries, the
changes in those middle years were not particularly dramatic. Long
periods saw the increased centralized control of the Roman Catholic
Church and the gradual separation of canon law from the law of the
individual states; the rise of the Germanic-Roman states and later those
of the Celts, the Slavs and the Hungarians; and the ultimate decline of
the Roman Empire. State boundaries changed almost overnight and
there were 'wars and rumours of wars'. The 'divine right of kings'
found expression often enough in the human greed of kings and their
courts. The golden age of Elizabeth brought exploration of new lands
and opportunities for new colonization and new trade. Nevertheless,
for the most part, the society of the Middle Ages and beyond was an
agrarian one. Power and prestige depended on the ownership of land.
Eventually, the entire feudal system was based on land ownership and
the various forms of tenure. Thus, in time, the main owners of land

---

1 *1 John* 2:15.

42

were the Crown, the nobility, the Church and, as we have seen, the monasteries. Senior officials were paid in landed property. This attachment to land ownership, particularly in Britain with its system of inheritance based on *primogeniture*, continued well into Victorian times and had its echoes in the law of property legislation of 1925 with its distinction between settled land and what had come to be known as traders' settlements.

Throughout the changing years, Christian attitudes also were changing and maturing. For the most part, however, it would seem that those changes were not by way of reaction to the changing environment, which was in any case a fairly slow process. Whereas nowadays a Christian voice would normally be raised somewhere against any new affront to Christian ethics, Christian attitudes in those middle years seem to have been inspired more by the outpourings of philosophers, theologians and senior clergy.

Troeltsch tells us that:

> From the standpoint of political and economic history the period of town civilisation which begins with the twelfth century is regarded mainly as a preparation and foundation for the modern world. At the same time this period, which is characterised by its great cathedrals and their intensive church life, its religiously consecrated guilds and corporations, its social and political efforts for the spiritual and material welfare of its citizens, its Christian parochial schools and its charitable institutions, its peace and its public spirit, has a direct significance for the history of ethics and of religious life and it constitutes the high watermark of the development of the Mediaeval spirit.[2]

For St Thomas Aquinas, man was naturally a town-dweller regarding rural life only as the result of misfortune or of want, although the town itself was strictly agrarian and supported its life by a system of exchange of goods with the surrounding country. It was Aquinas who identified and enunciated the basic principles of so-called 'Natural Law' founded primarily on what is 'reasonable' in society. For him, the principal concern of a theory of Natural Law was to explore the requirements of practical reasonableness in relation to the good of human beings who, because they live in community with one another, are confronted with problems of justice and rights, of authority, law and obligation.[3]

For Troeltsch ...

> ... the most important point to observe is the positive value assigned to work, to profit, to private property and the right of inheritance, coupled with the admission that, in accordance with Natural Law, it is an actual duty, both to oneself and to one's relations, to gain a sufficient measure of

---

2 Troeltsch, *The Social Teaching of the Christian Churches*, p. 255.
3 See John Finnis, *Natural Law and Natural Rights*, Oxford, Clarendon Press, 1980.

property which will ensure the maintenance of the family according to the standards of one's class ... (thus) the purely consumer's standpoint of the early Church has been discarded and the actual conditions of economic life are taken into consideration.[4]

However, (Troeltsch again)

... the self-restraint, the sacrificial spirit and all the traditionalism which are necessary if this system of Natural Law (Thomism) is to be maintained can only really be produced with the aid of the Christian virtues of love, humility and hope – a hope which is anchored in the real values of the future life.[5]

Unfortunately (in some respects) the world was changing and the growth of an independent lay civilization in the cities brought a new dimension and powerful competition to the previous world, which had been controlled by the Church and, more particularly, by the priests themselves. Accordingly:

A nascent capitalism with its monopolies, its practice of credit, its associations for trade, and its home industries, destroys the moderate recognition of natural requirements which were all that the simple, ecclesiastical ethic had known. The transformation of the conditions of life which was involved in the growth of possessions and in political independence created a civilisation of the senses which set aside the ecclesiastical principle of a love of the world which could be combined with religion.[6]

*   *   *

On the eve of All Saints Day in 1517, Martin Luther nailed his ninety-five 'Theses' to the door of the church in Wittenberg in Saxony. Although these theses were primarily an attack on the granting of indulgences in return for a confession of sins and a gift to papal funds, it has been said that to the Christian world as a whole Luther had 'announced his total dissatisfaction of a religious genius with late Mediaeval piety'.[7]

It was customary (according to Troeltsch) 'to describe Protestantism as the revival of the Pauline and Augustinian religion of grace in contrast to the Catholic religion of law'.[8] For Luther, secular

4 Troeltsch, *The Social Teaching of the Christian Churches*, p. 319.
5 Ibid, p. 321.
6 Ibid, p. 377.
7 David L. Edwards, *Christian England*, London, William Collins, 1983 and Fount Paperbacks, 1989, p. 309.
8 Troeltsch, *The Social Teaching of the Christian Churches*, p. 467.

institutions and natural possessions were appointed and ordained by
God. Thus, he was a dualist, 'a spiritual descendant of St Paul'. If for
Luther, as suggested above, the religion of grace was *in contrast* to the
Catholic religion of law, there appears to be a paradox in that
Lutheranism requires the spiritual Christian to live in utter love as the
servant of all to the entire exclusion of all personal interests whilst
regarding secular institutions and natural possessions as ordained by
God.

Lutheranism, as seen by Troeltsch, regarded labour with its toil and
its cares as being in itself contrary to nature. The fruitfulness of nature
and the minerals in the mountains were direct gifts of God and the idea
that these good things could only be appropriated by labour and
technical skill seems scarcely to have occurred to Luther. Private
property

> ought not to exceed the requirements of one's rank, yet pleasure in
> possessions even in gold and silver is allowed within the limits of a grateful
> frugality without any scrupulous consideration of measure of one's needs.
> The economic order consists essentially in this – to live within one's own
> class according to the social standards of that class and to regard it as a just
> claim on the government to be protected by it within this order. It is against
> all law, both Natural and Divine, to wish to rise in the world, to break
> through existing institutions on one's free initiative, to agitate and destroy
> Society by individual efforts, to improve one's manner of life or to improve
> one's social position.[9]

We are told that Luther's ideas were the same as those still held in the
early twentieth century by Catholics, conservatives and middle-class
people in general.

> Just as the latter fought against the stock exchange, the greed of the masses,
> the right of the workmen to form trade unions and against free competition,
> Luther fought against monopolies and against joint stock companies, against
> the demand for higher wages for day labourers and servants which was the
> result of the general rise in prices – against individualism which broke
> through class barriers.[10]

Close on the heels of Lutheranism, Calvinism became the chief
driving force in the development of Protestantism. The distinctive
feature of Calvinism was the doctrine of predestination and it was
inevitable that this should colour Calvinistic attitudes towards wealth
and economics. It has been said that:

> Since the Calvinistic idea of God is in many ways similar to the idea of
> Yahweh whose Being is Will the necessities of practical life led to an
> increasing use of the Old Testament.[11]

9 Ibid, p. 554.
10 Ibid, p. 560.
11 Ibid, p. 600(n).

And again:

> To people who have been educated on Calvinistic principles the lazy habit of
> living on an inherited income seems a downright sin – to follow a calling
> which has no definite end and which yields no material profit seems a foolish
> waste of time and energy – and failure to make full use of chances of gaining
> material profit seem like indifference towards God. From the Calvinistic
> point of view laziness is the most dangerous vice – it is hurtful to the soul
> from the standpoint of ascetic discipline and harmful to the community from
> the standpoint of social utilitarianism.[12]

The Calvinistic ethic was similar to the Lutheran view of work, i.e. a
practical exercise of a calling appointed by God and therefore an act of
divine worship. Both Calvin and Luther advocated labour as a
universal duty and abolished monasticism and mendicancy. Both
Calvin and Luther believed that poverty fostered Christian virtue more
effectively than wealth and the Calvinists introduced severe laws
against luxury. Indeed, Calvinism has been described as 'Christian
socialism' in that its

> social influence ... at that period was completely comprehensive in the sense
> that it moulded in a corporate way the whole of life in the state and in
> society, in the family and in the economic sphere, in public and in private in
> accordance with Christian standards.[13]

If Calvinism was Christian socialism it also saw the introduction of
what one might call Christian capitalism into the Calvinist ethic. Calvin
had first gone to Geneva in 1538 and returned there in 1541. He had
been commissioned to draw up a plan for the close, moral supervision
of the city and within this comparatively small and self-contained
territory Calvin was able to introduce some basic capitalist principles.
He urged the abolition of certain kinds of business which were
questionable from the Christian point of view (such as the manufacture
of playing cards), but it was at his instigation that, with the aid of a
state loan, the manufacture of cloth and velvet was introduced as a
home industry in order to give work to the poor and unemployed.
Later on, the manufacture of watches was introduced with the same
aim.

This fitted well with the early Protestant attitude to one's 'calling',
i.e. the exercise of one's energies in a service both necessary in itself and
appointed by God and one in which profit is regarded as the sign of
divine approval. This attitude permeated the world of commerce and
was no doubt the origin of what has since been called the Protestant
'work ethic'. For Troeltsch:

> It laid the foundation of a world of specialised labour which taught men to

---

12 Ibid, p. 611.
13 Ibid, p. 622.

work for work's sake and in so doing it produced our present day bourgeois way of life.[14]

Here perhaps we see the origin of modern Christian stewardship, viz.

Labour and profit were never intended for purely personal interest (in Calvinism). The capitalist is always a steward of the gifts of God whose duty it is to increase his capital and utilise it for the good of society as a whole, retaining for himself only that amount which is necessary to provide for his own needs. All surplus wealth should be used for works of public utility and especially for purposes of ecclesiastical philanthropy. Only 'productive credit' for business purposes is allowed, not 'usury credit' which is simply used for living on interest. From poor men or people who have been otherwise harassed by misfortune no interest is to be taken. The debtor ought to gain just as much from the money as the creditor.[15]

Thus, Calvinism became a major influence in the development of Protestant ethics.

Let us conclude this chapter with Troeltsch:

Thus this [Calvinistic] economic ethic became middle class, one might almost say lower middle class, capitalism and it bore all the signs of the results of the capitalistic attitude towards life – systematic division of labour – emphasis upon specialisation – the feeling for advantage and profit – the abstract duty of work – the obligation towards property as towards something great which ought to be maintained and increased for its own sake. The owner of wealth or property is 'the Lord's Steward' and administers a divine gift which has been entrusted to him.

This type of capitalism, however, preserves its special Christian character by its taboo on pleasure-seeking and self-glorification, the sense of the duty of work for the service of God, strict honesty and reliability, the humane obligation to make provision for the workers and to give respect to employers and the extensive use of wealth for philanthropic ends.[16]

14 Ibid, p. 645.
15 Ibid, p. 647.
16 Ibid, p. 812.

CHAPTER VII

The Quest for Wealth

Men are gaining possession without your knowledge.
Merchants ignore the interests of their sovereign and
are concerned only with their own commercial profit.
The Tsar of Russia (Ivan the Terrible)
to Queen Elizabeth (1571)

In the two centuries or so preceding the Industrial Revolution many events of significance for Christianity and business occurred in, or emanated from, England. An Elizabethan prayer referred to

The Commonwealth of England, a corner of the world, Lord, which thou hast singled out for the magnifying of thy majesty.

These years encompassed:

the accession of Elizabeth I (1558);

the defeat of the Spanish Armada (1588) which ensured the English dominance of the seas with the resulting commercial advantage, but which unleashed a wave of anti-Catholic persecution in this country;

the colonization of Virginia (1607) and the voyage of the *Mayflower* to Massachusetts (1620) – the Massachusetts 'government' was to become the standard American pattern, i.e. the puritan concept of 'a government of Christ in exile' composed of separate 'cities of God';[1]

the Civil Wars (1642-1651);

the influence of the Levellers from 1647 seeking a radical redistribution of wealth with communes taking over from the feudal manors and the stripping of the clergy of their right to tithes;

the Enlightenment in the late seventeenth century exemplified in the work of Isaac Newton (1642-1727) and John Locke (1632-1704) and in France by Voltaire (1694-1778) and Jean-Jacques Rousseau (1712-78) seeking to show 'that the present age is more enlightened than the past and that we understand nature and man best through the use of our natural faculties';[2]

the conversion of John and Charles Wesley (1738);

the emancipation of slaves (1833); and

the Declaration of Independence in the USA.

---

1 Alistair Cooke, *America*, New York, Alfred A. Knopf Inc., 1974.
2 Henry May, *The Enlightenment in America*, New York, 1976.

Here again, we are attempting to appraise Christian attitudes against a backcloth of considerable political and socio-economic change. We have borrowed our title for this chapter from Professor Asa Briggs's description of much of this period as 'the quest for wealth, power and pleasure'.[3] Certainly, as we have said, it was a time of exploration when, according to Adam Smith 'England purchased for some of her subjects, who found themselves uneasy at home, a great estate in a distant country'.[4] Such exploration was not necessarily altruistic. Sir Francis Bacon, himself an advocate of emigration, warned that 'planting of countries is like planting of woods and thus would take time to produce results'. He questioned the motives behind early discovery and colonization and claimed that they did not centre on the 'propagation of the Christian faith', but on 'gold and silver, and temporal profit and glory'.[5]

It was a period of great extremes of wealth. It seems incredible, looking back, that many died of starvation in this country in the early seventeenth century and in the years from 1500 to approximately 1650 inflation was rampant – food prices rose eight-fold whilst wages rose less than three-fold.

Earlier feudalism had left England with a dual structure in society. The only persons with social status in the seventeenth century were the peerage and the gentry. In the middle of that century, for example, there were 120 or so peers and 20,000 gentry representing approximately one in twenty of all adult males. Those without that social status were categorized according to their economic status, i.e. whether for example they were husbandman, cobbler, merchant, attorney or whatever. Gradually, however, from the mid-seventeenth century onwards those in the middle of society, possibly yeoman farmers or tradesmen, began to prosper. By producing a surplus over and above their own needs they could sell their produce profitably and continue to produce more with the aid of cheap labour. Thus, by the end of the century a middle-class group had emerged whose interests and wealth grew out of, but extended far beyond, their agricultural estates.

Meanwhile, the age of discovery and exploration continued. Back in the year 1600 the East India Company had been founded and it had been said that the English

> excelled all the nations and peoples of the earth in searching the most opposite corners and quarters of the world and ... in compassing the vast globe.[6]

---

3 Briggs, *A Social History of England*, p. 58.
4 Adam Smith, *An Enquiry into the Nature and Causes of the Wealth of Nations*, 1776.
5 Briggs, *A Social History of England*, p. 159.
6 Hakluyt, *Principal Navigations, Voyages and Discoveries of the English Nation*.

It has been suggested that it was during the period in which the Puritans were in command in this country that the seventeenth-century quest for power and wealth reached its peak.[7] It was Cromwell who had despatched convicts, rather than pilgrims, to colonize New England and the Long Parliament which had passed the Navigation Acts of 1651 which required that all merchandise imported into England from America, Asia and Africa should be imported in English ships. The Puritans emphasized the importance of hard work and towards the end of the seventeenth century Dudley North, in his *Discourses upon Trade* (1691), considered that 'the exorbitant Appetites of Man' were the main spur to industry and ingenuity and he continued (in an argument perhaps more familiar to our present day): 'Did men content themselves with bare necessaries we should have a poor world.'

What then was the attitude of the Church to this new-found quest for wealth and the resultant disparities?

Throughout the two centuries of this period the Church was very much concerned with its own affairs, its relationships with the Pope and with the monarch, its own forms and procedures, even its clothing, and its basic theology. Professor J.J. Scarisbrick writing in our own times described attitudes to religion in the sixteenth and seventeenth centuries thus:

> the impression derived from churchwardens' accounts is that altars, roods and lofts, statues and holy-water stoups and so on were taken down in Edward's reign, put back in Mary's and taken down again after Elizabeth's accession without great drama or disorder. And in the seventeenth century the monarchy itself was taken down and put back with limited participation by the people.[8]

Perhaps, however, we get a truer picture of the age from the preface to the first edition of *Christian England* by David Edwards:

> When lay folk did take sides in the religious controversies of the time they stayed out of trouble as far as they could and concentrated not on a close examination of the rival theologies but on matters more prominent in real life. Their questions, as we occasionally overhear them, are who now owns the land of the monasteries or has influence as the local squire or magistrate; whether one likes the present appearance of the parish church or the looks of those who never go near it; what one has to pay to the local parson or say to one's spouse or parents; why one eats fish on Fridays (or does not) or is proud to be able to read the Bible (or is not); where one happens to be born or to be listening when a faith was being taught attractively. Here is a people which is on the whole conservative and not only insular but also village-minded. It is a people which on the whole, during most of the sixteenth century, feels that the Catholic Church, with the priest at Mass, probably

7 Briggs, *A Social History of England*, p. 161.
8 J.J. Scarisbrick, *The Reformation and the English People*, Oxford, 1984, p. 89.

represents serious Christianity now as in the previous thousand years
(whether or not one is devout oneself). It is a people which on the whole
during most of the seventeenth century feels that (whether or not one is
deeply Protestant) the Pope and Catholic foreigners generally are a threat to
a nation which is beginning to prosper proudly. And it is a people which,
when the religious storms have blown themselves out during the eighteenth
century, on the whole settles down into the unenthusiastic acceptance of a
religion 'by law established', with tolerated minorities practising a religion
of much the same tone. It is a religion of reasonableness, honesty, duty and
respectability. It is not aloof from the world; it echoes Sir Toby's famous
question: 'Dost thou think, because thou art virtuous, there shall be no more
cakes and ale?'[9]

In the result, the 'Church of England' (established in 1559) seems to
have given little thought, and certainly no prominent lead, in the ethics
of economic life. The country prospered; the Church declined. Indeed,
it was left to the 'tolerated minorities' in the words of Edwards quoted
above, the Puritans, the Quakers, the Wesleyans and other Dissenters
to lead the way in a revival of Christian morality.

Such was the decay in the Church of England that by the early days
of the eighteenth century the main offices in the Church were all for
sale and the senior clergy received quite considerable revenues. Some
clergy held simultaneously three or four benefices which provided a
substantial income, out of which a curate would be paid a miserable
sum to look after a parish. Out of 11,000 livings in England there were
over 6,000 where the incumbent was non-resident.

These are also the years of a brutal penal code (there were 160
different 'hanging' offences). They were the years of acute infant
mortality (three out of four children of all classes died before their fifth
birthday) and they were the gin years. In 1750 alone up to eleven
million gallons of gin were reputed to have been drunk and in London,
in particular, out of 2,000 houses one in every four was a gin shop!

An intermittent preoccupation of the Church during the sixteenth
and seventeenth centuries was the Prayer Book. Mediaeval Christianity
had been primarily an emotional matter involving attendance at
Church ceremonies conducted by the priesthood. The emphasis was on
the mystery and the drama of the Church and its charitable role. This
was understandable in an age of illiteracy.

The first Book of Common Prayer, the work of Thomas Cranmer,
was to be published in 1549 – a book which provided for the Old
Testament to be read chapter by chapter each year and the whole New
Testament to be read three times a year.

A revised Book of Common Prayer came in 1552 with a more
Protestant emphasis and Forty-two Articles of Faith. Seven years later

9 Edwards, *Christian England*, Vol.II, p. 6.

(1559), however, Queen Elizabeth gave the Royal Assent to the Act of Supremacy and Uniformity taking the title of 'Supreme Governor' of the Church (a title which survives to this day) and introducing a further revision of the Prayer Book. This was to be the Prayer Book known to William Shakespeare which, along with the Bible, came 'first and most constant' of all the Bard's sources.[10]

On St Bartholomew's Day, 24 August 1662, the new Act of Uniformity (under Charles II) introduced the Book of Common Prayer which is still authorized for use in Anglican churches throughout the world at the present day.

This apparent diversion into the origins of the Church of England Prayer Book serves to illustrate one quite disturbing fact – that the Church, at least in public worship, had little if any concern for the temptations, the dangers and the proper uses of wealth and what we have called Christian economics. In Morning Prayer there is a plea that 'in health and *wealth*' her majesty may live long and in the Magnificat St Luke tells us that 'the rich He hath sent empty away'.

There is in fact in the Book of Common Prayer and in today's Alternative Service Book only one composed prayer (as distinct from Biblical lessons) which seeks grace to 'forsake all covetous desires and *inordinate love of riches*'. This is the collect for St Matthew's Day – appropriately enough for one who reputedly was a tax-collector!

Is the apparent detachment of the Church from the 'real' world a throwback or perhaps an extension of Thomasine ethics?

Whatever the truth of the matter a big sea-change was pending with the encroachment of the Industrial Revolution. As we approach industrialization we can leave the 'Quest for Wealth' with an anonymous prayer of more recent years.

> God, who givest to every man his work and through his labours dost accomplish Thy purposes upon earth: grant Thy blessing, we beseech Thee, to those who are engaged in the industries and commerce of this land. Inspire them with the knowledge that in ministering to the needs of others they are serving Thee; defend them from injustice and oppression, and give them the due reward of their labours ...

---

10 A.L. Rowse, *William Shakespeare*, London, 1963.

CHAPTER VIII

Industrialization

*Were we required to characterise this age of ours by
any single epithet, we should be tempted to call it the
Mechanical Age.*
(Thomas Carlyle, *Signs of the Times*, 1829)

It was the Mechanical Age because, for the first time on any large scale,
the so-called Industrial Revolution, a phrase reputedly coined by
Arnold Toynbee, author of *The Industrial Revolution in England*
(1884), is usually attributed to the years 1780 to 1820, but a degree of
mechanization had developed in England from the early days of the
eighteenth century. Indeed, Daniel Defoe in his *A Tour through the
Whole Island of Great Britain* referred to the

> New discoveries in metals, mines, minerals; new undertakings in trade;
> inventions, engines, manufactures, in a nation, pushing and improving as we
> are: these things open new scenes every day and make England especially
> shew a new and differing face in many places ... [1]

Every school child knew (or used to know) that Hargreaves's
Spinning Jenny invented in 1765 and John Kay's Flying Shuttle (1733)
had revolutionized the textile industry in England – by the mid-1780s
approximately 20,000 Spinning Jennies were in use in England. The
new industrialization involved the establishment of a factory system,
large-scale production, exploitation of water and steam power (largely
revolutionized by James Watt), the creation of a wage-earning class and
eventually the growth of large industrial towns. [2]

Historians generally agree that the birth of industrialization in
Britain, ahead of any other country, was due principally to (i) the
availability of local resources, coal, iron ore and steam power, (ii) the
availability of capital without the need to borrow abroad as other
countries found necessary when they, in turn, industrialized in later
years, and (iii) the availability of colonial resources, both in terms of
raw materials and foreign markets.

Whereas, as we have seen, the incomes of the poor during the
sixteenth and seventeenth centuries fell below subsistence level, the
Industrial Revolution brought about substantial increases in average

---

1 Daniel Defoe, *A Tour through the Whole Island of Great Britain* 1724-26.
2 See T.S. Ashton, *The Industrial Revolution*, Oxford, 1957.

incomes. The average income per head of the total population, which
had been around £8 to £9 a year in 1700, had risen to £22 by 1800
and doubled again by 1860.[3]

At the same time the population grew by leaps and bound. At the
first census of 1801 there had been only fifteen towns with a
population of over 20,000 inhabitants. By the end of the century there
were sixty-three.

In some respects the high water mark of the Industrial Revolution
was the Great Exhibition of all the Nations held in the Crystal Palace
in 1851. Of the 14,000 exhibitors, over one-half represented Great
Britain and the Colonies and Britain stood out as the 'workshop of the
world'. Prince Albert was to say on that occasion that:

> The products of all quarters of the globe are placed at our disposal and we
> have only to choose that which is best and cheapest for our purposes and the
> powers of production are entrusted to the stimulus of competition and
> capital.

This was the age of the factory and of the machine – the age of
family businesses and the age of individual ownership or partnership.
Notwithstanding the Companies Acts of the mid-nineteenth century,
which introduced limited liability, out of a total capital of £5,800
million of all British companies in 1882 only £64 million was quoted
on the London Stock Exchange.

Although, as we have said, *per capita* income grew significantly
during these years of mechanization, the rich benefited considerably
more than the poor. Optimistic Victorians saw the Industrial
Revolution as 'the betterment of the species' and Samuel Smiles (1812-
1904) saw industrialization as 'a harvest of wealth and prosperity'.[4]
The editor of a new periodical, *Engineering* wrote in 1866:

> Engineering has done more than war and diplomacy; it has done more than
> the Church and the Universities; it has done more than abstract philosophy
> and literature. It has done more than our laws have done to change society.
> Few of our middle class could be induced to exchange their homes and
> appliances for comfort for the noblest villas of Ancient Rome.

Nevertheless, there were many workers who were not better off in
absolute terms. In the textile towns the handloom weavers saw wages
and employment opportunities fall drastically as the powerloom took
over. Around 1830, one-third of the inhabitants of Colne in Lancashire
were subsisting on two pence a day, their main fare was meal,
buttermilk and potatoes with a few gills on Saturday nights.[5] Others
were more fortunate and, for some, real wages seemed to have

3 Briggs, *A Social History of England*, p. 189.
4 Samuel Smiles, *Self-Help*, 1859.
5 Briggs, *A Social History of England*, p. 190.

increased annually until around the time of the Great Exhibition in 1851.

The impact of industrialization within a timescale of, say, one hundred years was arguably greater and more concentrated than any other economic or cultural 'revolution' in history. It could be said that the industrialization of England changed the world and yet the eventual criticism of those years appears not to be on economic or social grounds, but on aesthetic ones. Ruskin, for example, foresaw that eventually England would be 'set as thick with chimneys as the masts stand in the docks of Liverpool' with 'no meadows, no trees, no gardens, no acre of English ground without its shaft and its engine'. It was through the attitudes of ordinary people to art and architecture that Ruskin challenged the political economy of his day.[6] His contemporary, William Morris (1834-96), the socialist artist and poet, believed passionately in beauty in everyday things and opposed what he saw as the ugly results of capitalism. He asked whether all was to end in a counting house on the top of a cinder heap with the pleasures of eyes having gone from the world.

It is perhaps unfair to label some of those early industrial entrepreneurs with the suggested evils of capitalism. Many of the industrial capitalists were not, as it were, a class apart – many were landowners and thus were already capitalists in mining, transport and property. Indeed, as we shall see, several of them became paternalistic employers applying what they saw as ethical considerations to the conduct of their business.

It is strange in retrospect, but the Government seems to have played a comparatively minor role in the industrialization of Britain. Parliament itself was unrepresentative of the population at large. In 1801, for example, nearly three-quarters of a million people in Yorkshire had only 2 county and 26 borough MPs, whereas in Cornwall the population of 188,000 had 2 county and 42 borough MPs. At the beginning of the nineteenth century only one in seven people in England had a parliamentary vote and, in any case, the process of getting into Parliament was very expensive. For the most part, Parliament was favourable towards capitalist landlords, for example with the passing of the Corn Laws of 1815, later to be repealed by Sir Robert Peel in 1846. Parliament did in fact introduce a system of factory inspection from 1833 dedicated to the task of 'correcting the great moral evils that had taken root and extensively spread in industry'. Another measure (with a familiar ring in present-day political discussion) was the Ten Hours Act of 1847 which restricted the working hours of women and children in textile factories.

---

6 See John Ruskin, *Unto This Last*, 1860.

Then there were the Factory Acts culminating in the consolidated Act of 1901.

Throughout those years, when 'machine power replaced muscle power',[7] the most significant development was that of the trade union movement. By the early 1890s there were approximately one and a half million trade unionists, 300,000 of whom were miners and another 300,000 employed in the retail trades. The early development of trade unionism reached its peak in or around 1834 when the Tolpuddle Martyrs were convicted of administering 'unlawful oaths' under the Mutiny Act of 1749.

According to Asa Briggs:

> It is to the later years of the nineteenth century and the first decade of the twentieth that we should turn for the making or re-making of the 'English working class'. The idea of class itself was a product of early industrialisation when, in the words of a contemporary 'operative workmen being thrown together in great numbers, had their faculties sharpened and improved by constant communication'. It was then that 'movements' were formed from below, some dedicated to reform, a few to revolution, all to 'union'.

> The limits to class-consciousness, which was not the only, nor necessarily the main, influence on thinking and behaviour in many parts of the country, were also revealed during these struggles. Old notions of hierarchy and deference survived even the deepest crises of early industrialisation and for all the growing sense of middle-class and working-class consciousness, it was probably the aristocracy and the gentry who in both good and bad times felt the strongest sense of identity: 'a common blood, a common condition, common pursuits, common ideas, a common dialect, a common religion and a common prestige, a prestige growled at occasionally, but on the whole conceded and even, it must be owned, secretly liked by the country at large'.[8]

The 'common religion' was of course the Church of England. But what had the Church to say about the long working hours, the exploitation, the extremes of wealth, the apparent submerging of human personality in mass production, the spoliation of the countryside, factory conditions and slavery?

Dr Hugh McLeod tells us that:

> The poor expected their priests to speak out on their behalf. Some did. But for the most part during periods of acute social conflict in the nineteenth century, the official clergy identified with the possessors.

And again:

> The Enclosure Acts ... so much resented by the rural poor brought prosperity to many clergymen. Tithe-holders were usually awarded large

---

7 An anonymous comment at the time.
8 Briggs, *A Social History of England*, p. 198.

amounts of land in commutation of tithes and many superb Georgian rectories towering above the houses of the parish ... were built on the proceeds. It was bad enough that the clergy were getting conspicuously richer at a time when the poor were getting poorer. To make matters worse many of them seemed to be putting on airs and mixing unwillingly with any but their social equals.[9]

It seems that the Church had little to say (not for the first time) to a world focused on economic conflict.

Many still identified work with religion, whether as paternalistic employers or as craftsmen. Indeed, many of the early craft unions held their meetings on church premises and it has been said that up to one-third of Methodist ministers left the Church to become trade union leaders. Nevertheless, as Dr McLeod points out:

> The logic of economic development was against them in the nineteenth century as ever larger firms took on an impersonal, bureaucratic character and human values got lost in the violence of the war between capital and labour.[10]

For the most part, the nineteenth century was a period of (i) disenchantment with the 'official' conservative Church, (ii) the development of Protestant dissent, and (iii) liberal, secular reform.

Foremost in the path of religious revival was the Methodist movement which took off after John Wesley's death in 1791 and had nearly half a million members by 1850. Wesley, himself a high-churchman, had sought to 'spread scriptural holiness throughout the land' and had not railed particularly against the industrialization of Britain, nor the resulting inequalities of wealth. Indeed, his famous dictum 'gain all you can, save all you can, give all you can'[11] was a challenge to both rich and poor and stands out as a non-Biblical encouragement to Christian stewardship. Dr McLeod tells us that these nonconformist movements

> continued to grow for most of the century. One essential was that they offered the craftsman and the peasant the chance of interpreting the Bible for themselves unhindered by an educated clergy or by persons of higher status. In their chapels the poor man (and sometimes a poor woman) could become a preacher, class leader or Sunday School teacher.[12]

Although the nineteenth century was a period of intense sectarian conflict reflecting the antagonisms between the land-owning class and others, there was also a degree of moral and religious consensus within the middle and upper classes of nineteenth-century Britain based on a common evangelical Protestantism.

9 Dr Hugh McLeod, *Religion and the People of Western Europe 1789-1970*, p. 25.
10 Ibid, p. 33.
11 John Wesley, *On the Use of Money.*
12 McLeod, *Religion and the People of Western Europe 1789-1970*, p. 37.

After the period of acute class tensions in the first half of the nineteenth century a new form of paternalism was precariously established in many of the factory communities of Britain during the prosperous 1850s and 1860s. It was part of the theory of this paternalism that a genuine comradeship was possible between 'respectable' people of different social classes on the basis of their common interest in the prosperity of their firm, their membership of the local community and common participation in local institutions and movements.[13]

Unfortunately, it may be argued, in the latter half of the nineteenth century this commonality of approach among employers and employed began to fade as modern capitalism became more widespread. 'Hands on' employers became less common as companies grew larger and shareholdings became more widely spread.

So one of the most distinctive forms of nineteenth-century middle class Christianity was dying out: as employers adapted to the pressures of the market and rejected the life of factory and community; while a growing body of their workers also repudiated the old ties.

Thus, as the century came to an end:

Neither employer nor employed needed to impress the other with his moral credentials: religion was no longer needed as a common language as personal communication between those at different ends of the economic hierarchy died out and as the economic elite became divorced from the industrial community, they ceased to support local religious institutions with their time or even their money.[14]

---

13 Ibid, p. 110.
14 S. Yeo, *Religion and Voluntary Organisations in Crisis*, 1976, pp. 106-7.

CHAPTER IX

The Church and Business

Before we move from the past to the present, it may be appropriate to consider the interaction of Church and business life over the years, and to reflect on the lives and work of those who, in comparatively recent times, sought to carry their Christian idealism into the world. Here then is a postscript to 'the past'.

The more the Christian movement closed its ranks and became an organised and unified body, the more it tended to regard the rest of life as the 'world'.[1]

Thus Troeltsch, writing in the early days of this century, gave expression, as many others have done, to the great gulf which existed between the Church and the world throughout most of Christian history and which arguably has become a yawning gap in our own times.

In these pages we have sought to outline the changing Christian attitudes to trade and business over the years from the relative absence of any precise guidance in the Gospels (other than the New Testament injunction to love one's neighbour) through the growth of the early Church with remarkably little interest in the trade routes, (which the Church development followed); the influence of Rome and the explosion of economic growth and the beginning of conflict between faith and money; the attraction of monasticism; the centralization of the Roman Church; the age of exploration; Thomism and Natural Law; the influence of Augustine, Luther, Calvin and Wesley; the work ethic and concepts of stewardship; the pre-industrialization quest for wealth and comparative detachment of the Church and then industrialization with widespread demographic change, the spread of capitalism, non-conformist movements and the twilight of the owner-employer era.

Are we right in thinking that the Church adopted a somewhat passive role in her relationship with the world of business? First of all, in the early years the problem probably did not arise. The first Christians recognized the worthiness of legitimate occupations – the first disciples as fishermen, Paul as a tent-maker (almost certainly a 'business' and not merely a part-time craft), Lydia the seller of purple and, in later years, the assumption by some Christians of high office in

---

1 Troeltsch, *The Social Teaching of the Christian Churches*, p. 100.

the administration of Rome. We may assume that those early Christians, for the most part born out of the Jewish faith, would have a healthy Hebrew view of work and a respect for God-given resources and the conservation of wealth within the family.

Also, despite the strictures of St James on the subject of business (see page 26)' and the other New Testament sources to which we have referred, it must be remembered that there was no single formal voice of the Church until the second century AD. As we have suggested earlier, the 'early Church' was a collection of like-minded communities drawn from various walks of life and existing in differing environments.

The more 'the' Church became an organized and unified body with its own system of law, the more it regarded itself as separate from the 'world', but within itself it became a centre of charity, a source of financial security for its members and undertook the financial welfare of widows and orphans and slaves. The Church's record of 'integrity with money' had a proselytizing effect on those outside the Church.

With the appointment of Gregory VII came the centralization of the Church in the Papacy, the enforcement of Canon Law, the administration of the Episcopal offices and, for the first time, the Church spoke with one voice throughout the then Christian world. On the other hand, as Troeltsch points out, the Church did not attempt to regulate the conditions and institutions in the world outside her own borders from the point of view of an ideal. On the whole, she accepted the conditions of the world and adjusted herself to them by means of the theory of relative Natural Law. However, for the system of Natural Law to be maintained it required the Christian virtues of love, humility and hope – a hope which is anchored in the anticipated values of the future life, as we discuss in the last chapter.

The advent of Protestantism saw the revival of the Pauline and Augustinian religion of grace in contrast to what has been called the Catholic religion of Law. It was left to Luther to emphasize the dualism of the Christian ethic. On the one hand, the 'spiritual' Christian must ignore everything which is not in keeping with the Christian spirit and temper – in utter love he must be the servant of all to the entire exclusion of all personal interests. On the other hand, he is called upon to observe the natural order around him, which means that

> the Christian may and should use law and compulsion, swear in courts of law, take part in divorce proceedings, strive to acquire wealth and property whenever such action is required by his official or social position or by the demands of the state or of the civil order.[2]

---

2 Ibid, p. 499.

This 'dualism' or dichotomy of the Christian life is as real for many people today as it was in the Lutheran ethic.

The doctrines of Lutheranism were to be developed and extended by Calvin, who was not opposed to private property nor to the endeavour to acquire wealth provided that all is done honestly, modestly and united with a generous charitable activity. It all serves the good of the community, of the Church, of the State and thus the glory of God. Indeed, according to Troeltsch (as we have already quoted),

> to follow a calling which has no definite end and which yields no material profit seems a foolish waste of time and energy – and failure to make full use of chances of gaining material profit seems like indifference towards God.[3]

So it was that both Calvin and Luther advocated labour as a universal duty and condemned monasticism and mendicancy. On the other hand, the Calvinistic economic ethic supported the 'anti-Mammon' spirit, a campaign it pursued with great severity in its laws against luxury. Nevertheless, we are told that Calvin 'quite approved of the fact that greater profits were made in trade than in agriculture since they were simply the reward of carefulness and industry'.[4]

It was Calvin's role in Geneva (see page 46) and the economic conditions which he introduced there which are regarded by some as the beginning of capitalism. Profit was the sign of the blessing of God on the faithful exercise of one's calling. But labour and profit were never intended for purely personal benefit. The capitalist is always a steward of the gifts of God whose duty it is to increase his capital and utilize it for the good of society as a whole, retaining for himself only that amount which is necessary to provide for his own needs. All surplus wealth should be used for works of public utility and especially for purposes of ecclesiastical philanthropy.[5]

It has been said that the theology of Luther and Calvin shaped Protestant Britain for the next four centuries.[6] We have sought to show in Chapter VII that, for the first 200 years or so of this period, the Church had been much concerned with its own affairs, its relationship with the Pope and monarch and the development of its own doctrines and patterns of worship. We have referred to the decay of the Church of England during the seventeenth and early eighteenth century and the way it was left to the 'tolerated minorities', the Puritans, the Quakers, the Wesleyans and other Dissenters to lead the way in a revival of Christian morality.[7]

Dr McLeod tells us:

---

3 Ibid, p. 611.
4 Ibid, p. 642.
5 See Ibid, p. 647.
6 See W.J. Sheils and D. Wood, *The Church and Wealth*, Oxford, 1987.
7 See Edwards, *Christian England*.

First in Britain and then in almost every other country, social and political changes were tending to sharpen the antagonism between rich and poor and to strengthen the class identities of both.

The most obvious of these social changes was the population explosion. Between 1750 and 1850 the population increased by three times in Britain.

The growth in the numbers of the poor and the increasing contrasts within the rural population were factors tending to exacerbate social antagonisms around the start of the nineteenth century and to render increasingly difficult the attempts of the official churches to act as a focus of social unity.[8]

We have discussed in Chapter VIII the impact of the Industrial Revolution which so changed this country and eventually the rest of the world. Until then the Church, from its earliest days, had experienced very little conflict or contact with business. The Church had itself accumulated considerable property and in what was primarily an agrarian society, agriculture was dominated by those whom Dr McLeod calls 'large-scale profit-orientated landlords and farmers' and 'for the most part, during periods of acute social conflict in the nineteenth century, the official clergy identified with the possessors'.[9]

In 1815, Reverend Richard Yates, Chaplain to the Chelsea Hospital ('by far the most influential propagandist of his generation'), published *The Church in Danger*, which was followed in 1817 by *The Basis of National Welfare*. Both pamphlets were addressed to the Prime Minister. Yates took the rich to task for failing in their obligations to the poor. They had built chapels for themselves and had not bothered with the working population and its spiritual needs. The first object of the proprietors was to obtain the highest possible rent for the pews. He was severe with those who had grown rich through the profits of the new industrial towns. For Yates, the solution to these ills lay in an Act of Parliament to furnish public money for the building of new churches in the populous districts, providing also for the easy sub-division of parishes and for the stipends and accommodation of the clergy to serve them. Yates's works achieved almost immediate success. Church building became a popular panacea for social evils.[10]

As the social consciousness of the churches was awakened, Friendly Societies and Savings Banks, intended to foster the habits of thrift and family responsibility among the working classes, were also founded by the clergy in many parishes. One parish priest (the Reverend Blackley, Vicar of King's Samborne in Hampshire) was moved to advocate a state scheme of compulsory national insurance for sickness benefit and

---

8 McLeod, *Religion and the People of Western Europe 1789-1970*, p. 22.
9 Ibid, p. 23.
10 Edward R. Norman, *Christian Businessmen: Church and Society in England 1770-1970*, Oxford, Clarendon Press, 1976, p. 52.

old age and in 1897 the Lambeth Conference Report on Industrial Problems recommended old age pensions.[11]

The same Lambeth Conference Report said:

Character is influenced at every point by social conditions and active conscience in an industrial society will look for moral guidance on industrial matters.

Some twenty years later, William Temple became the leading exponent of the view that Christian society – at least since the Reformation – had neglected to apply religious principles to economic and social relationships – that the great object of the Church in his generation was 'to be delivered from the poisonous heresy that business is business'.[12]

It has been said that 1924 was the watershed in the development of social teaching in the Church of England.[13] In April that year at an Assembly in Birmingham, 'The Conference on Christian Politics, Economics and Citizenship' (C.O.P.E.C.) was formed, principally under the guiding influence of William Temple.

The Reports of that Assembly covered a number of major social issues, including *Industry and Property*, from which the following is an extract:

It is not only repugnant to the principles of the Christian but revolting to the taste of an educated person that one class in a country, a small class of which the individuals are not necessarily distinguished above their fellow citizens for virtue or ability, should command more money than they can possibly spend in any rational or profitable fashion.[14]

In his book *Capitalists and Christians*, David Jeremy, Senior Lecturer in Economic History at Manchester tells us that:

the church in England has depended on the laity to endow it with property, to subscribe a portion of its income, advise on its investments, assist in its administration and much else. Even association with the rogues of business was seemingly unavoidable ... besides the difficulties of theological interpretation and the churches' reliance on wealthy laymen that made it hard for the churches to formulate a clear statement of their teaching about business. Industrial society had alienated many more poor than rich as it spread across the face of nineteenth century Britain.[15]

The years from the mid-nineteenth century to the early part of the twentieth century were characterized by the amassing of considerable wealth by families engaged in industry and commerce and by the needs

11 Conference of Bishops of the Anglican Community, Lambeth Palace, July 1897.
12 *The Guardian*, 29 November 1917.
13 Norman, *Christian Businessmen: Church and Society in England*, p. 279.
14 *Industry and Property*, C.O.P.E.C. Report IX, London, 1924.
15 David J. Jeremy, *Capitalists and Christians: Business Leaders and the Churches in Britain 1900-1960*, Oxford University Press, 1990, p. 54.

of the Church itself as it sought to extend its ministry into the newly populated areas. Other important characteristics of those years were (i) the families concerned were owner-employers and thus could dispose of their increasing wealth as they wished, and (ii) wealth was in comparatively liquid form in contrast to the estates of the old landed families.

In his exceedingly well-researched book David Jeremy identifies three target years, 1907, 1935 and 1955 and posed four major questions which may be paraphrased as follows:

1. To what extent have capitalists in twentieth-century Britain tried to introduce religion into an industrial context?
2. What have the churches taught with respect to business values, e.g. what standards, skills and social networks useful in business have they (the churches) provided?
3. What were the recognized limits to religion in business at the end of the nineteenth century? How extensive was paternalism?
4. What part have businessmen and women played in church life?

Over the years we may extract a fairly formidable list of Christian entrepreneurs who have, apparently, carried their Christian background and beliefs into business life. They include:

Sir Harold Bellman	(1886-1963)	Abbey National Building Society
Sir Jesse Boot	(1850-1931)	Boots Pure Drug Company
George Cadbury	(1839-1922)	Cadburys (Cocoa and Chocolate Manufacturer)
Jonathan Dodgson Carr	(1806-1884)	Biscuit Manufacturer
Arthur Chamberlain	(1842-1913)	Kynoch Limited
Samuel Courtauld	(1876-1947)	Chairman, Courtaulds
George Goyder	(1908-1997)	Scott-Bader Commonwealth
Lord Hambleden	(1868-1928)	W.H. Smith & Son
Sir John Laing	(1879-1978)	John Laing & Son (Holdings) Limited
Sir William Clare Lees	(1874-1951)	Bleachers Association Limited
William Hesketh Lever	(1851-1925)	Lever Brothers Limited, Soap Manufacturer
John Spedan Lewis	(1885-1963)	Retailer
Sir George Livesey	(1834-1908)	Chairman, South Metropolitan Gas Company
Lord Mackintosh	(1891-1964)	Confectioner
Viscount Nuffield	(1877-1963)	Morris Motors, Motor Car Manufacturer

Sir Alfred Owen	(1908-1975) – Chairman, Rubery Owen Group
Sir Joseph Pease	(1828-1903) – J. & J.W. Pease
Joseph Rank	(1854-1943) – Flour Miller
J. Arthur Rank	(1888-1972) – Milling and Film Magnate
Benjamin Seebohm Rowntree	(1871-1954) – Confectionery
Lord Stamp	(1880-1941) – Chairman, LMS Railway
Angus Watson	(1874-1961) – Skipper Sardines

We may look briefly (in alphabetical order) at a dozen or so of these Christian philanthropists, although no doubt there were many more such 'rich men furnished with ability ... honoured in their generations'.[16]

Sir Harold Bellman

We refer in Chapter X and again in Chapter XV to the growth of the building society movement, of which Sir Harold Bellman was one of the pioneers as Secretary, General Manager and subsequently Chairman of Abbey Road Building Society which became, by merger, the Abbey National Building Society. In his book, *Cornish Cockney*[17] he recalled his early days at a Wesleyan Chapel in Paddington:

> Sunday was the day for best clothes, buttonholes, music, happy fellowship and good cheer. I recall several men of distinction who passed through our home on these occasions. It was there in the Bible class and guild that I was encouraged to speak. I started by reciting at an early age and later read the lesson in church on an anniversary day, etc.[18]

Bellman was a close friend of fellow Methodist, Lord Stamp (see below).

George Cadbury

No catalogue of Christian philanthropists would be complete without the name of Cadbury. George was one of the sons of John Cadbury who, we are told, started the day at 7.00 a.m. with a walk across the fields in Edgbaston with dogs and children followed by breakfast and family Bible readings. When George and his brother took control of the cocoa and chocolate business they moved the works to Bournville, built houses on the adjoining land and founded the Bournville Village Trust. Cadbury was a practising Quaker in the days when there were

16 *Ecclesiasticus* 44.
17 C. H. Bellman, *Cornish Cockney*, London, 1947, p. 40.
18 Quoted in Jeremy, *Capitalists and Christians*.

The model estate laid out by Cadburys at Bournville, photographed in 1879 and reproduced here by kind permission of Cadbury Limited.

disproportionately more Christian businessmen of Quaker background than was true of any other denomination. David Jeremy tells us that by 1955 the Quaker representation in business was nearly thirty times the Quaker religious density throughout the country and a ratio nearly ten times greater than the Anglicans.[19] George Cadbury's Bournville Village was not a tool of the employer, as seems to have been the case with William Lever's Port Sunlight (see below). It was not a company town but a garden village. Cadbury was a deeply religious man and in 1906 he told a Committee of Church of England Bishops:

> Largely through my experience among the back streets of Birmingham, I have been brought to the conclusion that it is impossible to raise a nation morally, physically and spiritually in such surroundings and that the only effective way is to bring men out of the cities into the country and to give every man his garden where he can come into touch with nature and thus know more of nature's God.[20]

Throughout the thirty years or so of Cadbury's business life he began each day at the factory with non-denominational services of prayer.

In 1901, the Board of Cadbury Brothers Limited discovered that their supplies of cocoa from the Portuguese West African islands of Sao Tomé and Principe, off the coast of Equatorial Africa, were the product of slave labour. The Cadburys helped to finance the investigation into

---

19 Ibid, p. 112.
20 A.G. Gardiner, *The Life of George Cadbury*, London, Cassell, 1925, p. 107.

the truth of this situation and eventually boycotted the Sao Tomé producers in 1909, by which time most of the imported cocoa originated from the Gold Coast. In 1908, the *Evening Standard* accused Cadburys of profiting from the 'monstrous trade in human flesh and blood', prompting a libel action which was won by the Cadburys but resulting in an award of derisory damages.

The Cadburys and other Quaker employers led the way in trying to develop a Christian stance in the management of businesses and eighty Quaker employers assembled at the home of George Cadbury in Birmingham towards the end of the First World War in 1918, this being the first of four such conferences to consider what we should call today Christian ethics in business. At that first conference, Seebohm Rowntree (see below) passed on the view of the London Quaker employers that:

> It was probable that ultimately there would be a demand for a much wider participation in the control of business, but a great many of them felt they could not agree to that at the present time.

Here were the first stirrings of employee participation, but it was to be a long time before it became a reality. It has been said that Quaker employers were prone to the Utopian inclination,[21] but it might be argued that the Quaker employers' attitudes and discussions served as a model for other business leaders with Christian consciences.

Jonathan Dodgson Carr

Here is another example of Quaker influence in the building up of a business with a strong ethical background. Jonathan Dodgson Carr was the son of a Quaker grocer in Kendal who, according to legend, walked from there to Carlisle in 1831 to set up a bread and biscuit factory. Within ten years, he was producing twenty-one varieties and had been appointed biscuit-maker to Queen Victoria. It has been said that 'gain was not J.D. Carr's chief motive.'[22] He was in fact one of the great philanthropists of the Victoria era, dedicated primarily to feeding the poor and needy in Carlisle. Many of his workers were said to be illiterate and lived in slums. He provided them with a school and a library and local building societies to enable them to buy their own homes. His employees had to take a pledge not to touch alcohol and heavy fines were imposed for misconduct such as profane language or wasting time. When J.D. Carr was succeeded by his sons, of whom it has been said that 'both preferred religion to biscuits,'[23] workers were

---

21 Jeremy, *Capitalists and Christians*, p. 171.
22 Margaret Forster, *Rich Desserts and Captain's Thin: a family and their times*, Chatto, 1997.
23 Ibid.

called together to join them in prayer. Unfortunately, the heat of competition compelled them to incorporate the business as a limited company so that it became no longer an exclusive family affair. Today, Carrs of Carlisle are part of United Biscuits, but the strong ethical background continues.

Samuel Courtauld

Samuel Courtauld was a Director and eventually Chairman of the family textile company. He became known for his emphasis on the individuality of workers and the importance of spiritual values in industrial relationships. It may be argued that Courtauld was the most influential industrialist to join the Christian Frontier Council (CFC) founded by Sir Joseph Oldham (1874-1969) with the support of Archbishop William Temple, which grew out of the *Christian Newsletter* edited by Oldham. The functions of the CFC agreed in April 1942 were:

1. to create opportunities outside the sphere of organized religion for the discussion of Christian beliefs, standards and practice, and their application to current problems;
2. to examine the nature of the forces working in modern society in administration, industry, education, etc. and to endeavour to direct them towards a more Christian order; and
3. to understand the efforts being made by various groups to influence these forces and to co-operate with those of their activities which are contributing towards Christian ends.

We are told that Samuel Courtauld was moved by a characteristically Victorian vision of perfection and sought its realization in a harmonious middle way. High profit made him feel guilty.[24]

One of the business people to be greatly influenced by the CFC was George Goyder whose writings on the future of private enterprise inspired some of the more radical experiments, including the Scott-Bader Commonwealth. We return in greater detail to George Goyder's work in Chapter XIV.

Alongside Samuel Courtauld in the early days of the CFC was William Frederik Danvers Smith, Chairman of W.H. Smith & Son (see Lord Hambleden, below).

Viscount Hambleden

Hambleden was one of the first senior businessmen to become involved in the work of Joseph Oldham and William Temple. Within his

---

24 D.C. Coleman, *Courtaulds*, Oxford, 1969.

company, W.H. Smith & Son, he had earned a reputation for caring more about staff welfare than profits. In fact, under his father the company had developed a strong tradition of Christian ethics in the twenty years or so before the First World War. The company's labour relations were characterized by welfare measures which, to some extent, were ahead of their time and, for example, in 1894 a superannuation fund was set up for the salaried staff and a year later a pension fund was established for the 'non-clerkly staff' and union recognition was granted in the years before the First World War.

William Hesketh Lever

Although William Lever, first Lord Leverhume, is credited with creating one of the pioneering welfare schemes in this country, i.e. Port Sunlight, it has been said that he lacked a strong Christian faith and apparently a fellow Congregationalist, Angus Watson of Skipper Sardines has recorded that Lever had no faith in immortality and that 'material things meant much to him because the preparation for the spiritual life was after all secondary.'[25] Lever will no doubt be remembered partly because of his enormous business success, partly because of his considerable wealth (he was apparently worth nearly £3 million in 1912) and for his creation of the company village, Port Sunlight. Perhaps it may be said that his approach was that of paternalism rather than philanthropy. Of the 3,600 or so people who lived in the village in 1907, 3,000 worked in the factory. A company church was built in the village and Lever engaged his own minister. Anyone who lost his job with the firm had only one week in which to vacate his house in the village and he would be transferred to a separate communicant role distinct from the normal church membership. As we have seen, Port Sunlight differed from the Cadbury village of Bournville, which was a garden village designed primarily for working-class tenants. These were of course the days of company paternalism and it has been said that

> the paternalism of the family firm was vastly more important than is generally recognised ... and it was the paternalist employer who most successfully translated dependence into deference.[26]

Sir George Thomas Livesey

Sir George Livesey spent his working life with the South Metropolitan Gas Company, rising through the ranks to become eventually

---

25 Quoted in Jeremy, *Capitalists and Christians*, p. 4.
26 P. Joyce, *Work, Society and Politics*, Brighton, 1980, quoted in Jeremy, *Capitalists and. Christians*, p. 125.

Chairman of the company. He was a devout Anglican and at one time was a Sunday School Superintendent. He believed in profit-sharing for employees and that 'co-partnership is Christianity in business'.[27] It seems remarkable in retrospect that as early as 1886 he admitted foremen to a profit-sharing scheme and three years later in 1889 this was extended to the rest of the workforce. He arranged for their bonuses to be capitalized so that employees became shareholders and, in some cases, became members of the Board. Unfortunately he used the profit-sharing scheme as a means of breaking the power of the union and he caused a major two-month strike when he sought to limit the profit-sharing scheme to non-union members.[28]

Viscount Mackintosh of Halifax

Lord Mackintosh was one of the leading Methodists who took his Christian principles into his business life, but also took his business acumen into church administration. Indeed, over the years, only senior businessmen were admitted to the treasurerships of the major Methodist departments, e.g. J. Arthur Rank (Home Missions Department) and Sir Josiah Stamp (National Children's Home) and in the 1950s Lord Mackintosh became Treasurer of the Home Missions Department. In this he continued the tradition of earlier years when he had been President of the National Sunday School Union and President of the World Council of Christian Education and Sunday School Association (holding the latter post for no less than thirty years).

Viscount Nuffield

William Richard Morris (Viscount Nuffield) must stand high in any list of business philanthropists. He was not renowned for Christian works as such and, indeed, claimed to be 'not much interested in religion', but he is an outstanding example of ethical stewardship of wealth. It is said that he started out in business life (making bicycles) with a capital of £4.00 and over the years his benefactions for hospitals, medical research, medical schools and other medical services in this country and abroad totalled no less than £13 million.

Sir Joseph Pease

Joseph Pease was a Quaker (in 1882 he became the first Quaker Baronet) who took his Christian principles into the very considerable Pease empire of banking, mining, railway and textile industries and

---

27 Francis Goodall, *George Thomas Livesey*, (DBB).
28 Jeremy, *Capitalists and Christians*, p. 156.

was among the first employers in coal mining to accept the concept of trade union recognition. It is possible that his concern for his employees, and particularly his determination to keep them in employment, outweighed the group's responsibilities to its shareholders, especially in times of recession. When, in 1902, Barclay & Co. (being a merger of a number of Quaker banking partnerships) made an approach to take over the Pease Bank in Darlington, an audit of the books showed the Bank to be insolvent. (Indeed, in more recent years, some of us engaged in front-line finance have seen businesses going downhill, particularly in times of recession, partly because of an overweening and worthy concern to retain the workforce in employment.)

It has been said that the Quaker Pease family, in their collieries in the North-East, gave preference to Methodists as employees because of the relatively harmonious relations between employers and the mainly Methodist union leadership.[29] Apparently, however, by the early part of the twentieth century the Pease family had changed to a more comfortable lifestyle and had left the Society of Friends, a not untypical development in the years when many of the larger companies were moving away from the paternalism of owner-management.[30]

Joseph Rank and J. Arthur Rank

Here is another instance of father and son following in a great Christian tradition. As for the father, we cannot do better than quote again from David Jeremy:

> A particularly awesome father was Joseph Rank. Among his fellow Wesleyans he had the reputation of 'thorough, God-fearing uprightness' and that was vigorously relayed to his eight children, especially his three sons. Every Sunday morning, afternoon and evening, rain or shine, there were services at the Wesleyan Chapel when the family lived at Hull and Joseph Arthur Rank was too young to be sent away to school. At home, Joseph banished alcohol, forbade smoking and frowned on public dances and theatre-going. His passion to serve Christ occupied nearly every moment outside his business hours. Even within those hours he fearlessly told his employees what his religion meant: 'The business has been very successful. I don't put all the success down to myself. I put a lot of it down to God. I also put a lot of it down to you, that is office staff, millers, all of you.' In accordance with his Christian principles he closed his mills after midnight on Saturday until Monday morning. He gave generously of his income and his time to his church. Such a formidable example of piety his sons must have found difficult to follow. His youngest boy, however, never allowed fame and fortune as J. Arthur Rank, film magnate, to disturb his faith as a Methodist.[31]

29 McLeod, *Religion and the People of Western Europe 1789-1970*, p. 111.
30 Ibid, p. 111.
31 Jeremy, *Capitalists and Christians*, p. 77.

That youngest son, J. Arthur Rank, later Baron Rank of Sutton Scotney, did not indeed allow circumstances to disturb his faith. His Christian commitment began when he started Sunday School teaching in Reigate Wesleyan Methodist Chapel shortly after the First World War, in which he served in an ambulance unit. He became interested in religious films and in 1933 founded the Religious Film Society. He was later to establish Pinewood Studios and acquired control of Gaumont British Picture Corporation Limited and Odeon Theatres Limited. Until his death he maintained his link with the Methodist Church and was, as we have said, Treasurer of the Home Missions Department.

Benjamin Seebohm Rowntree

The father and son tradition was also seen in the Rowntree family. Joseph Rowntree (1801-59), a Quaker grocer in York, had become involved in the educational schemes of the Society of Friends. His two sons, Joseph (1836-1925) and Benjamin followed him in the business, of which the younger Joseph became Chairman in 1897. He took a particular interest in the welfare of his employees. Seebohm Rowntree followed his brother as Chairman in 1923, having served for three years as the Industrial Welfare Director of the Ministry of Munitions during the First World War. His publications include *Human Needs of Labour*; *Human Factor in Business*; *Poverty, a Study of Town Life*; and *Poverty and Progress*. It was Seebohm Rowntree who, as we have said, reported to the Quaker Conference in 1918 that 'there would be a demand for a much wider participation in the control of business, but a great many of them felt they could not agree to that at the present time.'

Josiah Charles Stamp

The last of this short-list is Lord Stamp, a leading Methodist layman who was to exercise great influence on the relationship of Christianity to business in the 1930s. He was a member of the Royal Commission on Income Tax in 1919, subsequently becoming a director of ICI, a member of the Court of the Bank of England and President of the London, Midland and Scottish Railway in the years 1926-41. Thus, he was Chairman (President) of the second largest employer company in the United Kingdom. He was an author of a number of books with an ethical content, e.g. *British Incomes and Property* (1916); *Wealth and Taxable Capacity* (1922); *The Christian Ethic as an Economic Factor* (1926); and *Motive and Method in a Christian Order* (1936). In that last publication he wrote:

No economic problems can be solved by Christian principles alone, though equally few could be solved 'without those principles as a powerful element in the solution'.

There was nothing wrong with wealth as such. 'Rich people are not intrinsically wicked by the possession of more than others, but by their attitude of mind towards their possessions.'[32]

Certain basic truths emerge from any study of what we have called Christian philanthropy. First, the early part of the twentieth century was the twilight for the tradition of owner/managers and family owners. The responsibility for management was gradually delegated to professional managers who were, and are, accountable to boards of directors, who in turn were, and are, accountable to shareholders. The entrepreneurs of earlier days were accountable only to themselves and, as many would see it, to their employees. Thus, David Jeremy tells us that:

> The interests of professional managers, whether their background was in accountancy or engineering, were not the same as those of family firm owners. Professional managers sought profits in order to build up their firms' organisational size and, with it, their own status and power ... They were much less interested in 'community based entrepreneurship' than in national or international organisational efficiency.[33]

In any case, if paternalistic employers, and in some cases their craftsmen, continued to relate their religion to their work,

> the logic of economic development was against them as ever larger firms took on an impersonal, bureaucratic character and human values got lost in the violence of the war between capital and labour.

Secondly, that tendency towards 'ever larger firms' made it increasingly difficult for the Christian employee to make any significant impact.

Thirdly, as we moved further into this century, perhaps because of the disruption of the war years, the seeds of Christian living were not so widely sown in Sunday Schools, church schools and even secular day schools. Thus, proportionately less of the latter-day entrepreneurs came from an ingrained Christian background compared with our specimen selection of Christian philanthropists listed above.

Nevertheless, in 1961, Bishop Wand was to write:

> If you ask (the average Englishman) whether he was a religious man, he would probably say 'no', but he would regard it as the greatest insult if you told him he was no Christian.[34]

---

32 Josiah Stamp, *Motive and Method in a Christian Order*, 1936, p. 129.
33 Jeremy, *Capitalists and Christians*, p. 17.
34 J.W.C. Wand, *Anglicanism in History and Today*, London, 1961, p. 179.

Around the same period approximately 90 per cent of the population claimed religious affiliation, viz. 60 per cent Anglican; 12 per cent Roman Catholic; 12 per cent Free Church; 1 per cent Jews; and 5 per cent other faiths.[35]

Despite the overt acknowledgement of Christian beliefs, the relationship between the Church and the business world has, it seems, diminished throughout the twentieth century. In the early part of the century, 28 per cent of laymen in the Church Assembly were company directors, but this figure had reduced to 20 per cent in the 1930s and to 17 per cent in 1955.[36] In the Methodist Church, there was traditionally a high proportion of businessmen among the senior lay preachers – as high as 77 per cent in the 1930s, but this dropped to approximately 50 per cent in more recent times.

Perhaps it is not surprising that Church and business drifted apart, bearing in mind that for two centuries leading up to the end of the nineteenth the notion of 'two kingdoms', i.e. religion and social ethics, had been tacitly accepted and kept resolutely apart. This was principally the influence of a protestantism which

> regards the secular and the religious aspects of life ... as parallel and independent provinces governed by different laws, judged by different standards and amenable to different authorities.[37]

This dualism was emphasized by Adam Smith, the father of modern economics, who in effect banished religion and morality and paternalism from business life, virtually relegating religion to the private sphere of the individual.[38] It was not until comparatively recent times that the philosophy of the 'two kingdoms' was gradually rejected and industry was to be seen as 'an instrument for establishing the Kingdom of God on earth'.[39]

It may be argued that the horrors and upheaval of the Second World War brought about new thinking in the relationship of Church to business and politics, but there is no doubt that it was William Temple and his associate, J.H. Oldham who led the way with the Christian Frontier Council (see page 68) and what some regarded as Christian Socialism, but by that time only a small proportion, somewhere between 5 per cent and 10 per cent, of leading businessmen were thought to have anything like the Christian commitment displayed by the Christian entrepreneurs described earlier in this chapter.[40]

That which we have called business includes trade, wealth creation,

35 John D. Gay, *The Geography of Religion of England*, London, 1971.
36 Jeremy, *Capitalists and Christians*, p. 287.
37 R.H. Tawney, *Religion and the Rise of Capitalism*, Penguin, 1939, p. 279.
38 S.G. Checkland, *Cultural Factors and British Business Men 1815-1914*.
39 Methodist Church Declaration of Conference on Social Questions, London, 1959.
40 See Jeremy, *Capitalists and Christians*, p. 412.

the profit motive, 'value added' and the economic environment in which business operates. In a recent article in *The Economist*[41] it is suggested that, whereas most people will admit their ignorance of physics or biology, 'the armchair economist is convinced that he knows exactly what he is talking about', but

> the public and their politicians are treated to perpetual squabbles about the exact effects of raising interest rates or of cutting capital taxes or whatever and concluded that economists disagree about everything and understand nothing.

It is not surprising, therefore, that over the centuries theology and economics have trodden different paths and that Archbishop Ramsey admitted that he was 'not versed in economics' and was 'unable to suggest particular economic policies'[42] and his successor, Archbishop Coggan considered that:

> *the Christian cannot, just because he is a Christian, lay claim to any special insight into the mysteries of economic problems.*[43]

---

41 *The Economist*, 23 August 1997.
42 General Synod Report, Spring 1974, Vol. 4, No. 1, p. 3.
43 Ibid. Summer 1974, Vol. 4, No. 2, p. 3.

PART II

The Present

CHAPTER X

Capitalism . . . or What?

Buying and selling are immemorial human activities found in every major
culture, but the geist (or spirit) of such activities varies. In the past there had
been commerce, banks, industries, factories for silk and other goods. What
then is different? In capitalist societies commerce is given a new meaning.[1]

The ending of the Victorian era and the beginning of a new century
provides us with a somewhat arbitrary line between 'the past' and 'the
present'. It is a tidy delineation because, as we approach the
millennium, it enables us to look at the twentieth century as a separate
epoch and to assess the impact of Christianity on modern business after
2,000 years of history. More particularly, the present century has been,
and is, a time of industrial development, international trade, instant
communication, population growth and technological advance far
beyond anything which could have been anticipated even one hundred
years ago.

We turn then to the predominant flavour of economic and political
life this century, viz. capitalism. But what is capitalism? We can say that
it is the use of physical, financial or human resources to produce
wealth. Within the limits of that definition capitalism is as old as
mankind. Even in pre-Biblical times the resources of the land and of
livestock were employed to produce a yield even if only sufficient for
everyday sustenance. Indeed, as we have already remarked, there is an
etymological link between cattle and chattels and capital.

Capitalism has come to mean different things to different people. In
modern usage, the term normally denotes a system of economic
management governing the production of goods and services in free
markets where the price mechanism reflects supply and demand with a
minimum of government control. According to Adam Smith,[2] it is a
matter of human propensity 'to truck, barter and exchange one thing
for another', words echoed to some extent in the above quotation from
Max Weber. Indeed, it was Weber who first associated modern
capitalism with the work ethic of Protestant Christianity. As we have
seen (page 44), it was in contrast to the Catholic emphasis on the
sacraments and dogma of the Church that Protestantism stressed hard

---

1 Max Weber, *The Protestant Ethic and the Spirit of Capitalism.*
2 Smith, *An Enquiry into the Nature and Causes of the Wealth of Nations.*

work, diligence and the concept of serving God in one's everyday vocation. Weber argued that these characteristics laid the foundation for business and the profit motive of our modern times. Whatever the accuracy of this it seems that, until approximately 200 years ago, capitalism as we now know it hardly existed. Whilst man may not have been happy with his lot, he did not necessarily strive to improve it. Economic growth was not sought after. The earth's resources went largely unexplored and in a predominantly agrarian society there was little scope for capital improvement.

Weber observes that his grandfather's linen business lacked the capitalist spirit. He did not seek to improve his business, but was content to make a modestly comfortable living from it. His eldest son caught the capitalist geist and opted for development. The essence of the capitalist spirit for Weber is its theme of sustained growth. The communism/socialism of the modern world was a reaction to the perceived exploitation of 'the masses' by the eighteenth- and nineteenth-century capitalists.

Writing from the vantage point of the early days of this century, Ernst Troeltsch tells us:

> This economic ethic [the work ethic] became middle class, one might almost say lower middle class, capitalist and it bore all the signs of the results of the capitalist attitude towards life – systematic division of labour, emphasis upon specialisation – the feeling for advantage and profit, the abstract duty of work, the obligation towards property as towards something great which ought to be maintained and increased for its own sake. The owner of wealth or property is 'the Lord's steward' and administers a divine gift which has been entrusted to him.[3]

Unhappily, this concept of stewardship did not carry far into the capitalism of this century partly, we suspect, because of the gradual separation of ownership from management, the increased incorporation of businesses, the diversity of shareholdings, the crossing of national boundaries and most of all the enormous growth of some corporations.

There have been many ethical objections levelled against capitalism. In his major work, *The Spirit of Democratic Capitalism* (a book which has already been translated into a dozen or more languages), Michael Novak, a former socialist, lists some of the more common criticisms of capitalism.[4] They are:

1. The corruption of affluence.
2. Advertising to appeal to the worst in people.

---

3 Troeltsch, *The Social Teaching of the Christian Churches*, p. 812.
4 Michael Novak, *The Spirit of Democratic Capitalism*, New York, Madison Books, 1991, p. 32.

3. Structural irresponsibility – the politicians pander to the desire of the population to live beyond its means.
4. An ambitious, adversarial class.
5. The decline of aristocracy with its tradition of patronage – the standards of the market are really the standards of artistic and intellectual excellence.
6. Envy.
7. Taste – described as bourgeois and philistine.

Over many years the objections of socialists to the operation of the market were (again according to Novak)[5]:

1. Markets resolve problems according to the purchasing powers of those who have money.
2. Modern advertising distorts the judgement of those who have money.
3. Large corporations are able to place administered prices on their goods.
4. Markets work in a way that the rich get richer, the poor poorer.

Novak is critical of Weber's failure to recognize the connection between economic liberty and political liberty. On the other hand, perhaps a weakness of *Novak*'s case is that he too closely identifies Christian motivation with democratic government – after all, the dominant party democratically elected at any one time does not have a monopoly of Christian virtue. Novak makes eight key points in his characterization and defence of capitalism as follows (the italics are ours):

1. The central theme of a democratic capitalist society is the triune structure in the division of the political system from the moral-cultural system and of the economic system from both. Each of these systems has its own special institutions and methods, disciplines and standards, purposes and limits, attractions and repulsions.[6] *It is difficult to disagree with this concept in a modern democratic society.*
2. A democratic capitalist society is essentially pluralistic. Among the systems known to humankind, only democratic capitalism has tried to preserve the sphere of the person inviolable. 'It glories in divergence, dissent and singularity.'[7] Because of the pluralistic structure of a democratic capitalist society, Novak rejects the

5 Ibid, p. 106.
6 Novak, *The Spirit of Democratic Capitalism*, p. 171.
7 Ibid, p. 65.

traditional view of a 'sacred canopy' because, he argues, at the
spiritual core of a pluralistic society there is an empty shrine. 'That
shrine is left empty in the knowledge that no one word, image or
symbol is worthy of what all seek there.'[8] *This has a certain appeal
because even the most evangelising Christian would not wish to
command the spiritual life of all around.*

3. The doctrine of 'unintended consequences' turns the eyes of the
political economist away from the moral intentions of individuals
and towards the final social consequences of their actions.[9] *This is in
contrast to Adam Smith's view that a system designed as closely as
possible to fit human character is best designed to unleash human
creativity.*[10] *The Christian may have difficulty in accepting Novak's
view – it is difficult to concede that the moral intentions of
individuals should be subjugated to the ultimate social aims.*

4. The creation of wealth: Novak draws a distinction between ancient
concepts of money as an identifiable, impersonal chattel (the miser
in his counting house) and the modern view of money with a time
value and a productive value. He quotes Walter Lippmann (*The
Good Society*):

> For the first time in human history man had come upon a way of
> producing wealth in which the good fortune of others multiplied their
> own. Money has become less materialistic. It is in part a symbol of social
> health and confidence in the future and it is linked to potential
> productivity ... It has come to be seen as the key to development and
> peace and justice.

Novak disposes of the assumption that there is a fixed 'pie' – that
one party can gain only at the expense of another, i.e. *the zero-sum
society. It is difficult to disagree that money has both a 'time value'
and a 'productive value': it may be arguable whether it has become
'less materialistic'.*

5. Many of the things today described as resources were not known as
such a hundred years ago. Wealth is created primarily through
practical intelligence. 'The cause of wealth lies more in the human
spirit than in matter.'[11]

> Economic activity is impossible in isolation since it consists in intelligent,
> voluntary transactions. The word 'commerce' means not only buying and
> selling but the coming together of peoples. Its transactions are reasoned,
> lawlike, contractual.[12]

8 Ibid, p. 53.
9 Ibid, p. 89.
10 Smith, *An Enquiry into the Nature and Causes of the Wealth of Nations*.
11 Novak, *The Spirit of Democratic Capitalism*, p. 103.
12 Ibid, p. 105.

Novak quotes Montesquieu's '*Esprit de Lois*':

> Commerce cures destructive prejudices. It polishes and softens barbaric morals. It makes men less provincial and more humane. The spirit of commerce unites nations. Commerce obliges nations to be pacific from principle.

On the whole we hope this may be so – but it is not a universal law. Commerce can be rough, unfair, one-sided, exploitive and prejudicial. Also there are those who would be deeply mistrustful of the economic self-interest of the majority.

6. Novak emphasizes the interdependence brought about by technology and trade, making the world more like a 'global village' and also what he calls the 'rich pattern of association' and 'community of values', thus producing a new type of human being, 'the communitarian individual'.[13] *We discuss communitarianism a little later, but so far we are a long way from a virtuous 'global village'.*

7. The family:

> ... each individual life being short, the most profound of economic motives is almost always family-oriented. This is the motivation that adequately explains herculean economic activities. This is the only rational motivation for long-range economic decisions. For in the long run – the individual economic agent is dead. Only his progeny survives to enjoy the fruits of his labours, intelligence and concern.

Novak might have been echoing the words of St James: '... riches last no longer than the flowers in the grass.' ...it is the same with the rich man: 'his business goes on; he himself perishes.'

8. There is a theology of democratic capitalism: Christianity has helped to shape the ethos of democratic capitalism but this ethos forbids Christians (or any others) from attempting to command the system.[14] There is a great gap between the word of God and systems of economic, political, social and cultural thought in modern societies.

> Many attempt to judge the present world by the standards of the Gospels as though the world were ready to live according to them. Sin is not so easily overcome.[15]

We can but agree.

Novak acknowledges that a free economy is not necessarily a Christian economy but concedes, quoting from J. Philip Wogaman's *The Christian Century, 1990,* that:

---

13 Ibid, p. 142.
14 Ibid, p. 68.
15 Ibid, p. 343.

Capitalism cannot be made to function in the human interest without a little love and human kindness.

Capitalism ... or What?

Are there any serious, Christian alternatives to capitalism? Since the Industrial Revolution only two politico-economic systems have claimed the allegiance of mankind, viz. capitalism and socialism. Socialism to many is an ideal, a vision of a better life, a better world of justice and equality. Out of the socialist ideal grew communism based on the ideology of Karl Marx and Friedrich Engels who, in the *Communist Manifesto* of 1848, saw communism as the final stage in the development of socialism with the abolition of private property and social exploitation. For Marx, an atheist, socialism could only be brought about by violence because the owners of the means of production could not be expected to give up their power and privileges without a struggle. In 1978, Leszek Kolakowski was to write:

> Perfect equality can only be imagined under a system of extreme despotism ... In real life, more equality means more government, absolute equality means absolute government.[16]

Just as simple capitalism can be seen in early societies, so socialism or communism was known to exist, to a degree, both in Old Testament and early Christian times. The Israelites knew a degree of common ownership because, as we have seen, the land and its resources belonged to God and no one could alienate in perpetuity the tribal inheritance. All that could be sold was the right to the crops for the remaining years until the next jubilee when the land reverted to its original tribal family. A degree of common ownership applied among the early Christians for, as St Luke tells us in the Acts of the Apostles:

> The faithful all lived together and owned everything in common; they sold their goods and possessions and shared out the proceeds among themselves according to what each one needed.[17]

And again:

> No one claimed for his own use anything that he had, as everything they owned was held in common.[18]

This commonality of property appears to have applied more in Jerusalem than among the other early churches and it took the form of a sale of assets and the sharing of the proceeds rather than common

---

16 Leszek Kolakowski, *Main Currents of Marxism*, Oxford, Clarendon Press, 1978, Vol. III, p. 528.
17 *Acts of the Apostles* 2:44.
18 Ibid, 4:32.

ownership of property in the accepted sense. Nevertheless, here are the seeds of a Christian form of communism.

Lord Griffiths tells us that:

> As an ideal, socialism is as old as civilisation. In the tradition of western philosophy there have always been those who long for a society in which injustice and poverty were abolished and people able to share their material possessions. In the *republic* Plato outlined an ideal social system within which private property was abolished... The experience of the early Christian community in Jerusalem in sharing their worldly goods is evidence for many of the material communism which is implicit in the great commandment 'Love your neighbour as yourself ...' In the mediaeval period numerous communal experiments were set up, a number associated with monasticism, which involved the adoption of their members of communist principles. Thomas More's vision of Utopia is that of a society in which private property would be abolished, in which the state would provide food, clothing, housing, education and medical treatment for all its members and in which the working day would be only six hours in length.[19]

Nearly 500 years after Thomas More, the once socialist Novak describes socialism in remarkably similar terms, viz:

> Positively, socialism once meant the abolition of private property; state ownership of the means of production through the nationalisation of industry; state control over all aspects of the economy; the abolition of 'bourgeois democracy' through the creation of a classless society; and an international order based upon a class analysis transcending national, cultural and linguistic frontiers. Socialism means the banishing of the profit motive which was judged to be the root cause of exploitation of labour.[20]

Despite the 'extreme despotism' (Kolakowski, above) of communism, there were those who clung understandably to its moral ideals. Thus, in 1974 Stuart Hampshire, joint editor of 'Epilogue in the Socialist Idea' (a report of a conference of leading socialists held in England) was still able to write:

> For me, socialism is not so much a theory as a set of moral injunctions, which seem to me clearly right and rationally justifiable: first, that the elimination of poverty ought to be the first priority of government after defence; secondly, that as great inequalities in wealth between social groups lead to inequalities in power and in freedom of action, they are generally unjust and need to be redressed by governmental action; thirdly, that democratically elected governments ought to ensure that primary and basic human needs are given priority within the economic system, even if this involves some loss in the aggregate of goods and services which would otherwise be available.[21]

Thus, there is to a degree a convergence to a point where many have

---

19 Griffiths, *Morality and the Marketplace*, p. 41.
20 Novak, *The Spirit of Democratic Capitalism*, p. 189.
21 Stuart Hampshire, *Epilogue in the Socialist Idea*, New York, Basic Books, 1974, p. 249.

regarded themselves as Christian socialists. A little surprisingly, however, Pope Pius XI described 'Christian socialism' as a contradiction in terms and held 'no one can be at the same time a sincere Catholic and a true socialist.'[22]

It is possible that what may be achieved among a small group of disciples or in the confines of a monastic brotherhood, or even in visions of 'Utopia', is not possible among nations or large corporations or multi-national institutions without virtually totalitarian government in control. The socialist dream of controlling the means of 'production, distribution and exchange' is possible only from the commanding heights – for communism to succeed it must have a monopoly of power. As we know, however, 'power tends to corrupt and absolute power corrupts absolutely.'[23] Absolute power also sows the seeds of its own destruction with its own elite, its malign control, its secrecy, its corruption and its greed. To quote Kolakowski again:

> Wherever communism is in power, the ruling class transforms it into an ideology whose real sources are in nationalism, racism or imperialism. In this way communism has produced its own grave diggers.[24]

To the Christian, there is the additional concern that totally planned economies leave little room for personal Christian stewardship.

There was a telling comment by the business philosopher, Charles Handy in the Spring 1996 edition of the London Business School *Alumni News*. Professor Handy suggests that the premise of Anglo-American capitalism will not hold up in the world of today. That premise is that the people who provide the money own the property, i.e. own the company. But now people are really the companies' assets. Some companies are worth ten or even thirty times more in the market place than the value of their tangible assets. This is the market's assessment of the intellectual property contained in the people in the business – their competence, their experience, the research, the knowledge and expertise. 'In what sense,' asks Charles Handy,

> is it moral and in what sense is it practical for the people who provide the money to own the people who work in the business?

He asks:

> What is it all for? In the new sort of economics, wealth does not trickle down like it used to. In the new economics, you get richer by employing fewer people and wealth stays at the top.[25]

22 Pope Pius XI, *Quadragesimo Anno*, para.120.
23 The oft-quoted words of Lord Acton (1887).
24 Kolakowski, *Main Currents of Marxism*, p. 529.
25 Professor Charles Handy in *Alumni News*, Newsletter of London Business School Alumni Association, Spring 1996.

Self-Help and Mutual Benefit

Capitalism is inevitably associated with the profit motive, whether in the wider field of macro-economics or the more personal and domestic life. As we have seen, profit as such is not condemned in either the Old or New Testaments, but in Britain from the late eighteenth century onwards there developed a number of associations of a non-profit-making nature, many of which survive to this day. This was partly a manifestation of the non-conformist conscience and partly perhaps a general distaste for the concept of joint-stock companies and, in later years, the 'casino' (as some would have it) of the stock exchange. For the most part, however, these non-profit organizations grew out of a spirit of self-help, not least for those people who might otherwise have been passed over by the growth of capitalism. Typical among these institutions were the building societies, the mutual life offices, the friendly societies, the credit unions and, in time, the co-operative societies.

The first building society was established in Birmingham in 1775. All the early societies were 'terminating' in the sense that they were designed to terminate at a fixed date or when some other objective, specified in the rules, had been attained. Nowadays, all modern building societies are 'permanent'. In the early societies, which were small and local, the members would subscribe funds which would be used first to buy some land and then to build a house. Further money would be used to buy further land and build further houses. The houses would be allocated by ballot among the members or, in some cases, the right to a house would be sold by auction among the members. In time, money was subscribed by other people who had money to invest but did not necessarily wish to buy a house through the society.

By 1900, there were 2,286 building societies in existence, but by the mid-1990s the number had been reduced by mergers and conversion into banks to approximately eighty societies.

There were two remarkable aspects of building societies. The first is that the public showed such confidence in, and respect for, the various societies that by the 1980s they accounted for over 50 per cent of all personal savings. The second remarkable fact is that, although building societies made profits, these were always ploughed back into the society and never distributed to members (with the exception of the mergers and conversions to public liability companies in recent years), notwithstanding that the members legally owned the societies. No investor ever lost money in a building society despite one or two mishaps. As well as being a safe haven for savings, these non-profit-making organizations were largely responsible for the comparatively high level of house ownership in Britain today. One could make a strong ethical argument in favour of mutual societies.

A similar mutual concept led to the formation of life assurance societies. The oldest survivor of the life assurance offices was founded in 1762,[26] made possible by the work of James Dodson, FRS who, in or around the year 1750, made a study of the ages of people on gravestones and constructed the first mortality table. Although, in modern times, a number of mutual life offices have converted, or are in process of converting, to public liability companies (or merging with existing insurance companies), the main reason for this is the availability of additional capital by the process of listing on the stock exchange. Nevertheless, for many societies the concept of mutuality holds good and the profits are shared with the policyholders, not with outside shareholders.

In similar vein, friendly societies came into being under an act of 1793 and are governed in their modern form by the Friendly Societies Act, 1992. These benign, mutual, non-profit-making societies were described in the original Act as:

> Societies of good fellowship formed for the purpose of raising by subscriptions of the members or by voluntary contributions, a stock or fund for the mutual relief or maintenance of the members in old age, sickness and infirmity or for the relief of the widows and children of deceased members.[27]

These somewhat stringent requirements continue with some modification to the present day, their value being recognized by the degree of tax exemption which they enjoy.

Yet another form of non-profit organization is the credit union. In the United States, credit unions have enjoyed considerable popularity and there are believed to be over forty million members. They have not been so widely accepted in this country, but there has been a modest surge in the numbers of credit unions since the passing of the Credit Unions Act of 1979. These non-profit-making mutual organizations were sometimes referred to as 'do-it-yourself banks'. A credit union is a financial co-operative which accumulates members' savings and provides the members with low cost credit. They come under the overall supervision of the Chief Registrar of Friendly Societies and the members must be united by some common bond, e.g. members of the same trade union or club or residents in the same area or employees of the same firm. The maximum permitted membership is 5,000 and the maximum permitted savings per member is £3,000. A member may borrow up to the amount of his personal investment plus £2,000 and

---

26 The Society for Equitable Assurances on Lives and Survivorships, forerunner of the Equitable Life Assurance Society of the present day.
27 Friendly Societies Act, 1793.

the rate of interest is limited to 1 per cent per month on the outstanding balance of the loan. Traditionally, they have sought to meet a social need, not only in the provision of loans but in an educational and advisory way on matters of finance.

Outside the field of finance, the Co-operative Wholesale Society enjoyed considerable growth, again until recent years, the profits being divided among the members according to their respective levels of expenditure in the co-operative stores. Out of the Co-operative Wholesale Society's banking department grew the Co-operative Bank, which is now among the major banking institutions of this country and which has in itself sought to pursue a course of ethical business (see pages 132 and 170).

There remains 'communitarianism', a grouping together of people with a common origin, or common language, or common heritage or a common philosophy or religion. In many cases groupings arose from 'the need for identity and mutual support'.[28]

According to Dr Hugh McLeod, by 1907 there were twenty different languages and dialects spoken in the Ruhr and many of the workers, attracted there from other countries, sought to establish churches similar to those they had left behind.

Sometimes the 'community' is that of the small village in which all share the same values. In the United States, local communities would often depend on ethnic origins, e.g. the Irish, the Italians, the Spaniards, the Poles, etc. Novak writes of the co-operative and fraternal nature of daily activities. Families helped each other in putting up barns, building churches and schools, roads and bridges.[29]

In earlier times, this communitarianism had overstepped the mark when the colonizing Puritans in America sought to establish the 'City of God' where the civic franchise depended on membership of the Church. In more recent times, Novak has looked for the community spirit in world development, the business corporation, the interdependence of nations and the ethos of co-operation, i.e. a community of values among varying cultures. Herein lies the seed of the 'global village', the subject of which we shall return to in Part III. In general, however, attempts at Christian communitarianism, other than pure monasticism, have failed and it is often an escape from the realities of life. Strange to say, even the most isolated community appears to need the profit motive for, as Dr Johnson remarked:

Man is never so innocently occupied as when he is getting money.[30]

---

28 McLeod, *Religion and the People of Western Europe 1789-1970*, p. 76.
29 Novak, *The Spirit of Democratic Capitalism*, p. 135.
30 James Boswell, *The Life of Samuel Johnson*, London, James Blackwood & Co., 1791.

CHAPTER XI

Contemporary Concerns

No-one wants to do business with anyone they think is unprincipled.[1]

These words spoken by Andrew Buxton, President of the Chartered Institute of Bankers, at the President's Dinner in January 1997 go to the very heart of modern business ethics. Mr Buxton went on to say:

> What is ethical practice in one place may not be ethical in another and we must be guided by the belief that context matters when deciding what is right and what is wrong.

It follows that trust and ethics go together and that businesses with high ethical standards generate a feeling of trust. We will refer a little later in this chapter to the ethics of banking, but there is little doubt that across the entire business spectrum increasing importance is attached to ethical standards and an increasing awareness of the need for 'trust' in business life. Andrew Buxton tells us that 90 per cent of the top 500 companies in the United States have written codes of conduct. In our own country, nearly 150 leading companies have introduced codes of business standards.[2]

The list of subjects in which business standards have come to be important is almost endless. It includes advertising, bribery, charitable giving, competition, conflicts of interest, conservation and environmental responsibility, donations and gifts, human rights, insider dealing, responsibilities to shareholders, customers and employees, pension fund provision, remuneration, safety at work, tax evasion and 'whistle-blowing'. In days gone by, many of these ethical standards were taken for granted and some may think that (Andrew Buxton again) 'an ethical code merely re-states motherhood with a bit of apple pie thrown in.'[3]

There is little doubt that the modern preoccupation with business ethics exceeds anything found in history. This is partly because some age-old standards have been taken down and dusted, but more particularly modern business has become more complicated, more global and, in some areas, more specialized so that fraud, manipulation

---

1 Andrew Buxton, Chairman of Barclays Bank and President of the Chartered Institute of Bankers, speaking at the President's Dinner, 15 January 1997.
2 *The Institute of Business Ethics*, London, 1996.
3 Andrew Buxton, op. cit.

and unjust enrichment are not always apparent above the surface. Here then are some examples of present-day concern about ethical standards in business.

In November 1994 a MORI poll found that two-thirds of young people aged from fifteen to thirty-five were experiencing a moral crisis and moral leadership was found to be most lacking among business leaders, newspapers and politicians. Out of concern for such declining standards, the National Westminster Bank, jointly with *The Times*, introduced a Business Ethic Essay Competition inviting undergraduates of any discipline to answer the question 'Can a Competitive Business be Ethical?' In a more recent year, the subject was 'Would you, as the Managing Director of a construction company, build a controversial by-pass through an area of outstanding beauty?'

It is significant that environmental considerations have assumed much greater importance in present-day corporate philosophies. Here, there are echoes of the Old Testament where land was seen as an inheritance from Yahweh (see page 21). In the financial world, perhaps no bank more than the Co-operative Bank has championed environmental causes. In recent times the Managing Director, Terry (now Lord) Thomas, has written that:

> The Co-operative Bank is committed to environmental best practice, having contributed £1 million to set up The National Centre for Business and Ecology, which aims to provide an environmental service for the small and medium enterprise.[4]

Perhaps of wider significance is the work of Business in the Community. In the 1995 Report, Mr Colin Sharman, Senior Partner of KPMG, wrote:

> Today, business relationships are not merely driven by economic factors. Profit, technological advance, employee participation, production location – all have ethical and moral dimensions. They affect the quality of the environment, the use of natural resources, the safety of consumers and the hopes of families.[5]

How significant that Mr Peter Hunt, Head of Community and Regional Affairs at Shell UK, should be able to write in the same Report:

> There has been a fundamental shift in the way business organisations are viewed over the last two decades. We have moved from a concept of ownership to one of stewardship and that raises important issues of legitimacy for companies.

Here is a theme to which we shall return in the closing chapters when

---

4 *The Times*, 14 September 1996.
5 *Business in the Community*, Foreword to the Annual Report, 1995.

we consider the corporate structures of business and the stakeholder concept of corporate responsibility.

There is perhaps a touch of irony in the fact that Shell itself, at its 1997 Annual Meeting, was confronted by a shareholder resolution calling on the company to establish new procedures for dealing with environmental and human rights issues. This was consequent upon the sinking of the Brent Spar oil storage rig at sea and the alleged record of the company in its environmental and human rights policies in Nigeria. The shareholder group concerned consisted of eighteen public and private pension funds, five religious institutions, an academic fund and individuals from a pressure group called the Ecumenical Committee on Corporate Responsibility.

There are increasing signs that more and more companies wrestle with their consciences over what they regard as their shareholder interests. Many companies have ethics committees, ethics officers and, as we have said above, ethics codes. Problems arise, however, particularly among multi-national companies when strategic decisions have to be taken regarding investment in countries with repressive regimes or, by western standards, unacceptable attitudes to child labour, slave labour, safety at work and so on. But, according to *The Economist*,

> to expect firms to behave well is easy; defining good behaviour is much harder. The allegation that multi-nationals are exploiting the third world is often misguided. Usually the 'exploitation' consists of letting developing countries make use of what economists would call sources of comparative advantage – cheap labour, say, or a greater tolerance of pollution. That is how poor countries grow less poor. Often, people in the rich world who rail against the exploitation of the poor are mere protectionists in disguise, afraid that competition might steal their own jobs.[6]

In America, in particular, there is an increasing outcry against what is regarded by some as the exploitation of female and child workers in developing countries, especially at a time when American executive salaries are soaring. On the other hand, Irwin Stelzer, writing in the *Sunday Times*, argues:

> It is doubtful that workers in developing countries would be helped if American companies were to curtail their overseas manufacturing. An executive of a company making coat hangers in China said the wages he pays, now averaging $25 per month, have made his workers the richest people in their villages.[7]

Meanwhile, in the United Kingdom at least one charity, Christian Aid called on supermarkets to draw up a code of practice for their

---

6 *The Economist*, 20 July 1996.
7 The *Sunday Times* – 'Sweatshops Put Heat on Bosses', 28 July 1996.

suppliers and to mark clearly the countries of origin of their own-brand products. In a report published in October 1996, the charity claimed to have uncovered punishing work conditions, pesticide poisoning, low wages and discrimination on farms and plantations in countries such as Brazil, South Africa, Thailand and Peru. The charity urged supermarkets to adopt a twelve-point model code stipulating standards such as minimum age for workers, working hours and conditions and union representation.

In the first year of its campaign, Christian Aid maintains that consumers have become aware of 'their enormous spending power, viz. £52 billion a year in the major supermarkets'. In May 1997, a MORI poll showed that 92 per cent of British consumers thought British companies should have a minimum standard of labour conditions for their Third World suppliers. The charity has reported that seven out of the top ten supermarkets, with a combined turnover of approximately £50 billion, have now adopted ethical policies and six supermarkets have agreed to draw up codes of conduct which, they have agreed in principle, will be externally verified. In the meantime, more than a quarter of the United Kingdom's imported food and drink comes from developing countries.[8]

However, some of the United Kingdom's leading companies rate highly in the up-to-date list of Europe's most respected companies. The list is based on a survey of Chief Executives and Investment Analysts throughout Europe and is not based on what we would regard as exclusively ethical standards. Nevertheless, the leading companies[9] are rated, in part, on the high quality of their products and services, and the balance of interests of shareholders, customers, employees and the community. The top ten names in the 1997 Annual Survey are:

ABB	Engineering and Metals	Sweden/Switzerland
British Petroleum	Oil, Gas and Mining	UK
Nestlé	Food Processing	Switzerland
British Airways	Transport	UK
Tesco	Retail Services	UK
AXA-UAP	Insurance	France
BMW	Cars and Aero Engineering	Germany
Carrefour	Retail Services	France
Unilever	Food Processing	Netherlands/UK
Daimler-Benz	Cars and Aero Engineering	Germany

Another league table which commands wide interest is that which

8 Christian Aid, *The Global Supermarket*, October 1996 and *Change at the Check-out*, October 1997.
9 *The Financial Times and Price Waterhouse Survey* – 'Europe's Most Respected Companies', September 1997.

shows the level of corruption in various countries throughout the world. This Annual Report is issued by the Berlin-based Transparency International Group, which was set up in 1993 and draws its conclusions from a number of international surveys of business people, political analysts and the general public. It is of particular concern that Britain, usually near the top of the list for integrity (and where bribery and corruption are usually met with cries of 'sleaze'), has dropped to fourteenth in the international league. The anti-corruption table,[10] in which marks out of ten are awarded, is as follows:

1.	Denmark	9.94
2.	Finland	9.48
3.	Sweden	9.35
4.	New Zealand	9.23
5.	Canada	9.10
6.	The Netherlands	9.03
7.	Norway	8.92
8.	Australia	8.86
9.	Singapore	8.66
10.	Luxembourg	8.61
11.	Switzerland	8.61
12.	Ireland	8.28
13.	Germany	8.23
14.	United Kingdom	8.22

Perhaps some comfort can be taken from the fact that the Organisation for Economic Co-operation and Development has recommended that member states make bribery a criminal offence.

It is not our purpose here to list the poorest performers in the league table except to say that the lowest twelve in the table have less than three points out of ten. It must be borne in mind, however, that the level of corruption in some Third World countries is accentuated by the actions of some multi-national companies offering bribes to secure contracts in those countries.

The impact of multi-national corporations on Third World countries is the subject of comment in Chapter XII where we report the discussions with leaders in Church and business. In an article in *The Economist* in July 1996, it was suggested that, in the eyes of their critics, the sin that these firms have committed is to have invested massively in countries with repressive regimes, so helping to keep them in power, to which the reply of these multi-international corporations would be that

---

10 Source: Transparency International Group and *The Economist*, 2 August 1997.

less scrupulous firms would take their place if they were to quit and that foreign investment is likelier in the long run to improve rather than worsen the lot of local people.

It is suggested that companies, unelected, have no obvious right to throw their weight around in politics, whether local or global and that companies were not designed for making this sort of moral decision – indeed, it is put forward that, given their duty to shareholders, such action could be *ultra vires*.

Notwithstanding this welcome present-day emphasis on business ethics, it appears from a recent survey by the Industrial Society that there is still a large 'ethics gap' between what senior management say businesses should be doing and what they are actually doing. It was found that there was a gap between theory and practice as far as ethics and the ethical management of people were concerned. More than 50 per cent said that ethical standards had become more of a priority over the past three years, but 40 per cent said that they had never consulted their employees on ethics.

> Key ethical issues may vary across sectors, but all managers must feel confident in their ability to make ethical choices so they can distinguish between hard bargains and sharp practice.[11]

Our concern here has been primarily with ethical business judgments in the broadest sense as seen from the top down, i.e. as determined by the decision-makers in modern business. What then is the view from the outside among those who may be inclined, or perhaps disinclined, to invest in particular enterprises?

In a recent advertisement, Friends Provident claim to have managed 'the UK's first and largest range of ethical investment funds', which invest in companies 'which make a positive contribution to society' and they seek 'to avoid companies which harm the world, its people or its wildlife' – very worthy aims but not a very precise science because (Andrew Buxton again) 'one man's ethics are another man's eccentricity.'[12]

In investment matters it is particularly difficult to follow one's heart. There is a long list of business practices, several of which would be a stumbling block to some investors. They include, for example, companies involved with tobacco, alcohol, armaments, gambling in various forms, environmental damage, 'slave' labour, animal-tested cosmetics, pornographic literature and so on. Unfortunately, in these days of multi-national activities and multi-faceted groups, even companies which appear to be 'clean' on all these issues may be involved in one or more of them in the outskirts of the group. On the

---

11 *Managing Best Practice*, No. 26, Industrial Society, 1996.
12 Andrew Buxton, op. cit.

whole, however, so-called ethical funds have performed as well as others. For example, leading companies which exclude tobacco, alcohol and gambling (but include armaments) achieved a three-year rolling return to May 1996 which, on average, was 1 per cent per annum better than the FT-SE All-Share Index.[13] At the time of writing, there are approximately sixty retail funds specializing in ethical or environmental investment. However, one report dismisses ethical investment as 'a fad' and considers it is 'another name for fashionable causes'.[14]

The Church Commissioners and other Christian charities are known to be selective in their choice of equity funds and in February 1996 the investment bank, Flemings introduced an equity investment fund for Islamic investors. Generally, under Islamic law, investment in debt and, in most cases, equities, is not acceptable with the result that Islamic money generally was invested in leasing agreements and commodity transactions. Mr Ossama Nassar, Head of Flemings' Middle East operations, has said:

> Over the last four years there has been a change. More and more scholars have looked deep into the matter and most Charia Boards now accept equity investment, although some do not.[15]

So much for business ethics without the 'Christian' prefix: and yet many a Christian will recognize in these ethical precepts an overriding concern for good neighbourliness, honesty of purpose, the conservation of God's world and the relief of poverty and injustice. Many of these concerns have their origins in Judaeo-Christian traditions. Indeed, the Institute of Business Ethics, to which we have referred, was founded by the Christian Association of Business Executives.

In addressing the Institute some years ago, Father Francis McHugh, Director of Christian Social Ethics at St John's Seminary, Wonersh, said:

> The difficulty that the Christian faiths have in approaching a business ethic lies in their need to balance out in some way spiritual and temporal values. ... The Old Testament has a useful ethic about wealth and economic life and about business. It approves of it and we also in our Roman Catholic, and I think also in other Christian traditions, include a strong element of approval of the process of the creation of wealth and of the activities of business.[16]

And again:

> I cannot find a text in the New Testament that praises wealth or money or

---

13 The *Financial Times*, 15 February 1997.
14 *The Social Affairs Unit Research Report* 21, 1996 – 'What has ethical investment to do with ethics?'
15 The *Financial Times*, 3 February 1997.
16 Father Francis McHugh, Paper delivered at the Conference of the Institute of Business Ethics, London, 21 October 1988.

business or economic life ... I think that the teaching of Jesus was so concerned to get over the spiritual values that He simply did not have time to go into the other side of the story.[17]

In enunciating six principles for business ethics, Father Francis McHugh concludes:

It is wonderful that the churches at the moment approve the creation of wealth, that business is coming at us with codes of ethics, but I think we have to think a little bit more about where the law fits in all this and how we can make it stick.[18]

We shall address this subject in our closing chapters.

Let us return then to the subject of banking – for money and ethics have always been uncomfortable companions. In Chapter I we have outlined something of Old Testament attitudes to banking's forerunner, viz. usury and its subsequent development in Britain. In the New Testament there is remarkably little guidance on the subject. Indeed, all twelve references in the Bible to usury are found in the Old Testament except for the parable of the talents. Usury in the Bible means the taking of interest, in any form, in return for the loan of money or goods. The just man is 'he that hath not given forth upon usury, neither hath taken any increase'. It seems that the Mosaic prohibition of usury left a somewhat unclear position well into the Middle Ages when we are told that the canon law, 'the first systematic attempt to apply the principles of right and wrong to the economic sphere'[19] came out with a clear prohibition of usury, which was said to be present in any contract or loan which called for a fixed rate of gain without corresponding risk to the lender. Usury was officially defined in England in an Act of 1495 (II, Henry VII, ch.8) as

taking for the same loan anything more besides or above the money lent by way of contract or covenant at the time of the same loan, saving lawful penalties for the non-payment of the money lent.

An Act of 1545 permitted loans carrying interest up to 10 per cent per annum. This Act was repealed in 1552, but in 1571 a further Act was passed, which provided that all contracts for payment of interest of over 10 per cent were to be null and void. Thus generally, religious opinion after the Reformation did not differ very much from that of earlier days in the condemnation of usury.

That which became known as 'interest' was originally a penalty exacted for non-repayment of a loan on the due date. Throughout the subsequent history of banking, interest on loans has been partly a measure of the risk and partly the cost or deprivation to the lender. It is

---

17 Ibid.
18 Ibid.
19 George Goyder, *The Just Enterprise*, 1989, p. 99.

not without significance, therefore, that in our own time the Chairman
of Barclays Bank tells us that:

> Increasingly, environmental risk and indeed reputational risk need to be
> considered alongside the old criteria connected with the balance sheet and
> the business. A company that is polluting the environment clearly carries a
> greater risk to the lender. Clear ethical values and guidelines can reduce a
> company's exposure to risk and should provide a way of streamlining
> decision-making by setting a framework within which those with devolved
> responsibility can work effectively.[20]

It is arguable, however, that ethical constraints on bank lending have
diminished over the years. Years ago, anyone seeking a personal loan
for the purpose of backing the winner of the Grand National would
have met with a stark refusal. Nowadays, however, many loans are
agreed by post, usually on a system of credit scoring, with little regard
to the eventual use of the money. As to corporate lending, Andrew
Buxton points out that all the banks look seriously at such issues as
arms trading, environmental policy and corporate governance, in
addition to normal commercial judgments.

In the December 1984 issue of *Banking World*, Bishop Hugh
Montefiore considered that there were grave moral objections to some
modern loans and rates of interest (see page 124). The Bishop was
writing particularly of loans to under-developed countries. Nearer
home, there have of course been widespread criticisms of banks and
building societies for the apparent ease with which mortgage finance
and consumer credit generally have been made available to the public
and not always to the borrower's advantage. Lord Sudeley has written:

> In this country, banks (and building societies) lend largely without risk to
> enable (sic) mortgages, which has driven up the price of housing to artificial
> levels. Out of this, no wealth has been generated at all.[21]

Some of the building societies have acknowledged that the
availability of mortgage finance fuelled the rise in house prices in the
1980s, resulting ultimately in a large number of repossessions and a
great block of 'negative equity'.

The enormous increase in consumer credit in general has also
prompted criticism in that it has been regarded as inflationary and has
encouraged consumer borrowing by credit cards, personal loans, etc.
beyond the capacity of the borrowers to service the loans. Writing on
the relationship of law and morality in these matters, Sir Gordon Borrie
has said:

> ... the law seems to distance itself from morality in credit matters. If you
> are pushed by clever, persistent and insistent marketing into being over-

20 Andrew Buxton, op. cit.
21 Lord Sudeley in *Country Life* – 'Banks are to Blame for Inflation', 30 May 1996.

committed, then as long as there has been no misrepresentation, duress or undue influence, the agreement is binding. Yet it is at least open to question whether it is moral for a lender to promote credit aggressively, often aiming at those already in financial difficulties, with only minimal enquiry into the borrower's track record or existing commitments.[22]

In fact, the whole question of consumer credit, including the economic and social aspects, was considered by the Crowther Committee which reported on 24 March 1971[23]:

> The Committee found no reason to view with concern the growth of consumer credit. Moreover, the evidence examined showed that the proportion of borrowers who get into difficulty with their payments was very small and did not provide grounds for restrictive measures. The Committee considered that the correct line for economic policy should be to allow consumer credit the maximum freedom to develop under competitive conditions induced by increasing the amount of information available to the consumer, especially by mandatory disclosure of the effective rate of annual interest (including all charges), and by stimulating the education of consumers in the use of credit.

> From the social aspect, users of consumer credit should be treated as adults capable of managing their own financial affairs. There should be no restriction on the freedom of access to credit but measures should be taken to prevent debtors from falling into default and to assist those who do.[24]

In the far wider field of what one might call social economics, Sir Gordon Borrie argues that there 'has long been a strong case for an extension of law to enforce higher standards of morality in the marketplace',[25] but he acknowledges that: 'Regulations and law can go too far.'[26] It seems appropriate to conclude this chapter with Sir Gordon's comment:

> *Moral standards without legal underpinning will be inadequately supported. But I suggest that a society that leaves nothing to an individual's own sense of what is right and moral would no longer be a free society. Where the balance should be struck between freedom and regulation is of course a perennial problem that every new generation has to tackle in the light of changing patterns of behaviour. There is no final answer.[27]*

---

22 Sir Gordon Borrie, *Law and Morality in the Marketplace: Ethical Conflicts in Finance*, The Association of Corporate Treasurers, Blackwell, 1994, p. 48.
23 But see the discussion with the Rt. Rev. Dr Peter Selby in Chapter XII.
24 D.G. Hanson, *Dictionary of Banking and Finance*, London, Pitman, 1985, p. 179.
25 Borrie, *Law and Morality in the Marketplace*, p. 58.
26 Ibid, p. 61.
27 Ibid, p. 61.

CHAPTER XII

Selected Interviews

Miss not the discourse of the elders.[1]

In this and the following chapter, an attempt is made to probe further into the contemporary interaction between Christian ethics and business theory and practice. This has involved two methods of research – first, a series of face-to-face interviews with leaders in Church and business, as described in detail in this chapter and second, a postal survey among the Chief Executives of 500 leading companies and one hundred medium-sized companies, as detailed in Chapter XIII.

The personal discussions covered a number of salient aspects of 'Christianity and business', but we did not slavishly follow an agenda in any particular order and indeed, it was most noticeable how some 'answers' arose naturally from the thread of discussion without the need to pose the questions. In particular, our thoughts were centred on the following aspects:

1. The compatibility or otherwise of Christian love and the profit motive.

2. Christians and 'the world'.

3. What is true discipleship?

4. What is meant by the Kingdom of Heaven?

5. Can Christians change the world through business?

6. Can corporations have a Christian conscience?

7. Can we move away from the impersonal 'company' structure?

8. What is the role of the Church?

The discussions with the leaders in Church and business ranged over the entire field of our basic subject, i.e. the relationship of Christianity to business. The various discussions are reported here under the names of each contributor. To do otherwise and, for example, to take each individual subject with up to twenty or so comments and opinions, might be exhaustive of each subject but somewhat *exhausting* to the

---

1 *Ecclesiasticus* 8:9.

reader. Also, by taking each interview in turn, it is possible to omit items which would otherwise be repetitive and, more particularly, to introduce in other parts of the text those subjects which have been especially illuminated by some of the participants. For example, the conversations with Mr Roger Sawtell and Lord Thomas are very relevant to the discussion on co-operative business in Chapter XIV.

The sequence in which the following names appear is arbitrary and is, in fact, the order in which the discussions occurred. That order was largely determined by geographical considerations, summer holidays and pressures on individual diaries. Nevertheless, it had the advantage that certain themes emerged which could be developed in the light of earlier discussions. Biographical details of the participants are set out on pages xvi to xviii. We come then to Bishop David Jenkins.

The Rt. Rev. Dr David Jenkins

Dr Jenkins considered the profit motive perfectly compatible with Christian love and thought it was a proper form of stewardship. He recalled the time when he was working for the World Council of Churches and was Theological Adviser to the Christian Medical Commission. An American running Rockefeller Health in Thailand had posed the question: 'What is the statistical equivalent of theological compassion?' In other words, as the American had put it: 'I am supposed to love my neighbour, the person who ends up in a ditch and

The Rt. Rev. Dr David Jenkins

so on. Now in Thailand I've got hundreds of thousands of people in ditches. How do I decide how to get resources and apply them and so on?' In Dr Jenkins's view, if we are going to care for our neighbours in the world as it is today, we must have due regard to the resources of technology, energy production, accounting methods and circulation of capital.

But what about accumulating wealth for oneself? In the Bishop's view, different opportunities arose for people making different amounts of money and 'the mere making of money is not itself a good thing or a bad thing.' It does, however, affect the next level of stewardship, i.e. what you do with the wealth you acquire.

But are there not winners and losers in business? Is one person's gain not another person's loss? Yes, there are winners and losers in each, what you might call, trading episode and the theory is that the wealth so produced will cascade widely to the benefit of others. The Bishop agreed, however, that despite the cascading of wealth there was a growing disparity between the haves and the have-nots, both in our domestic economy and internationally. The Bishop agrees that it is a very grave question and is inclined to the view that it is getting worse, not better. There are those who consider that Adam Smith has 'rescued us from having to be bothered about self-interest because we now know that self-interest is the thing that drives ... But then people now seem to say: "I don't have to worry about consequences."' That, in the Bishop's view, would be clearly contrary to stewardship 'because stewardship involves responsibility, including of course responsibility for creation and the whole exploitation of the world's resources... this is the sort of thing that Christians should introduce into the whole argument, not saying: "Oh, it's always wicked to make money or to make a profit." '

The question remains, however – should Christians withdraw from the world or seek to change the world? Is one likely to change the world through business? Very much so, suggests Dr Jenkins – 'much of it for ill rather than for good.' Thus:

> each generation has its own challenge and so we may very well be at a point where we have been seduced by what I call the amazing growth of the nineteenth century and I think it is very important to make the point that, for the whole of the two thousand years of recorded history, life was nasty, brutish and short for most people. Then from about 1790, it began to appear that all the peasants were being called to a heavenly banquet. So you can well understand people feeling now that we have got our destiny in our own hands, heaven is round the corner if we produce enough and share enough, and so you have got this amazing growth of the nineteenth century and I like to put it that we have been seduced into thinking that that's also amazing grace, but it doesn't work just like that. So now we have a challenge of the fact that this turns out to be, in one sense, much more

limited and questionable than we thought ... so we have really got to think much harder and return to notions like stewardship, neighbourliness, responsibility and citizenship.

If the Christian's task is to change the world, is it right to join a 'worldly' organization in order to do so? 'I think, in a sense,' said Bishop Jenkins,

the only way you can avoid belonging to a worldly organisation is by committing suicide or going to live in the desert. Of course, the second one is a proper Christian witness, but ... most of our forms of witness are pretty impaired.

On the subject of discipleship,

people think that as long as you *believe* you are all right, that is to say you have a sort of a bit of a disciple in your head and a framework in your mind, and as long as you think that that is there and perhaps perform a certain few routine acts, well that is good enough. I think the business of actually sweating it out on the ground in the face of all the difficult questions that are raised, is not thought to be part of discipleship and the notion exists that what Church is really for is to comfort people at points of stress and enable them to feel comfortable at home and friendly and all the rest of it, which is essential to belonging to a community of course, but it is a community of disciples and anyone who has read either the Old Testament or the New Testament, whether it is the people of God in the Old Testament or Christ and his disciples in the New Testament – it's not like that. It is precisely the creative wrestling with the unanswerable problem.

What, then is the role of the Church?

To be more understanding and anxious to support people and back them up than it is on the whole. It seems that far too much of the Church's attitude to all this is far too privatised, individualised and internalised.

But has the Church not trodden its own path, not being unduly concerned about commercial and economic forces in the world? In the Bishop's view, it was not until the late eighteenth century that commerce and trade became a power in the world (although of course there was banking from the sixteenth century and millionaires from about the fourteenth century onwards). Thus, it was not until comparatively modern times that one sees the 'inordinate power, excessive power of capital, industry, factory work, let alone the huge financial network. Everything was subordinated to agriculture.'

But in our own day, we are moving increasingly towards the multi-international way of life, the global village. Is it just possible that we are moving towards a more ethical Kingdom in this world?

Yes indeed, in a sense God has caught us out. Just when we thought we could manage without Him and get on with our own affairs, we've suddenly discovered we have become one world. It just goes to show that we are one world: we are indeed, as it says in the Book of Samuel, all bound up in one bundle of life. Therefore, this business of who are my neighbours and how you treat them becomes much sharper than it has been for a long time.

On the subject of corporate structures, Bishop Jenkins referred to recent research into alternatives to shareholder control, for example credit unions and co-operatives – a subject to which we return in Chapter XIV. The Bishop considered that such notions had to be entertained and thought, in fact, it would become more and more urgent to look at the actual operations of the market and especially the financial markets. We had got to the point where, in order to attract capital, you had to contemplate such a quick and high return that one would not be able to afford it. 'Is not one of the reasons for unemployment that people are asking too much for capital? Thus, we have to think of different forms of organisation whereby people would be content with a much lower rate of return on capital.'

Mr Michael Blackburn

The reference to interest rates leads appropriately to the discussion with Mike Blackburn, Chief Executive of the Halifax, which only recently had undergone a period of conversion from being the largest building society into one of the largest banks in the country. The discussion turned naturally to the subject of wealth creation. Essentially, in Mr Blackburn's view:

Mr Michael Blackburn

Wealth creation means adding value. If society works on the premise that it is better to go forward rather than backward, then wealth creation and improving the lot of individuals must be a good thing. Going on from that, the issue is how the wealth is to be used. In that context 'the camel through the eye of the needle' is not irrelevant.

But, despite so much wealth creation, has the gulf between rich and poor not increased? Certainly, it appears that the divide has grown bigger between the Western World and the Third World. But, queries Blackburn:

Is the Christian world less or more extreme in the division of wealth in its societies? Is there not a bigger gulf between the haves and the have-nots in other cultures and religions?

However, if improving the lot means going back to the basics of food and shelter, the lot has been significantly improved in the First World as opposed to the Third World.

Turning to the apparent paradox of Christian love and profit-making, Blackburn posed the question: 'What is Christian love?' and continued:

Is it, as we have got in our own mission and values statement (see Appendix) to do with valuing and respecting each other? We are essentially a business about – and for – people. We do not have big capital assets, plant and so on. We are a business that employs some thirty-six thousand individuals, dealing with twenty million customers. So, the people dimension, their behaviour and the inter-personal relationships in our business are very important. As a consumer in other areas of business, I certainly want to feel that those organisations I deal with have integrity and would do 'the right thing'. I would also like to think that the employees of organisations with whom I deal are subject to employment policies and practices which are 'good'. So, in this business, I want to see employment policies and practices which are, and which are seen to be, shining examples of good practice. There are two reasons. First I think it is right. Second, I believe that we are more likely to create more wealth for more people by doing things that are 'right'.

But is business not concerned with winning and are there not reciprocal losers?

Business is about success and if success equals winning, are there reciprocal losers? That would imply a zero-sum game which I do not think is the case. If an organisation is succeeding faster than another organisation then, in that sense, the second organisation is 'losing' – but only relative to the first.

But is not the success of a business quite often at the expense of someone else?

It depends what we mean by 'the expense of'. New technology has succeeded at the expense of old technology. New chemicals and fabrics have created new jobs at the expense of Lancashire cotton mills. In that sense, success is at the expense of someone else. I see that as being inevitable and part of 'progress' which most of us want.

Mr Blackburn considered the question whether or not a corporation could have a Christian conscience, to which he replied:

> A corporation can have *values*; those values can have a Christian base or context. And just as Christians can fail to live up to their values, so too can corporations.

What, however, is a corporation?

> It is certainly the board, the managers and the staff. It is the shareholders. It is the brand. Is it the customer base, the suppliers to the corporation or the communities in which the corporation operates? Probably not, vitally important though those are to the success of the corporation.

On the subject of ultimate statutory responsibility, Blackburn posed the question: 'Do we acknowledge only one stakeholder or a range of stakeholders? When push comes to shove the shareholder is *primus inter pares*, but somewhat distant.' Nevertheless, he instanced cases in the commercial world where both shareholders and customers had been exceedingly vociferous and thereby able to induce significant changes in the direction of a company.

Was there some possibility of a wider stakeholder concept and perhaps a wider mutuality of interest?

> There was certainly a mutuality of interest in the original building societies, the terminating societies. Arguably, that principle died when permanent building societies were established in the nineteenth century. We have not seen many mutual building societies or life assurance businesses created in this century.

Is it not possible that the enterprising Christian would be more at home in the mutual world than in the one that is rigorously controlled by shareholders?

> Certainly a mutual constitution is more comfortable, less taxing than a PLC constitution. But as to the question: 'Am I more likely to exercise a moral influence in a mutual context than if I were in a PLC structure?' the answer is: 'No, I don't think so.'

Mike Blackburn's comments on wealth creation find an echo in the first part of the discussion with Bishop Alec Graham.

The Rt. Rev. Dr Alec Graham

On the subject of wealth generally, Bishop Graham reminds us that there is a good deal in the New Testament, and in the Epistle of James in particular, about disparities of wealth and the way in which people

The Rt. Rev. Dr Alec Graham

of different social and money backgrounds are treated by the Christian community. In many respects, the New Testament section is untypical from that of the subsequent Church. But one also has to look at the material in the Old Testament where there is a great deal about the creator God, who made the world in a certain sort of way and why it has indeed gone askew. Nevertheless, society cannot survive in any sort of fashion that is going to allow humans to live a tolerable life without virtues of hard work, planning, thrift and discipline. There is a lot of that in the wisdom literature, but not only there. A great deal of it underpins the law and has to do with right relationships in a trading community.

The Bishop considered that there is in fact room for people who have a very particular calling and he said this with some feeling because he had just ceased to be the Visitor to the Community of the Resurrection. He had seen 'quite a bit about the whole matter of renouncing one's possessions. Some are called to do this and, in fact, it is a very important witness, particularly in today's society where you are not considered normal or fulfilled unless you have accumulated money or you use it in a flamboyant way, but to keep going you have to have your own economic arrangements.' The Bishop did not doubt that very many people are attracted by what one might call the somewhat dazzling and romantic view of abandoning everything, but actually they are led on to what is a much harder way sometimes and that is of discerning how to put this into practice in a world which is very largely grey.

Bishop Graham recalled that 'marvellous text' in Ecclesiasticus about all sorts of people like labourers, masons and agricultural labourers, people who by their labour maintain the fabric of the world. He said it is a marvellous text because it really expresses the whole insight of the Wisdom tradition that the Creator God has made the world in this way, and the truly wise person perceives how it is made and co-operates and furthers it.

Bishop Graham was referring to the words from Chapter 38 of Ecclesiasticus:

> All these put their trust in their hands,
>   and each is skilled at his own craft,
> A town could not be built without them,
>   there would be no settling, no travelling.
> But they are not required at the council,
>   they do not hold high rank in the assembly.
> They do not sit on the judicial bench,
>   and have no grasp of the law.
> They are not remarkable for culture or sound judgement,
>   and are not found among the inventors of maxims.
> But they give solidarity to the created world,
>   while their prayer is concerned with what pertains
>   to their trade.

But did not the early disciples and the apostles leave their employment and go into the world to preach the Gospel? Would they have suffered martyrdom for the sake of a business career? 'We know very little about them,' replied the Bishop, 'but, yes, somebody must have maintained them.' Was that not the communism of the early Church? 'Yes, but it did not mean to say that every disciple has to be, as it were, provided for by his colleagues.'

Are the saints of the present day not called to a life of complete dedication to Christ? 'Well,' questioned Bishop Graham,

> do you want, as it were, the saint to be parasitic upon the rest of the universe? ... one would want to say that the saint is the person who pursues his Christian vocation in the place and circumstance to which he or she has been called, and most people do not have much opportunity of choice. You take what comes your way and most people in the pews are people who really have not got much option about how they earn a living ... if you want work, you take what's there.

Thus, Bishop Graham spoke with great realism about the worthiness and integrity of all legitimate occupations, and the difficulty in this present age of abandoning the plough or, as it were, one's fishing nets and setting out to change the world.

This sanctity of secular vocations arose almost spontaneously in the subsequent discussions with Bishop Richard Harries.

The Rt. Rev. Richard Harries

The Bishop considered that:

> from the Christian point of view, any secular vocation which is genuinely useful to our fellow human beings and to the maintenance of the fabric of a civil society can be a legitimate vocation and Luther took it as far as thinking that you could be a Christian hangman, which some of us might disagree with. I think the principle is the same, but then it comes down to a question of individual vocation and individual discipline and whether a person feels that he or she can genuinely live out a Christian life in a particular part of the secular world where they are operating, and I think it is true to say that there are some areas which are more difficult than others. But I think that one of the areas that has gone wrong, ever since certainly the romantic movement, is that Christians have thought it was legitimate to be doctors and nurses, teachers and clergymen and have been less able to champion, in a fully Christian way, a life in business or industry. I think perhaps Non-Conformists were better than Anglicans, but I think, in this country in particular, there has been a lot of romanticism on the one hand and snobbishness on the other so that everybody's ideal has been to make enough money quickly enough so that they can retire to the country and pursue a life of leisured reflection.

Is making money, whether quickly or not, i.e. making money for its

The Rt. Rev. Richard Harries

own sake, incompatible with Christian love? The Bishop did not think a profit was necessarily made at other people's expense because,

> if one goes back to the simplest kind of market, a market in a village or in a jungle clearing, then we have certain people bringing produce for which they will get something in return. In a pre-cash society it would be barter and in later years it would be cash, which would enable them to buy for some of their own needs, and this is entirely compatible with love because it should be a mutually beneficial arrangement and, indeed is a foundation for any community living together, and one could probably justify this from St Paul's concept of different gifts within the body. Not every limb is the same, but every limb is different and one could extend this from Christian people to Christian gifts and from Christian gifts to the gifts which make the world go round.

In the Bishop's view the Christian Church has always recognized, right from New Testament times, that Christians have to earn their living in the world in the same way as everybody else and St Paul severely castigated those people in the Church at Thessalonica who downed tools in expectation that the end was very near. So Christians have to take their proper place in the world earning a living and making their contribution to society. One of the great strengths of the Reformation was that it recovered the whole concept of lay vocation. In the fourth and fifth centuries with the rise of the monastic movement and, to some extent, the flight from the world, there were those who tended to grow up with the idea of duty as first-class Christians who did not get married, who then became monks and did not own any possessions and second-class Christians who did marry, who did work in the world and, as it were, jogged along on the bottom of the Christian life. Now Martin Luther swept all that away quite rightly.

Does that concept of first-class and second-class Christians still apply today? Is there not still a sense of 'dualism' so that the Christian has to choose between renouncing the world or becoming active in the world? Bishop Richard replied that there is a genuine tension, a genuine dualism which goes right back to the New Testament itself and arises from the fact that, as Christians, we live between the time of Christ rising and Christ coming again. We live literally with our feet in two worlds – our feet in this continuing world and, therefore, with all the necessity upon us, moral obligation upon us, of maintaining the fabric of this world so long as it lasts and at the same time the pressure of the eschatological, i.e. of last things when everything will be new, and this tension is there in the New Testament.

The Bishop continued:

> I don't think there should be an absolute dualism, but I think there is a genuine tension. Luther lived with dualism – the world of the Kingdom and the world in which we live. St Augustine lived with it in another way – this

world and the City of God. I do not think any Church has finally resolved it, nor do I think any Church should finally resolve it and I think that, in a way, as Christians we should live with that tension. In other words, if one decides to become, let us say, a Christian financier, not only should one seek to do good through one's secular work as a Christian financier, but one also ought to be open to the possibility that one might very well be called to move on to something very different, and that if a Christian loses the sense that, as it were, all may be required of one, then we have lost something fundamental – what it is to be a Christian.

What advice, therefore, would the Bishop give to a young man or woman embarking on a career, but being a convinced and practising Christian? In the Bishop's view, people should ask themselves three questions. First of all, questions about their own gifts and what they actually enjoy doing and what they are good at. 'I am sure that's a perfectly proper place to start.' Secondly, he thought that people should ask themselves from a Christian point of view whether what they intend to do will be of a genuine use to other people and he did not think people should interpret general use in too narrow terms. 'There are lots of ways of being of general use.' Thirdly, in the Bishop's view, one needs as a Christian to bring the problem to God in prayer for there is such a thing as vocation. 'When one has assessed one's gifts and weighed up whether what one is considering will be of use to others, there is still the ultimate question of whether this is that to which God is calling one.'

If the Christian is to seek first the Kingdom of God and his righteousness, what meaning should we ascribe to the 'Kingdom of God'? In the Bishop's view, the Kingdom of God should literally mean

God's rule rather than the place where God rules. ... it is that ultimate state of affairs where God will be all in all, but I think that ultimate state has been brought amongst us in Christ and, therefore, God's Kingdom exists in Christ crucified and risen, and Christ's Kingdom exists in an anticipatory sense where Christ is acknowledged and obeyed by Christians. So I think it has a dimension of the past, the present and the future.

So the Kingdom of God is within you?

No, I think most people would now say that that is not actually how, first of all, the Greek should be translated. It should be translated that the Kingdom of God is amongst you and Jesus referred not to the eternal Kingdom, but to the presence of himself and his teaching and his miracles, and this was the Kingdom of God breaking into this world.

But did he not say: 'My Kingdom is not of this world'?

Indeed, he said that in the fourth Gospel in the dialogue with Pilate and that is certainly an important aspect in that it points at the contrast between the kingdoms of this world, which are of course dominated by power, usually ruthless and aggrandising power, and the Kingdom of God's just and gentle rule, and that is God's Kingdom ... and if one asks where it is, it is in Christ crucified and risen and where Christ is acknowledged and in that ultimate state of affairs. The reason why people should resist the idea that it is simply within us is because God's kingship embraces the whole universe and God's kingship is concerned with the whole totality of human existence, not just the inward and spiritual side.

The discussion turned to mission statements of the kind drawn up now by approximately 200 companies in this country. The Bishop's comments were, we believe, very realistic and down to earth, viz.

First of all, I think the mission statement needs to be drawn up with the company as a whole participating in the process and not simply dashed off by the chairman on the back of an envelope during a boring moment in a meeting. I think drawing up the mission statement needs to be by genuinely participating persons and secondly, from the outset, there needs to be some clear understanding of how the performance of the company is going to be reviewed in relation to the mission statement, and at the moment certainly the latter probably does not take place in many companies, and I think that is the next step. I think that unless a company pays attention to the consumer, to the supplier and increasingly to the wider community and the wider environment, it will suffer in so many ways. The company that literally only pays attention to the shareholder, I think will very quickly come a cropper.

Finally, in business and in the law we use words such as reasonableness, fairness, business ethics, honesty, integrity, fair play, fair competition and so on – words which do not necessarily have a Christian connotation. Are they not, however, derived from an inherited Christian background?

Yes, I think that is right. I think that the word 'inherited' is important to draw people's attention to because the fact that these virtues are prized in our society is, to some extent, a legacy of our Christian past. It is Christianity which has shaped and moulded our society, but I see nothing wrong myself in a kind of common language of morality which can be owned by all people. For Christians, there will be a difference in that they won't simply see it in moral terms, but they will see that morality, as it were, being under-girded and impelled and inspired by their religious beliefs. So there will be a religious motivation. So Christians won't just talk about what is right, but they will talk about trying to do God's will.

The relevance of Christian accountability is well demonstrated in the booklet *Business Values*,[2] written jointly by the Bishop and Lord Laing of Dunphail, who in turn had the assistance of a distinguished working party. The booklet, written primarily for business people in the Oxford Diocese, brings out the fact that nearly two million people live in the

2 The Rt. Rev. Richard Harries, Bishop of Oxford and Lord Laing of Dunphail, *Business Values*, Oxford, 1996.

Diocese and 'practically everyone benefits directly from business, whether through employment, pensions or stipends.' The booklet is written from a distinctively Christian perspective – 'serving Christ in the economic sphere is no less significant than serving Him in a monastery' and 'there is a Christian vocation to be found in ministering to any legitimate wants.'

The authors continue:

> Whilst it is true that the Bible and Christian tradition most certainly warn against allowing wealth to become a god, the Apostle Paul writes that God 'richly provides us with everything for our enjoyment'. In this, Paul reflects the widespread teaching in the Hebrew Bible which sees wealth and prosperity as a proper reward for industry, and among the blessings which God has for his faithful people. The legal codes in the Hebrew Bible endeavour to ensure that 'wealth creation' takes place only in ways which benefit the community as a whole and are amazingly relevant to the problems of today. For example, the Book of Leviticus addresses the issues of ecology and land conservation by placing restrictions on over-intensive arable farming.

Throughout the text, the emphasis is on the Christian's accountability to God in every aspect of life, including business affairs. The Christian, whether in business or not, must seek to honour the commandments, from both the Old and New Testaments, to love God and one's neighbour, and

> the move from personal conviction and morality to a corporate commitment may not be an easy one to make, but it is an essential bridge to cross if a business is to be inspired by ethical principles.

The authors make a plea for explicit guidelines, whether in the form of mission statements or codes of ethical conduct, recalling that in the 1980s there was, in this country and in other countries, an increasing recognition of the importance of efficient wealth-creating business:

> At the same time, serious concerns emerged about what seemed to be a narrowly commercial approach to business with inadequate regard for its wide impact. The expansion of international companies, which tended to separate decision-makers even further from those affected by their decisions, added to the worries. We believe that if industry is to respond effectively, firms must underpin their business objectives with explicit ethical guidelines. As for Christians, we would affirm that these should be based on Christian teaching.

Nevertheless, no moral code will effectively influence the behaviour of an organization unless it is accepted and respected by the whole membership of that organization, and it is no accident that in this area 'the conviction and commitment of the Chairman and Chief Executive, whether Christian or not, has been a force in identifying and building most successful structures.'

This emphasis on leadership from the top was stressed in our discussions with Sir Leslie Fielding.

Sir Leslie Fielding

From a vantage point of international experience, Sir Leslie considered that, whatever the corporate objectives of a business may be, much depends on the personal predilections of the Chairman, the Chief Executive and his key people around him. Whatever the legal position may be, there are dominant individuals in a corporation who will swing things one way or the other and square it with the statutes.

Sir Leslie continued:

> Their motivation can often be Christian or, if not overtly and creedally paid-up communicant-church-member-Christian, at any rate, without any insult to them, sub-Christian, that is informed by Christian values, and I do not think one should sneer at that and one does meet such people regularly who have got an eye to a buck and a bottom line and to read a balance sheet, very determined and aggressive leaders of men, but who are capable in moments of sentimentality or spiritual reflection of nuancing their decision in the light of an undeclared, ethical assumption and that is good. I do not know how much longer it will last as that sub-Christian culture erodes.

But does not the quest for wealth feed on itself so that, as the businessman gets richer, he tends to want more? 'Greed', said Sir Leslie,

Sir Leslie Fielding

is a thing that we now have to watch. Now we have a situation in which people are no longer secure, do not have jobs for life, can be 'right sized' or 'down sized' or chucked out whenever it is convenient to do so. On the other hand, others at the top draw advantages which seem to me to be excessive by any commercial criteria. I think particularly of the privatised water companies, the rewards some of those have which are quite excessive and also excessive by my Christian standards. I do not think this kind of personal greed is compatible with Christian or sub-Christian stewardship of the affairs of a corporation.

On the other hand,

we cannot expect the world to be run like a monastery or some Sunday School isolated from the need to protect the planet, keep the air clean, deal with crime, prevent the invasion of the realm, raise money for hospitals, old age pensions and all that sort of thing. Rather it seems to me that the world is, as in the Bible and in our experience and is as seen through history, a very, very imperfect and sin-ridden kind of place in which the Church struggles to proclaim an item of good news which makes sense and finally comes into its own at the end of the world, the end of the universe, in the last days. Meanwhile, perfection is not to be found.

Sir Leslie had referred on a previous occasion to 'the kingdom of grab'.[3] Sir Leslie had quoted from St Luke, viz. 'Beware! Be on your guard against greed of every kind, for even when a man has more than enough his wealth does not give him life.'[4] The late Duchess of Windsor had apparently said 'You can never have enough money,' and, said Sir Leslie: 'In my own experience, however much folk have they seem to want more.'

I do not know how far ordinary people have really yet taken in the dimensions of what Joe Rogaly of the *Financial Times* calls 'the kingdom of grab' ... but certain high principles must now be brought to bear in the kingdom of grab. I do not mean greater disclosure to shareholders of executive rewards, or more restraint and discrimination over who gets the cash – although I agree with both. Nor tighter control over dishonesty and malpractice in the City of London – although society needs that too. The basic fact needs to be loudly proclaimed that greed is greed, sleaze is sleaze – they corrode and ultimately destroy everything and everyone with which they come in contact: they distort the economy and corrupt society: they often do tragic harm to those who practise them.[5]

Thus, Sir Leslie spoke of greed as a 'very important and dangerous basic sin'. But can corporations be greedy? We posed the question to Sir Leslie as we had to others – can a corporation have a Christian conscience? 'In many ways,' he replied

3 Sir Leslie Fielding, KCMG, *The Kingdom of Grab*: a Sermon in commemoration of the. Founders and Benefactors of Durham Cathedral, 2 November 1994.
4 *Luke*, 12:15.
5 Sir Leslie Fielding, KCMG, *The Kingdom of Grab*.

... corporations seem to me to find it easier to act with a Christian conscience than the individual entrepreneur or the very small niche firm because the individual entrepreneur and the niche firm are fighting for survival in a very Darwinian sense, usually with a very, very narrow optic. The great corporation, on the other hand, has established itself. They go up, they go down, but broadly for a period of decades or a century or more there they are at their peak and they acquire a sense of their own dignity and responsibility in the world, which extends beyond the narrow business of manufacturing and marketing a widget, which then flows up to committees and individuals and budgets – which I rather commend ... the larger you get, the more organised you are ... sooner or later the questions of conscience and the placing of the company in society tend to raise their ugly heads.

Despite that apparent ability on the part of corporations to maintain ethical values, does not the co-operative or mutual structure of business, particularly in former days, present the Christian with a less 'greedy' and arguably more participatory business structure? Sir Leslie agreed that

the remarkable concept of mutual help, often among working class, non-conformist Christians, was a wonderful thing. However, it may well be that, in terms of ability to provide goods and services in modern market conditions, you cannot keep a mutual organisation going against market conditions because you are then creating a Jurassic Park. Accordingly, if things which were splendid in the nineteenth century and early twentieth century had a lot of good qualities to them, the qualities assigned to these commercial self-help phenomena were identical really to a well-run religious community – not necessarily an Anglican or a Roman Catholic one, but a gathering of devout Protestants. The Taizé community was founded partly as Protestants and there is the Iona community. But any community can be found at its best and its sublimest (which perhaps does not last very long in the corporate organisation) among such organisations as a great university or college or in a good regiment at a particular stage in a war where they are bonded together to help each other, to assume risk together, to bail each other out and not to count the personal cost.

In other parts of this work we have posed the question: 'What is the young Christian to do if he or she contemplates a business career?' If any person, young or old, is called by the process of a conversion or evolution in the Christian life to follow Christ utterly and completely, can they in all conscience move into a world of business which is based on profit-making? Sir Leslie considered that in this, as in other respects, there is a lot to be said for the priesthood of all believers – 'that the ordained clergy, despite my great respect for them and who are of course absolutely vital, are not the Church and all of us are required to carry the good news and to try to live with Christ in the world that God has given us'.

Most of us are Christians some of the time, a few of us are Christian a lot of the time. I don't know anyone who is a Christian or is the image of Christ all the time, although some people come very close to it. So it is not so difficult, one need not be too fastidious because we are of the world, of the earth, earthy as well as being of the spirit, the spirit received as the charisma of baptism, confirmation and communion.

Sir Leslie did not think that the Christian who is in business need feel that he struggles under a most oppressive burden unknown by any other Christian in any other walk of life. Of course, a Christian will not agree to break the law, a Christian will not agree to do something flagrantly dishonest, a Christian will not agree to be vindictive and cruel in the handling of a personnel dispute. On the contrary, the Christian should be, if he is a manager, a charismatic personnel manager, firm, tough-minded but with a gentleness for the individual and a sense of what is going to happen to that individual. In negotiations he may be as cunning and manipulative as one can be in a negotiation, but without the lie and without the dirty trick, not to break the law, not above all to cloud his better judgement by considerations to do with his own personal enrichment and our Lord is very, very clear about the dangers of greed.

The discussion of discipleship arose again in our meeting with Bishop Ronald Bowlby.

The Rt. Rev. Ronald Bowlby

The Christian, said the Bishop, must always be very clear that in the final analysis he is trying to do the will of God, which is, in very broad terms, trying to implement whatever he understands by God's love and justice. The Christian has to make up his or her mind about particular issues and that may sometimes mean that if the firm that he or she works for has changed course, that may put a big question mark against whether it is right to continue working for that employer. Of course, this raises extremely difficult issues for people whose livelihood is then at risk.

But is Christian love compatible with the profit motive? In the Bishop's view, the consistent teaching of the New Testament is that you must not make Mammon your god – we came into this world having nothing and we are going to leave having nothing. But more importantly, we are here to glorify God above all else and so it is from that point of view that we have to be able to criticize everything else and examine our motives accordingly. The Bishop sees the profit motive as being much more to do, in the end, with efficiency – 'effectiveness is perhaps the better word'. The Bishop does not think the Christian ought to have any difficulty in saying that he wants to

The Rt. Rev. Ronald Bowlby

make the best product, or to offer the best service, or to be a wise steward of the resources of the world for the sake of other people and all to the glory of God – but the Christian cannot accept that being in business to make a profit is the sole motive.

But if we are true disciples, ought we not to give over the whole of our life to the work of the Kingdom? The Bishop recalled his own earlier days in the North-East trying to help young 'blue collar' workers in the shipbuilding industry to see how fundamental Christian values might apply in relation to the jobs they were doing. It seemed to him 'extraordinarily important to have people, to put it no higher, of integrity and compassion in senior positions in political life, industry or whatever as anywhere else in the life of the community', and continued:

> If I was talking to a young person, someone sufficiently educated to have choice, then I would say 'You must think very carefully about what is the best way to use your particular gifts and you may well decide that there are certain things that it would be better to do than others, and you can then choose to do them.' An awful lot of people have very little choice and the question for them is what is the best way in which to make use of what they will be forced to do anyway.

The discussion turned on how a young person should work towards the coming of the Kingdom of God. The Bishop used the analogy of the iceberg, i.e. what we experience here in this life is part of something much bigger. In the end, a community of people who are living in the world in a way in which God wants them to live and becoming the people that God wants them to be, based on those values which are derived in the end essentially from Christ's teaching, but also drawing on the whole Jewish tradition in the process – the Kingdom would be about people treating each other justly ... essentially that is what love has to be in terms of working it out in personal relationships.

The Bishop continued:

> It is interesting that going right back to somebody like St Benedict who was the great founder of monastic communities, he was very clear that part of faithfulness to the Kingdom was doing manual work, or managing the affairs of the Benedictine Abbey and its lands efficiently, and thus the whole idea that prayer and work were intimately connected was part of the concept of the Kingdom ... The Kingdom of God is within you because in the end we have to discover the values of the Kingdom for ourselves and we have to incorporate them into our own inner being, but that is not to say that they are not to be applied and worked through in our ordinary life and our relationships with other people.

And again:

> Someone who always influenced me very much is St Francis. People ask what Francis meant by poverty and whether it is realistic to embrace the concept of total poverty. I think that those who have been touched by Francis's spirit have always felt in the end that we have to translate that whole emphasis on poverty into what we would probably call simplicity, but recognizing that what Francis was referring to was that extremes of wealth divide people from each other. I would want to say, as a Christian, to people who are high earners – will you not consider very carefully not so much that it is 'wrong' to earn a tremendous amount of money if you are a very gifted and able person, but that there comes a point where to go on earning more and more divides you from people and you will be the poorer at a very deep level for that.

Bishop Bowlby considered that so much of modern business 'is more to do with financial services in one form or another than it is to do with production'. Having worked in London and in the North-East, the Bishop was often asked about the difference between the two. He replied that he felt that in the North-East, even during periods of decline, there had been a community spirit which drew its strength from common involvement in producing ships, coal, steel and so on, and this applied to the 'white collar' workers who were solicitors or bankers, who felt they were part of this community effort, but

> I came to London and realized that I had come to a world where, on the whole, many people now are employed to move other people's money about, and who make judgements about people's performance in other parts of the country based, for the most part, on whether they are delivering 8 per cent

rather than 6 per cent or whatever, and I think that makes a big difference to people's whole attitude to the work they are doing and what it is for.

What has been the attitude of the Church?

I think the general feeling among people who have worked in business and industry until recently has been that the Churches have been very antagonistic to any sort of worthwhileness about what people do. The Church has seemed hostile, and I think that we really have to look at that again and say that it is as proper to be a good businessman or industrialist as, for example, to be a good farmer.

The Bishop considered that the Christian Churches ought to have made it clear that they affirm the work of people who are enabling the wheels of industry to turn. It is all part of serving God's world in its modern forms. But also, the Church ought to be saying that as many people as possible should be able to have a quality of life which is human and dignified. Whilst capitalism appears to be the most effective way of achieving the aims of industry and production, it, capitalism,

must always be subject to the restraints and constraints that enable it to deliver a better standard of living to as many people as possible, not just to a proportion, and the biggest failure of unrestrained capitalism in our present world is that, so often, it still fails to do that even when it could.

On the subject of business structures, Bishop Bowlby regretted the demise of the mutual and co-operative concepts and we return to this subject in Chapter XIV. One of the principal advocates of the co-operative movement in our own day was, and still is Roger Sawtell.

Mr Roger Sawtell

A large part of our discussion with Mr Sawtell was on the subject of business structures and will be covered more particularly in Part III.

Our opening discussion arose from a key theme of this dissertation, viz. Is Christian love compatible with the profit motive? Are there not winners and losers? On the first point, Mr Sawtell saw no great problem of incompatibility. The concept of the market economy, which is competitive, is mirrored to some extent in other walks of life, indeed in the whole of life, not least in the individual family and in the life of a community. On the subject of winners and losers, Mr Sawtell replied: 'I do not know a society where there are not winners and losers – and business is just one part of that.' To him, the size of a business was a matter of more concern because

... the question of size is absolutely critical. There are these steps, you know, when you get a group of people – perhaps up to twenty (and I am sure Jesus knew just what he was doing when he had twelve disciples rather than twelve hundred). A group of that size can meet round a table and learn

Mr Roger Sawtell

to trust each other. With a group of more than twenty, another stage becomes inevitable; each group has a representative and, therefore, the maximum size becomes 20^2 which is 400, a medium-sized business. The next stage goes to 20^3 which is 8,000, a large organization with at least three levels of administration. So, when a business reaches about twenty people, the structure changes and there is no doubt that the winners and losers are more sharply defined for stage two and even more so for stage three.

What happens, however, to the Christian in the 200^3 category – does he not find himself (or herself) as a small cog in a very big wheel? Mr Sawtell's reply was that 'all change comes from individuals.' In fact, changes in the world have only been brought about by small groups of people. Thus, if someone is working in an organization of 50,000 or so, it does not mean that he or she is not in a position to change it, particularly as one rises to a more senior position. If, however, the Christian comes to a point where something is quite unacceptable, there must be times when to resign is the only possibility.

As businesses become not only larger, but more multi-international, does it not become increasingly difficult for the Christian to influence the course of events? Roger Sawtell thought this may be so, and considered that there was a greater field for those who felt the need to work in smaller businesses. In some of those smaller businesses, electronics for example, it has become possible for a small group of people to do many more things than they could even ten years ago.

Is it possible, however, that as business becomes more international and we move more towards the 'global village' that there will be a greater harmony and greater co-operation among nations – not exactly the Kingdom of God, but is it a move in the right direction? Mr Sawtell thought it was and instanced the message of St Paul to the Colossians that we should all be one in Christ – something which could only be achieved as we move towards the global village.[6]

What should the Church be doing or saying in all this? Unfortunately, in Sawtell's view, the Church says very little or nothing. They say 'It is not our expertise,' but they hope to see you on Sunday in the pews. He would be happier if Church leaders were to say:

> Well, we are not too worried whether you are in the pews or not, but we will support you in what you are doing, working out a theology for the Kingdom in industry and commerce, and structures and groups within that because that is the Church in industry. It is not only here in my cathedral or whatever it may be. So, in that sense, Church leaders do have a part to play.

Roger Sawtell is a businessman who has forsaken the more traditional business vehicles in order to promulgate the co-operative ideal. In contrast, our next meeting was with an old friend who had spent something over forty years with one banking institution and, like ourselves, had seen many changes in both the structure and indeed, ethics of banking. We come, therefore, to our conversation with Sir Philip Wilkinson.

Sir Philip Wilkinson

Sir Philip was doubtful about the degree of influence which a Christian could have on a large institution. In his experience, Christians tended to 'hide their lights under bushels' and, in some cases, it could be some time before one came to know the Christian position, or otherwise, of even close colleagues. In any case, the influence of a junior member of the staff was very slight and if a Christian made a particular stand it was usually in terms of his or her own behaviour rather than any attempt to change the direction of the business.

In other chapters we have discussed mission statements and the recurrence of the word 'integrity'. In those earlier days in banking, integrity was taken for granted and any departure from the straight and narrow would have resulted in dismissal. In Sir Philip's words, people with whom one worked in those days, whether they were practising Christians or not, 'had a deep sense of what was morally right and what was morally wrong'. Has that changed? He thought it had to a degree. There was now 'a tremendous emphasis on profit-

---

6 *Colossians* 3:11.

Sir Philip Wilkinson

making' and perhaps less consideration given to the way the profits were made.

What about the nature of bank lending – has that not also changed? 'Yes,' agreed Sir Philip,

> I think that much of it was character lending in those days. If the person was someone you did not trust by his actions, if he had let you down or told you untruths and such like, he would not have been someone to whom you were inclined to lend money. You could not trust him, whereas I think now a lot of personal lending is done on a credit rating basis, which means the integrity of the person does not necessarily come into play.

What about the *purpose* of bank loans. Sir Philip agreed that, in all the text books, the purpose of an advance was a very crucial part of lending. Does this more relaxed attitude encourage consumer borrowing?

> Yes, but nowadays there are so many temptations to borrow. In our young days, there were temptations to take up hire purchase, but we held back because the rate of interest was often considered to be exorbitant. Nowadays, one might be encouraged by the power of advertising to purchase a new car with what purports to be two years' free credit. These days, there is also in-store credit, personal loan schemes and perhaps most important of all, credit cards. This is where the banks have really not behaved very morally. Often, if they see someone using their credit card to a good extent, they increase their limit, which always seems contrary to what we were taught, i.e. that here might be a danger sign that they were using

the credit card to finance purchases all the time and we would have thought: 'Well, we had better watch this person.'

In the wider field, what about so-called 'Third World debt'? Sir Philip agreed that this was a very difficult issue.

A lot of it has grown up because of the misuse of genuine loans for development purposes in Third World countries – the loans have been misused and sometimes have disappeared – how they are going to be dealt with is a great problem and some of this debt has got to be forgiven.

Nearer home, Sir Philip regretted the passing of the mutual, co-operative and self-help societies which had developed during the eighteenth and nineteenth centuries. Many of these had been Christian-inspired and had started as local groups within churches. Many had become defunct or demutualized and the alternative was shareholder control under the Companies Acts. Can incorporated companies have a conscience? 'I think they attempt to have one,' said Sir Philip.

They have to work very hard at it. There are many examples of conscience being combined with mission statements and many companies have set up trusts for charitable purposes, usually with a very small percentage of their profits and thereby appeasing their 'conscience' in the process.

But can a corporation have a *Christian* conscience? Can a company love? 'No,' was the reply, 'not in that strict sense, but it can have values and often it is the influence of Christian directors that has brought that about.' Did Sir Philip agree that a company's values emanated from its board of directors? 'Yes, indeed and thus, if the board changes the values can change.' In fact, 'we can all probably call to mind an example of where that has happened – the board changes and the company changes.'

The discussion with Sir Philip, primarily on banking matters, called to mind an article (already mentioned in Chapter XI) in the *Banking World* magazine in 1984 by the then Bishop of Birmingham.[7]

The Rt. Rev. Dr Hugh Montefiore

The Bishop considered that there were grave, moral objections to some modern loans and the rates of interest which were charged, particularly in relation to loans to underdeveloped countries. The whole question of debt, both domestically and internationally, is discussed later in this chapter.

Leaving that aside, Bishop Montefiore could see no difficulty in reconciling Christian love with the profit motive. He could see nothing

7 The Rt. Rev. Dr Hugh Montefiore in *Banking World* – 'Is Interest Immoral?', December 1984. See also Hugh Montefiore, 'The Ethics of Making Money', *Chartered Banker*, May 1998.

The Rt. Rev. Dr Hugh Montefiore

wrong with the profit motive in itself. 'It is when it gets out of control that it is wrong and when it is exercised in such a way that people do not care about others.' Wealth creation is just as important as wealth distribution. 'It is too easy for the Church to concentrate on *distribution* – fair distribution – but I see the need for creation of wealth and that is what business does. I am not saying,' continued the Bishop, 'that there should not be fairer distribution, but if you concentrate on distribution you will be the despair of industry and you fail to realize that it is as necessary to create as to distribute.'

But, in the result, has it not meant a greater disparity between the rich and the poor, both domestically and internationally? 'Most certainly,' agreed the Bishop, 'what has happened is that the poor have lost out or stood still while other people have got richer.' Also, he found it very distressing that 'money is used to make money' (a subject referred to elsewhere throughout these discussions).

In the process of wealth creation, are there not winners and losers? Yes, replied the Bishop, and it must be appropriate that people who cannot compete to produce articles to service the needs of people at competitive prices should perhaps seek other kinds of employment.

> But what I think is very wrong is that you now have huge conglomerates which have a larger income than many states and then they shift their production to another country and cause chaos in so doing.

The Bishop recalled a saying that 'a business run on New Testament lines is likely to be much more successful than one that is not.' What does that mean, 'New Testament lines'? 'It means,' replied the Bishop,

> a caring business, making your employees happy, co-operative partnerships. These are all things that Christians ought to do in industry as well as being very profitable – producing better goods at lower prices for other people.

But can very large institutions be 'caring' businesses?

> No, I think this is one of the problems. I do think these huge institutions tend to be soulless and they tend to take on a momentum of their own and they are beginning to drive out the small firms because of their power. But that does not mean that someone should not try to rise to the top of large institutions and try to make them more just. I do think in the world of industry justice is the form of love that is most necessary. It is necessary because people who fall on bad times, and their families, need to be treated with compassion (and that does not necessarily mean that you have to suffer fools gladly) ... in the industrial world, justice is the form that Christian love should most take.

But does not all this become a matter of conscience – is that not difficult for a corporate body? Bishop Hugh considered that, if directors can be conscious that they have not behaved as they should have done and can change their ways, which in the individual is called repentance, and can even apologize and sometimes without the use of the Courts make up for it with justice, then yes, they are being conscientious – but of course the next lot of directors may be very different.

In theory and, for the most part, in practice a board of directors can only do those things which are to the advantage of the company, which means the shareholders.

> Well, yes. My own view is that this is wrong. There are three parties at work – there are the shareholders, there are the directors (and I have to say that a great deal is done in order to boost the ego of directors and that the share price in the City redounds on them) and thirdly, the employees – they are the people who make the thing work and so they have a natural interest and concern, and usually, if treated right, are extremely sensible. You must realize that it is not just the fault of the shareholders – it is the egotism of the directors and alas, sadly, they are concerned with short-term benefit rather than the long-term horizons because short-term benefits are reflected in the share price and the share price reflects their own success.

And again, very much on the same theme:

> It is a very curious thing that everyone wants to enlarge a successful business and that seems to be wrong and doubtful. It is for personal aggrandisement usually and it is not necessary. It is true to a certain extent that, unless you go forward, you go backwards in business and it is accepted that one must innovate. But I am sad that there is such a desire for aggrandisement because it often means that the ethos of the business is lost, just as the building

societies have been swallowed up, and I do think that Christianity could have a lot to say about financial aggrandisement, but does not say it.

We suggested that the growth of many companies had led to multinational business and the concept of the global village. Could this be the beginnings of a better world? 'It should be,' replied the Bishop,

> but then people are sinful. What matters is the intention of the human heart in business. Without that, no regulations in themselves will make the world a better place unless people have their heart in the right place.

Bishop Hugh is particularly concerned about the environment and considered that business should be more concerned about environmental problems. There were some instances where globalization had helped – for example, the restrictions agreed on global warming gases and the like. But he did not see globalization being an unmitigated good for everyone. He did not think, for example, that globalization through the International Monetary Fund had done much good, nor had the agreement on tariffs (GATT).

Unfortunately, another feature of globalization had been the facility for 'playing' the international securities markets – another example of making money out of money rather than providing goods and services for the benefit of all, a subject linked, at least in part, with *Faith in the City*,[8] published by the Church Committee, of which the Chairman was Sir Richard O'Brien.

Sir Richard O'Brien

Before we came to *Faith in the City*, our discussion with Sir Richard centred on the subject of competition. Sir Richard acknowledged that the imperatives of the Gospel, however you interpret them, are difficult to reconcile with the requirements of competitive life. Competition he regarded as both inevitable and virtuous in the sense that it was the only way to keep people 'up to the mark', to keep them active and alert and so forth. On the other hand, it could be the cover for all sorts of brutal, or near brutal, behaviour patterns in industry. Sir Richard suggested that industry is not necessarily about wealth creation, but is really about 'survival' and therefore about long-termism with all its implications for investment, industrial relations and indeed, everything in industrial life. In business, one has a job to try and survive in a decent manner, behaving yourself with regard to price policy and local environment policy, and perhaps we do not emphasize enough the survival element.

We asked Sir Richard how he would advise a young person today – a

---

8 *The Report of the Archbishop of Canterbury's Commission on Urban Priority Areas*, Church House Publishing, 1985.

Sir Richard O'Brien

young Christian determined to serve Christ and to seek his Kingdom in all things. Could Sir Richard, himself an experienced industrialist and adviser to companies, recommend the young person to go into the business world? 'Oh absolutely.' But should he or she be advised to go into the so-called caring professions? 'Not necessarily so.' Sir Richard continued: 'Indeed, there are very good and Christian aspects of industry – it is enormously stimulating and exciting – making things, whatever those things are. There are huge opportunities, even in the firms which do not present a Christian face to the world. There is nothing debilitating or wrong with industry.'

> I would say to such a person, first of all you have to be on top of your job, i.e. you have to be a good professional. I am not interested in your promotion of the Christian virtues as such. I am interested in your doing your job well. As a result of doing your job well, you acquire influence and you can use your position to begin to make whatever comments you feel proper about the Christian religion in your situation.

But would Sir Richard agree that, in a large number of cases, particularly in the early years, there is not much opportunity to influence the course of events in large organizations and the actual work for many people, whether it be pushing a pen or turning a spanner, might not be terribly creative? Sir Richard, himself a leading figure in the car industry years ago, replied that:

> The way round ... is what we discovered years ago in the motor industry,

which is that if you have people working at deadly, repetitive jobs on their own so that they cannot communicate with other people, either because of noise or lack of propinquity – if they are in that situation then they become very discontented, miserable, unhappy, bored and so forth. But if you create a situation, that is by organizing the pattern of work in the workplace so that you are not working alone, you are in co-operation with others, perhaps you are making a contribution of your own and passing the piece or part to the next person and he or she can pick it up, or you can talk easily and naturally as you are doing your job.

Can a large concern have such a Christian conscience? Sir Richard, through his association with the Confederation of British Industry, had been in touch with a large number of firms and he instanced the case of ICI for the serious manner in which they approached their responsibilities. Of course they were serious about making profits, but they were also serious about the achievement of the workforce and

> the achievement of the workforce was of a kind which brought very closely together the Christian ethic, however you interpret it, and ICI's managerial policy towards its employees. Opportunities were given to the workforce in regard to advancement and so on.

Thus, in Sir Richard's view, though we cannot say that a corporation has a soul, we can say that the manner in which it performs its duties and responsibilities can vary, and is wholly compatible with the efficiency of ICI in the long run.

Was that the same as saying that a board of directors has a conscience? Sir Richard thought it was so, but one must remember that 'the first job of a firm is not to promote Christianity.' In practice, in Sir Richard's view:

> ... the responsibilities which the directors ought to have, which spread widely over the corporate entity, are not defined as widely or as clearly as they should be. They are very often behind the interpretation which many directors, and I think an increasing number now, put upon their own responsibilities. I reflect on the atrocious policy which a number of boards have had in recent years towards the acquisition of share options, the pursuit of money for the sake of money, not in any way justified by what I have said about the need for 'survival' of the firm. Monstrous behaviour, grossly selfish – but this is life.

Let us return, therefore, to *Faith in the City*. This was the title of the 400-page Report published in 1985 by a Commission set up by the Archbishop of Canterbury on the subject of urban priority areas under the chairmanship of Sir Richard O'Brien. The Report concluded with sixty-one recommendations covering such matters as urban policy, poverty and unemployment, housing, health, education and law and order in areas where there was need and deprivation in a large number of towns and cities throughout the country.

Of particular interest to us here is the question posed in the Report: 'Is wealth creation the answer?' We cannot do better than to quote paragraph 9.28 of the Report, viz.

> If the national standard of living is to grow, the process of wealth creation must be supported wholeheartedly. The pursuit of efficiency in industry is to follow the Biblical insistence on the proper stewardship of resources – providing, that is, such a pursuit does not become a short-sighted and selfish exploitation of human and material resources and that ... it is accompanied by the fair distribution of the wealth created. To affirm the importance of wealth creation – as we do – is not enough. Economic policy should be as concerned with the distribution of income and wealth as with its creation. What seems to be lacking at present is an adequate appreciation of the importance of the distributive consequences – for cities and regions, and for groups of people – of national, economic policies.

The Report goes on to say that business management in today's complex world is a 'challenging calling' for many Christians and the authors of the Report shared the view of Business in the Community that 'the principal way businesses can help is to stay in business and secure a healthy, economic base.' Further extracts from the Report are set out in Appendix I.

We can move from the wider group of towns and cities covered in the Report to *the* City, viz. the 'square mile' of the capital city of London with its financial institutions where our discussion is joined appropriately by the Rev. Dr Leslie Griffiths.

The Rev. Dr Leslie Griffiths

As Superintendent of Wesley's Chapel in City Road, Dr Griffiths frequently finds himself as host to leading figures in the City as well as various professional bodies. One of Dr Griffiths' principal concerns is the need for better regulation – some kind of regulatory activity that would stop things 'going radically wrong'. He considers that there is a lot of evidence from recent years, and especially since globalization and the 'Big Bang', that some things have gone wrong which might not have gone wrong if there had been an adequate regulatory body or mechanism. Dr Griffiths does not worry about business activity as such. He thinks it is 'perfectly possible to discuss the right relationship between profit-making and the common good' and he believes that

> all of us, at our individual levels as well as at our corporate activity levels, need whatever help we can get to keep us from simply taking advantage of opportunities in ways that are greedy and self-indulgent.

Dr Griffiths expressed stringent views about the behaviour of some multi-national companies. For example,

The Rev. Dr Leslie Griffiths

my feeling is that the multinational experience is all about moving capital and resources to where the maximum profits can be gained and sometimes by going into cahoots with repressive regimes in order to exploit or to have monopolistic access to their raw materials. ... it seems to me that our experience of the multinational company goes in the opposite direction from the ideal of world government or world co-operation.

How can the dedicated Christian change all that? By becoming a parson or joining the caring professions? Dr Griffiths had noticed that some of the finest minds of the younger generation are themselves choosing not to go into certain business activities because they feel they would be 'dirtying their hands' and they are looking for a more satisfying and vocational sort of life. But

I have always believed that a Christian lives in a fallen world and is part of that fallen world, and cannot pretend that he or she is above it all, beyond it all, or holier than it all, and the sooner we get involved with the business of rolling up our sleeves and trying to show integrity and behave with integrity and to ask the hard questions within an environment that might raise difficult questions – that is the only effective way.

And again:

I would not feel it right, just because you are a Christian, not to get involved with what you consider to be a dirty activity. I think that really you are leaving the field to people who make it dirty and dirtier if you do that. God did not forbear to send His Son into this world and I presume that it was open to God to achieve His purposes in other ways, but He chose 'the Word became flesh' ... for those people who have a vocation, I honour them for it. But I do not think that, by definition, certain activities are excluded as realms where Christians ought not to be seen. I have a friend who at this moment is walking up those parts of Soho where gay and exploitative sex are diminishing human beings and impoverishing their lives, and he takes the risk of being identified with, or sucked into, all kinds of things that are definitely dubious by any standard. He takes that risk because, by being there, he has a chance of engaging with somebody whom he might have the opportunity to help whereas, if he were not there, that opportunity would not exist.

Dr Griffiths continued:

I am prepared to work with people who are not Christians and people who are people of goodwill, who are not people of faith at all and I recognise that sometimes in the pluralist, democratic society, I may have to compromise – I do not mind compromising so long as I am in a dialogue with people. In other words, I think that there has to be a far less purist view of social outcomes for theological insights, recognizing that we live in a society with all kinds of other people. What you cannot have is a theocracy. You cannot have simply the imposition of a kind of packaged Christian and ethical framework that comes down like a parachute from the sky. I want the outcome to be as consistent with the Christian insights as is humanly possible, but in achieving those outcomes I have to debate with all kinds of people who will not necessarily come from where I am coming. I think we have to be prepared to take risks and it is possible at the end of the day we will not like ourselves for having compromised more than we intended. But I would rather that we made the effort, even if we fail, than that we simply stand on the outside wagging fingers. I do not think wagging fingers does anything.

Did Dr Griffiths think the Churches should take a more active role or were they in danger of just wagging a finger. Yes, he replied, he was quite sure that the Churches should take a more active role and the Church should find more ways of affirming Christians who are working in the difficult, financial sector. Dr Griffiths mentioned a friend who had just produced a book of prayers, in which professions such as accountancy and banking are prayed for. The author said he was 'fed up' with having nurses and teachers prayed for all his life, but accountants and bankers very rarely – and so we come to a banker who, whether prayed for or not, has arguably led the field in matters of conscience.

Lord Thomas of Macclesfield

Lord Thomas, better known to his contemporaries as Terry Thomas, Managing Director, until recently, of the Co-operative Bank has sought, perhaps more than most, to introduce ethical values into the banking

Lord Thomas of Macclesfield

scene. Lord Thomas recalled that the founding father of the 'Co-op' was Robert Owen. He himself was not a Christian and indeed, did not believe in God, but his fellow-shareholders were Quakers and

> they were the only shareholders he could find that would allow him, as the principal shareholder and as the manager, to operate in a way that he believed was a reflection of nature.

That was 200 years ago and the Co-operative Bank, itself a subsidiary of the Co-operative Wholesale Society, was founded 125 years ago. Lord Thomas posed the question:

> Have we been faithful to the values that have been stitched into our institution and are we today building on what we as people inherited from that earlier work, and are we passing on to future generations something better than we inherited ourselves?

By the autumn of 1992, the Bank felt ready to launch publicly their ethical stance under the umbrella of their original mission statement.[9] Very high in the ethical stance of the Bank was that they would not be financing companies to sell arms to dictatorships or Third World countries, which 'really should not be arming themselves to the teeth'. Thus, humane issues and the dignity of mankind came first and foremost in the whole question of ethical issues. Second on the list were

---

9 The first mission statement was in 1988 and this was followed by the Ethical Policy Statement in 1992 (See Appendix).

environmental matters – 'the world is just a village and if you pollute one part of the village, the whole village is polluted.' The third area was concern for animals –

> if you are cruel to animals, it is only one step away from being cruel to people and we should respect them as different species, particularly in areas where we are exploiting them and being cruel to them.

Lord Thomas's view on ethics might well be echoed in many quarters, viz.

> Ethics is not like the Ten Commandments. The Ten Commandments are absolute and will last for all time. Ethics reflect the ignorance or the understanding at any one point. An example we used in our research was that the Bishops of England voted in favour of slavery in or around 1820 and voted against it as being unethical in the 1840s. We prefer to use the word 'values' – values are the shining light and we must keep on recharging the light so that we continue to learn and understand, and then evolve our decision on whatever it might be.

Lord Thomas claims that the Co-operative Bank started the campaign for the banning of landmines worldwide, beginning with the campaign 'Pledge 100', which was actively supported by many leading names throughout the country and Diana, Princess of Wales herself wrote to the Bank, saying: 'I want to be associated with' the campaign. With her support and that of the Red Cross, the campaign gathered momentum throughout the world with the result that over one hundred countries signed the Convention outlawing anti-personnel mines.

But how do you measure the rights and wrongs of a potentially ethical issue? Lord Thomas explained that this was not something which the Bank did on its own initiative. Decisions are taken on the basis of surveys among their customers and the Bank does not take a particular stance unless at least 70 per cent of those responding consider a particular issue to be significant. Thus, as mentioned above, ethics (at least in the Bank's view) are not absolute.

Questioned on whether or not other banks, in general, were on the right or wrong side of ethical values, Lord Thomas was fairly scathing and indicated that in his own, earlier banking days there was

> no feel or semblance or identification with any moral values at all. ... anything was OK as long as, first, it was legal and, second, you could be sure of getting your money back.

But he considered that the banks were beginning, reluctantly, to come back to the view that 'there are ways of doing business and there are ways of not doing business and still make good profits.'

Quite apart from such ethical considerations, Lord Thomas has been a leading advocate of the co-operative concept, having been elected in the past as President of the International Co-operative Banking Association. We continue the discussion with Terry Thomas, therefore, in Chapter XIV on various alternative forms of corporate structure. Meanwhile, we turn to Bishop John Brewer.

The Rt. Rev. John Brewer, Roman Catholic Bishop of Lancaster

As it happens, the theme of banking ethics was taken up by Bishop Brewer who regretted the 'great emphasis on profits'. 'Profit,' he suggested, 'is the only thing that counts.' He mentioned that in his diocese he had quite a number of people who had left banking because it had ceased to be a service to the public and had become a service to the shareholders.

The Bishop spoke of the fundamental difficulty of reconciling Christianity with business because 'the kingdom of this world is in conflict with the Kingdom to come' and 'the history of the Christian Church is the history of people opting out.' Nevertheless, one has to see God even in the business world and there are so many different examples – little shafts of light where somebody in business has managed to create something that is of service. The creation of wealth, considered the Bishop, and the creation of things in the manufacturing world have been of inestimable value to the human race –

The Rt. Rev. John Brewer, Roman Catholic Bishop of Lancaster

God is working through that and our job is in fact to help people who are working in these fields to see that they have got a mission to allow them to find God where they are because he is deep down there somewhere.

The Bishop spoke of *The Common Good and the Catholic Church's Social Teaching* published by the Catholic Bishops' Conference of England and Wales in 1996. In that document, suggested the Bishop, the emphasis all the time is on the value of the human being – it must remain there and everything else, the business world, public life, everything that goes on in life in general, must be at the service of the person.

The Bishop recalled 'the best epitaph' he had ever heard. He was on a bus on the way to Rome on the night that Pope John XXIII died and the bus driver turned to the passengers and said: 'He was a Pope who made me feel a person.'

There is much in *The Common Good and the Catholic Church's Social Teaching* which is germane to our theme in these pages and thus, some relevant extracts have been included in Appendix II. In the meantime, we quote the following on the dignity and humanity of the worker:

> Work is more than a way of making a living: it is a vocation, a participation in God's creative activity. Work increases the common good. The creation of wealth by productive action is blessed by God and praised by the Church, as both a right and a duty. When properly organized and respectful of the humanity of the worker, it is also a source of fulfilment and satisfaction. At best, workers should love the work they do. The treatment of workers must avoid systematically denying them that supreme measure of satisfaction. We would oppose an unduly negative view of work even from a Christian perspective, which would regard it purely as a burden of drudgery; or even worse, a curse consequent upon the Fall. On the contrary, even before the Fall human work was the primary means whereby humanity was to co-operate with and continue the work of the Creator, by responding to God's invitation to 'subdue the earth'. [para. 90]

As we continued our discussion, the Bishop spoke warmly of the work of the Archbishop of Milan who has a meeting with a large group of young people for five hours each month. They are given work to do and they have a diet of prayer and Scripture reading and for twelve months – no television. At the end of the time, they have to write to the Archbishop and say what they have decided to do for the rest of their lives. The whole purpose is to assist young people in the decision-making process.

But then, for us, a key question – would Bishop Brewer encourage a young person of a Christian persuasion to go into business? 'Yes', he replied,

> I would very much encourage them – it would be fatal to say 'that is not a

world for us' if we want to retain our Christianity – that is where we find it, that is where we come across the hard knocks. But it is steering a course and trying as best we can within the limitations of our position and our abilities to have some sort of influence over others.

The Bishop has very kindly allowed us to quote from a talk he gave to the Conservative Christian Fellowship in October 1995.[10]

> The struggle to live in the world, but not of it, is as old as Christianity itself. Even in the earliest days of the Christian Church, as we know from the Acts of the Apostles, they decided that the only thing to do was to opt out of the rat race and form an alternative society. They sold all they had and lived in common. But this did not last long. They were forced back into the world because 'God sent His Son into the world not to condemn the world but so that, through Him, the world might be saved.'[11]

Thus, the problem of a businessman is as old as Christianity and in the sixteenth century Thomas More wrote about the ideal Christian state, heaven on earth, in which all its citizens would be able to live truly honourable and satisfying lives. He called his book *Utopia* – a word which means 'Nowhere'.

> I believe that if we are expected to carry the cross behind Jesus, the problem of being a Christian in an alien world is part of it. In the early Church the only ones regarded as saints were martyrs. Somehow, if you had escaped martyrdom you had served two masters – God and the world.

The Bishop continued:

> The problem about our age and political systems and science and technology is that you can so easily be reduced to a number, a statistic, a quantity. They talk about shedding jobs, not people, three hundred laid off, two million unemployed – all figures. Monetarism talks about value for money. Hospitals, schools, residential homes for the elderly – closed for want of money. Everything is judged in economic terms – including the value of the human person. Being a Christian means putting people before policies. Christ never said: 'Follow my system,' but 'Follow me.' The tendency to quantify human beings is very old and Christ himself was born at Bethlehem and was immediately simply a statistic because they were conducting a census of the Roman Empire.

The Bishop drew our attention to Hans Küng's *On Being a Christian*.[12] This is very much a book for our times. It was written, according to the foreword,

> for all those who, for any reason at all, honestly and sincerely want to know what Christianity, what being a Christian, really means ... and for those:
>> who do not believe, but nevertheless seriously enquire;
>> who did believe, but are not satisfied with their unbelief;

---

10 Conservative Christian Fellowship at the Conservative Party Conference, Blackpool, October 1995.
11 *John* 3:16.
12 Hans Küng, *On Being a Christian*, Collins, 1977.

who do believe, but feel insecure in their faith;
who are at a loss, between belief and unbelief;
who are sceptical, both about their convictions and about
    their doubts.

Bishop John's words, quoted above: 'Christ never said: "Follow my system," but "Follow me"' have an echo in the words of Küng:

'Following' means 'walking behind him'. It is a question of being active, no longer visibly accompanying him around the countryside as in Jesus' lifetime, but of binding oneself to him in the same spirit of allegiance and discipleship, of joining him permanently and making him the measure of one's own life. This is what following means: *getting involved with him and his way and going one's own way – each of us has his own way – in the light of his directions.* This possibility was seen from the beginning as the great opportunity: not a 'must', but a 'may'. It is, therefore, a genuine vocation to such a way of life, a true grace, which requires us only to grasp it confidently and adapt our lives according to it.[13]

The theme of Christian responsibility in business life was expanded in our discussions with the Rev. Dr Michael Quicke.

The Rev. Dr Michael Quicke

As Principal of Spurgeon's College, Dr Quicke has been supportive of the Jubilee Centre in Cambridge where work continues on relational justice and a Biblical understanding of business life.

Dr Quicke considered that 'so often those of us in the Christian leadership are extremely naïve about the issues of being a Christian in business life today.'

Were there any particular concerns which troubled Dr Quicke as an observer of the business scene? 'On the one hand', he replied,

there are great pluses when, for example, one talks about work as being a partnership with God and obligations to the community – one can honour those who, in their business lives, have kept a clear balance between the ability to create huge personal wealth but to be concerned for employees and the community.

On the other hand,

the downside for me is associated with the abuse of power that would go with wealth and the fact that, in some churches (and this has sometimes been said to be the main curse of free churches), we have venerated wealthy people and given them a great deal of power in our local structures. Though we have very few of the benefactors that we used to have, I am nevertheless concerned that some people take the platonic view and separate their spirituality, their singing of their hymns and so on from their practices

---

13 Ibid, p. 545.

The Rev. Dr Michael Quicke

throughout the rest of the week. I personally know business people who very much resent the Church doing anything other than enabling them to worship in ways that do not disturb them. Therefore, you get a split between sacred and secular, between Christian life and the real world of business, and I see that accelerating because I think that Christianity has been individualized and privatized so that the market place now is somewhere where, if you happen to hold a Christian view, it can be regarded as something akin to astrology or whatever else. The thought of a God who claims all of life is rapidly being eroded and that is all to do with post-modernism, loss of absolutism and the relativism of everything. And, therefore, you get quite gifted, thoughtful business people claiming that what they do is in order so long as they do not hurt too many people. To stay private and individualistic is allowing an increased selfishness.

How can that situation be changed? 'It seems to me,' replied Dr Quicke, 'that there is now a move to talk about values and to work on values.' He thinks it should be recognized that

the people who work are involved actually in a mutual enterprise and that, therefore, there is to be a value in people, a value in serving through the products or services which are being offered.

Did Dr Quicke think that the churches generally gave sufficient support to those who are leading the field in redressing the situation? 'No, I don't,' replied Dr Quicke and continued ...

If I talk about the Baptist Church because local churches clearly have within their own aegis all the responsibilities of leadership, you tend to demand a very great deal of people and it would be far better sometimes to release those who are Elders or Deacons or whoever and understand that their key role is to be a top-rate employer rather than all the time drag them into church issues. I think we are poor at preaching on issues to do with the market place. We have individualized and spiritualized too quickly. I think we are very poor at honouring our top people and making sure that their work in the market place is regarded as Christian work rather than thinking that, really, Christian work only goes on in the local church.

Dr Quicke explained that one of his colleagues, a former ICI chaplain, would claim that all ministers should invest a great deal of their energy in getting out to their people. All the time one comes to people with a great deal of Christian sympathy, but they have been alienated because the Church has either made immediate financial demands ('You've got the money – we need it to repair the church'), or the fact that what is said on Sunday bears no relationship to Monday. That is the most critical issue, the total irrelevance.

Dr Quicke concluded:

All sorts of people are becoming concerned to think through issues of wealth creation. The Church has too often allowed a separation between a kind of spiritual worship, comforting, counselling, reactive mode and too rarely pro-actively encouraged its bright young people to work in business with a view to making a difference in the valuing of people.

We think most people would agree that there are few, if any, large business organizations which have done more to 'value people' than the John Lewis Partnership. Thus, it was particularly helpful to meet Kenneth Temple.

Mr Kenneth Temple

As Chief Registrar of the John Lewis Partnership, Kenneth Temple has a particular responsibility for the smooth working of the Partnership's employee ownership arrangements. The structure and basic philosophy of the John Lewis Partnership is set out in Chapter XIV as an example of what we might call a co-operative form of business.

Did the original concept of the 'Partnership' have a Christian origin? Mr Temple thought not, although one might see a religious dimension in Spedan Lewis's sense of guilt when, during a long convalescence after a riding accident, it was borne in on him that his father, his brother and he were taking more out of the business of John Lewis than the three hundred employees put together. When Spedan Lewis was given the opportunity to control Peter Jones (which was run separately from John Lewis) he began to develop a business philosophy with two linked concerns. On the one hand, he considered that if the

Mr Kenneth Temple

employees of a business felt involved in it and that their fortunes were more directly connected with the fortunes of the business itself, then they would be more efficient and thus, the business would improve. The linked premise, which Spedan Lewis sought to test, was that employees should be encouraged to feel fulfilment, happiness and belonging.

The eventual transfer of the John Lewis shares to a trust and the arrangements for employee profit-sharing are outlined in Chapter XIV. Why is it, given the outstanding success of the John Lewis Partnership, that more organizations have not followed suit? Mr Temple suspected that Spedan Lewis, if he were alive today, would be disappointed that his idea had not caught on. To some extent, he had seen a political dimension to the new concept and had written a book in 1954 entitled *Fairer Shares: a possible advance in civilisation and perhaps the only alternative to Communism.*

Mr Temple agreed with us that only rarely would the owner of a large business be so philanthropically minded as to hand over the entire business to other people, but there was another reason in Mr Temple's view:

> For quite a while through the sixties and the seventies and maybe even the eighties, we have tended to keep ourselves to ourselves and regarded our concern as being the development of our own business, and we have not engaged as actively as we do now with other people who have similar ideas.

There is also perhaps a third reason – there are other ways nowadays where owners of businesses can involve employees in tax-efficient methods by share-owning schemes, share options and the like.

Is the 'Partnership' form of business essentially more ethical than other, more normal business structures? Mr Temple thought it was more ethical, not least because there is such

> open and full accountability in the Partnership ... managers are accountable on a regular basis through the democratic structures – the branch councils and the central council and so on ... and we have this system of anonymous correspondence where anyone can write in to our Gazette, which is our in-house journal and, provided it is not libellous, an answer has to be supplied by the appropriate director.

Has the Partnership had problems of redundancy on a significant scale? The approach taken to redundancy in the Partnership is that it is not people who become redundant, but rather the jobs that have become unnecessary or superfluous. 'In any dynamic organization, which is improving in terms of productivity and technology, there are going to be some jobs that disappear.' Always the Partnership tried to offer alternative positions, but sometimes 'we do have to say goodbye to people on redundancy terms'. Mr Temple, as a former Personnel Director and as a Christian, sometimes found this very difficult.

We referred to the fact that, historically, capital, i.e. the investors, owned the employees – was it time for a reversal of these roles? Mr Temple said that Spedan Lewis's driving motivation was that the rewards of the enterprise should go not to the providers of capital, but to those who provided the labour. Thus, the Partnership had been financed by loan capital and preference shares, etc. – 'the rewards without limit should go to the employees because the employees are employing the capital.'

The Rt. Rev. Dr Peter Selby

The idiosyncrasies of road and rail transport between home in the Lake District and the Bishop's House at Hartlebury Castle prevented a face-to-face discussion, particularly on a rather foggy day. We are indebted, therefore, to British Telecom and the Post Office for the ensuing 'discussion' and the word 'indebted' is fortuitously appropriate because these discussions coincided with the publication of Dr Selby's book *Grace and Mortgage: the Language of Faith and the Debt of the World.*

It has been borne in upon us throughout our own deliberations that no consideration of money matters is complete without deep thought on the subject of banking, consumer debt, international debt and

The Rt. Rev. Dr Peter Selby

money-lending in general. We have touched on these matters throughout these pages in our discussions with a number of eminent bankers, but we are particularly fortunate in having the benefit of *Grace and Mortgage*. The reader is treated here to a masterly survey of consumer debt in this country and so-called 'Third World' debt set against Dietrich Bonhoeffer's question 'Who is Jesus Christ for us today?' In the Bishop's view,

> We have made it possible for ourselves to worship God (religiously) and Mammon (economically) by simply allowing ourselves two separate kinds of language and not letting them interact in any way that would confront our dependence on the economy of credit.

(To a considerable extent that same dichotomy has been apparent in our own researches and discussions leading to this present work.) Perhaps this is a reflection of the Church's own attitude in these matters. We have repeatedly posed the question 'What should the Church be doing?' 'First of all,' suggests Dr Selby, 'it will require the breaking of the long and destructive silence within the Church's life about the matter of money.' He admits that

> in years of attending worship and of preaching, the subject of money seems to figure only when it is time to raise the question of 'Christian giving'.

The Bishop considers that human beings, and particularly those who profess Christian faith, will have come to a decision whether or not they will continue to 'collude' with structures that so manifestly destroy life and 'elevate money from being an instrument to being a divinity'. He touches on the possibility of inventing alternative structures like credit unions, which 'will enable lending and borrowing to become humane again'. This is very germane to the discussion in Part III on other possible business structures. It must be recognized, however, that such alternatives can come only from small beginnings at grass roots and often within limited boundaries. However, do not let that deter anyone.

Let us return to the Bishop's principal strictures on the level of both domestic, i.e. consumer debt and that of Third World borrowings.

We have referred (see page 99) to the Report of the Crowther Committee in 1971 and its basically optimistic view of consumer credit, but in the ensuing twenty-five years the situation changed dramatically, principally because of the introduction of credit cards. As the Bishop points out, in the decade from 1978 to 1988, the number of credit cards increased from eight million to twenty-five million. Over approximately the same decade, consumer debt in general increased from around £11 billion to approximately £43 billion and mortgage borrowing increased fivefold to a figure of £300 billion by the end of the 1980s.[14] It was not surprising, therefore, that the 1990 Report of the National Consumer Council, *Credit and Debt: the Consumer Interest*[15] suggested that there were serious casualties on the road to 'financial sophistication'.

Drawing on our own experience, we know that there were a number of factors resulting in this quite horrendous credit boom with its attendant casualties. First, there is the desire to have today what one might otherwise not be able to have until some date in the future. The Bishop recalls the Access slogan 'Take the waiting out of wanting'. (This, on the whole, was quite contrary to the Victorian and post-Victorian adage that you did not buy today what you could not afford until tomorrow.) Second, it must be remembered that it takes a very strong-willed person not to purchase something on credit if for no other reason than to 'keep up with the Joneses'. Then again, Dr Selby refers to the enormous increase in the amount of income earned from the lending of money – a sevenfold increase in the two decades to 1990, a period in which average wages had generally only doubled. It should be borne in mind, therefore, that in the case of credit cards, despite the huge increase in the number of cards issued, the profit is made from the granting of credit. This, in a sense, is a pity because the

---

14 The Rt. Rev. Dr Peter Selby, Bishop of Worcester, *Grace and Mortgage: the Language of Faith and the Debt of the World*, quoting from Michael Wolfe, *Handbook of Debt Advice* (London Child Poverty Action Group, 1996).
15 London, HMSO, 1990.

plastic card is a very efficient method of paying for goods and services, but there is no profit to be made from the annual charge for the card nor from the merchants' charge – the profit is not made from the consumers who pay their credit card bills monthly, but from those who take extended credit. Thus, the credit card houses have a very real interest in encouraging their cardholders to borrow on credit.

Turning to house purchase, there were enormous incentives to take out maximum mortgage loans. House ownership was encouraged by governments, banks and building societies, and to pay a rent for one's house was regarded as 'money down the drain'. Inflation was the dominant factor. When, in the early 1970s, inflation nudged 26 per cent, there was every temptation to borrow up to the hilt in order to buy the house of one's choice. The loan was a fixed amount and the value of the house was rising – thus, inflation paid off the loan. 'Negative equity' was unthinkable and repossessions negligible. As the Bishop points out, in the years from 1980 to 1991 repossessions increased twenty-five times, i.e. from 3,000 to more than 75,000. In fact, by 1995 negative equity in the housing market reached the incredible level of £6 billion.

However, there is a noticeable improvement in the overall attitude to consumer debt. The recession and the attendant uncertainty of employment and the gradual disappearance of 'jobs for life' because of technological advance have all contributed to a more cautious approach to long-term borrowing. Meanwhile the banks and building societies have themselves introduced more stringent control – they have no wish to see a further wave of repossessions. Nevertheless, Peter Selby rightly concludes that:

> the credit and debt economy has taken such a hold on our society that making any substantial inroads into its territory will take time and commitment.

As for world debt, the picture is even more alarming. There were times in our banking days when it seemed that loans to some Third World countries were a case of 'throwing money away'. There were, of course, some corrupt and oppressive regimes, to which the Bishop refers.

> Their love of prestige projects, whatever the relevance of these projects to the actual needs of their people, their resort to high levels of military expenditure, not least to ensure their own survival and their practice of financial self-aggrandisement have all been part of what has saddled their countries with burdens of repayment which they have no prospect of being able to bear.

In fact, the situation is far worse than that. The loans made to developing countries have, in some cases, retarded their development.

The rate of interest has, at times, increased to three or four times the original rate. The interest payments can be met only by impoverishing the people of the very countries which were to be supported. In the result, maintains the Bishop, whole families have become impoverished, children are dying, slave labour is common and, in some cases, the West is exploiting the cheap labour of the East to a point where competitively priced exports are hopelessly inadequate to meet the interest payments on the loans. We may add that the principal argument in favour of Third World loans in earlier days was that underdeveloped countries would become more affluent with higher standards of living and, therefore, better markets for the goods and services of the Western countries. The result, in our view, has been just the opposite and Dr Selby agrees.

Perhaps we may conclude this part of our discussions with the Bishop's words:

> ... for all the difference there undoubtedly is between the economies of the Biblical period and of our own, the reality of debt and its power to enslave were well perceived by our forebears in the faith, and the Bible and the early Christian centuries furnish us with much upon which to reflect in the process of liberating our economy from the power of debt.

A recurring theme in Dr Selby's book, and indeed throughout the discussions leading to this current work, is that of the inequalities between rich and poor, North and South and between the Western World and the Third World. There is little doubt that the gap between rich and poor has domestically and internationally widened in the last few decades. *The Economist* magazine[16] in 1994 argued that the biggest increases in income inequalities had occurred in countries such as those of America, Britain and New Zealand where free market economic policies had been pursued most zealously. It was argued that the market economy 'has no moral sensibility' because income inequalities arise from the independent actions of individuals with different skills and different assets, who are rewarded according to whatever consumers and producers are prepared to pay.

In America, for example, the top 20 per cent of households in 1992 received eleven times as much income as the bottom 20 per cent, the multiple having increased from seven and one-half in 1969. This gave the richest 20 per cent of households no less than 45 per cent of the country's total net income and the poorest 20 per cent only a 4 per cent share.

In Britain, also, the gap between rich and poor continued to widen from 1977 onwards. In that year, the income of the richest 20 per cent of Britons was four times the income of the poorest 20 per cent, but by

---

16 *The Economist*, 5 November 1994.

1991 the multiple had increased to seven. According to the article in question, inequalities of income in both America and Britain had become larger by 1994 than at any time since the 1930s and this trend has continued since.

Approximately two years later in 1996, the United Nations Human Development Report forecast that if the yawning gap between rich and poor continued to increase, the world would become 'gargantuan in its excesses and grotesque in its human and economic inequalities'.[17] The Report illustrated, for example, that the world has 358 billionaires whose combined assets exceed the total annual income of 45 per cent of the world's population. Although in a number of countries the human development index, a barometer of the 'quality of life', has improved over the past three decades, economic decline has affected no less than one hundred countries, home to one-quarter of the world's population, thirty-five of which countries have suffered a deeper decline in income per head than that seen in the 1930s.

There are various factors contributing to this increasing disparity between rich and poor. In part, it may be exploitation, as suggested earlier in this chapter – more particularly, intense competition keeps wages at low levels in some parts of the world – improved technology has resulted in higher unemployment – and there is an increasing gulf between skilled workers and the unskilled at the bottom of the pile.

It seems appropriate to quote the following from the White Paper presented to Parliament by the Secretary of State for International Development in November 1997:

> This White Paper sets out the Government's policies to achieve the sustainable development of this planet. It is first, and most importantly, about the single greatest challenge which the world faces – eliminating poverty. It is about ensuring that the poorest people in the world benefit as we move towards a new global society. It is about creating partnerships with developing countries and their peoples, on the basis of specific and achievable targets, to bring that about.
>
> We shall work closely with other donors and development agencies to build partnerships with developing countries to strengthen the commitment to the elimination of poverty, and use our influence to help mobilise the political will to achieve the international development targets.[18]

✻   ✻   ✻

---

17 Dr Richard Jolly, *The United Nations Human Development Programme's Report*, 1996.
18 *Eliminating World Poverty: a Challenge for the Twenty-First Century*, Cmnd. 3789, November 1997.

SOME CONCLUSIONS

It is difficult to arrive at a meaningful summary of these various discussions, partly because the agenda was widely based and partly because any attempt to paraphrase or reinterpret, out of their immediate context, any quotations from the discourse may be inaccurate and even misleading. Nevertheless, we can highlight some particular subjects and seek to arrive at a consensus of opinion.

Business and Christian Love

There was near unanimity that the business world and Christian faith were not necessarily incompatible. There was perhaps an undue emphasis on the making of money for its own sake and certainly greed should be discouraged. In the quotation from *The Common Good*: 'Work is more than making a living.' It was generally accepted that most people nowadays have little choice as to the way in which they earn a living and a secular vocation was acceptable so long as it was genuinely useful to fellow human beings. Serving God in an economic sphere was 'no less significant than serving in a monastery'. Yes, there is a degree of 'dualism' between the Christian life and business life, but Christians should not stand aside and leave the economics field to others – the Christian may 'see God in the business world'.

Are there not Winners and Losers?

There was broad agreement that there were 'losers' in every walk of life just as competition came in many forms. There was not necessarily, however, a 'zero-sum' economy and one person's gain was not always another person's loss. All agreed, however, that there had been a growing disparity between rich and poor, both domestically and internationally. And there was a clear view that underdeveloped nations had impoverished themselves in their endeavours to meet the obligations of 'Third World' debt and that, in many cases, those debts would have to be forgiven.

The Emphasis on Money

There was general acceptance of the need for wealth creation and, in the words of *Faith in the City*, the process of wealth creation 'must be supported wholeheartedly'. If living standards are to be improved, wealth creation, it was suggested in our discussions, was as important as wealth distribution. There was, however, almost universal condemnation of an undue emphasis on money. For example, the comment was made that 'earning more and more' divides one from other people. There was general regret at the use of money 'to make money', particularly in the field of the more esoteric securities dealing. Similarly, there was some disapproval of the considerable profits made from the lending of money, a serious departure from Old Testament ethics, as discussed in Chapter I.

A recurring theme was that of 'stewardship'. It was generally accepted that in the process of wealth creation and in the deployment of that wealth, the Christian should seek to do the will of God.

Career Choices

There was some suggestion that in past years the Church had encouraged its members to take up careers in the so-called 'caring' professions, e.g. medicine, teaching, missionary work. However, little support for that view came through in our discussions. There was virtually unanimous agreement that young people should choose those careers for which they felt best suited according to their natural gifts and abilities, and to take their Christian faith with them.

It was accepted, however, that a young Christian's influence was likely to be very small in the large business conglomerates of the present day.

The Corporate Conscience

Contrary to the findings in our next chapter, it was generally accepted among our participants that a corporation could not have a conscience and, even less, could it have a specifically Christian conscience. It was the general view, however, that corporations could have 'values' and there was a suggestion that a corporation could acquire over the years a sense of responsibility greater than might be the case with an individual. A number of participants regarded large corporations as 'soulless'. They accepted that the values of a corporate body tended to be those of the board and senior executives, but there was the suggestion that management was too often concerned with short-term benefit.

The Demise of Mutuality

In almost every case, the participants in these discussions expressed regret at the passing of those mutual organizations which were more common in former days. These of course include building societies, friendly societies, mutual life offices and co-operatives. Our discussions on these business structures spill over into Chapter XIV.

The Kingdom of Heaven

Our discussions on the nature of the Kingdom are summarized in our final chapter 'The Kingdom and the World'.

What is the Responsibility of the Church?

There was some agreement that the Church in past years had done little to build bridges with the world of business and economics, and that the Church should seek to play a more active role in the market place. It seems appropriate to conclude with the recent words of Matthias Petzoldt, Professor of Systematic Theology in the University of Leipzig:

> *The Church itself has an economic existence; it is itself an economic factor. As such, the Church must be self critical. Furthermore, the Church must be aware of its role as economic-political opinion-former. This economic-political mandate can be played out in public pronouncements by church committees (for example, in church memoranda or explanations published by Synods or church executive bodies) as well as in church services and study themes in community projects and seminars. Christians should be kept well informed in matters of economics in order that they may be able to form their own opinions.*[19]

---

19 Matthias Petzoldt, *Studies in Christian Ethics*, Vol. X, No:2, T. & T. Clark, p. 75.

CHAPTER XIII

A Survey of Attitudes

All you need say is 'Yes' if you mean yes, 'No' if you mean no.[1]

The aim of the survey was to discover, if possible, the extent to which leading business people are influenced by Christian beliefs and principles in the conduct of their business affairs. The individual questions and the analysis of the responses are set out below.

The world is tired of intrusive surveys, whether by clipboard or post. We are told by those familiar with market research that a typical response is often around 10 per cent and that anything in excess of that is regarded as something of a bonus. We were diffident, therefore, about intruding on the time of busy people with a questionnaire which was both personal and philosophical. The approach was made to the Chief Executives of 500 leading companies and of an additional one hundred or so medium-sized and smaller companies, as defined in the Companies Acts, viz. those with less than 250 employees.[2] Out of the overall total of 600 approaches, replies were received from just over 30 per cent. Of these, approximately thirty-five were very courteous letters conveying good wishes, but indicating that the director concerned preferred not to complete the questionnaire (and indeed as a matter of company policy no longer responded to *any* surveys).

Thus, out of the total number canvassed, 24 per cent responded fully to the questionnaire and many of these made helpful comments, some of which are incorporated here, or sent additional material on which we have been able to draw throughout this work.

We come then to the first question in the survey.

Q.1 Would you describe yourself as a committed Christian?

Of those who responded, 55 per cent considered themselves to be 'committed Christians'. Apparently this is rather higher than one would normally expect but, on the whole, one would probably expect this answer from those who take the trouble to respond at all. On the

---

1 *Matthew* 5:37.
2 Companies Act 1985, s. 247.

other hand, the word 'committed' is challenging and may account for a proportion of the 45 per cent who answered 'No'.

It is not without interest that in a survey of 1,093 adults conducted by the Bible Society in 1996 in England and Wales, only 49% of the respondents claimed to be Christian and 46% were apparently of no religion.

Q.2 Are you a regular churchgoer?

Of those responding, nearly two-thirds (63%) replied that they were *not* regular churchgoers. What is perhaps more significant is that the remaining one-third profess to be regular churchgoers – a proportion considerably higher than the general level of church-going in this country, usually pitched at a maximum of 9% of the adult population. Perhaps of greater interest to the Church is that, out of all those respondents who would describe themselves as 'committed Christians' (Question 1), 37% admitted they were not 'regular churchgoers'. That, perhaps, is something which should be of concern to the Church.

Q.3 If the answer is 'Yes' to either of the previous questions, would you say that in your case it is a matter of Christian faith which guides your business decisions?

Of those who answered 'Yes' to either of the first two questions (and, as one would expect, most, but not all, of the 'regular churchgoers' described themselves as 'committed Christians'), 40% considered that it was Christian 'faith' which guided their business decisions.

Q.4 If the answer is 'No' to this last question, do you consider that your business decisions have their root in basic Christian teaching?

Out of all the respondents who replied 'No' to the third question, no less than 76% considered that their business decisions had their root in basic Christian teaching.

In the result, some 80% of those responding to Questions 3 and 4 considered that Christian faith guided their business decisions, or at least that those decisions had their root in basic Christian teaching.

Q.5 Alternatively, do your business decisions have their root in some other religious faith?

Only five respondents answered 'Yes' to this question and others indicated by letter that they were of a different religion. Altogether, the sample is too small to draw any conclusions, but this is not surprising in relation to the Christianity-based nature of the survey.

The next question is no doubt of greater interest.

Q.6 Do you find that your ethical considerations in business are sometimes varied by the need to arrive at a consensus among your colleagues?

This was obviously a very searching question and no less than 52% of respondents indicated that their 'ethical considerations' are sometimes varied by the need to arrive at a consensus among colleagues. There were a number of qualified answers among the 'Yeses' and the 'Noes'. For example, there was one response: 'no, but rarely'. And another respondent indicated that there were some matters which were 'non-negotiable'. Another replied in the affirmative, but 'not in major practice'. And another: 'There are always judgmental lines to be drawn.' One respondent indicated that ethical considerations would be varied 'not so much by need: more as a result of hearing of the ethical views of others'.

One gets the impression that in some board rooms Christian principles are somewhat flexible but not perhaps, as indicated below, to the point of undue conflict.

Q.7 Do you consider that an incorporated company (being a separate legal person) can have a Christian conscience?

A remarkable 62% of respondents answered 'Yes' to this question. There were a small number of qualified answers such as: 'It depends on the vision and values of those leading the company,' and 'Some companies exist to proclaim Christian values.' and 'Yes, a conscience but not necessarily a Christian one.' One qualified 'No' was that a company could not have a Christian conscience, but could have an ethical code.

It is difficult to see that a company, being a legal, i.e. non-human person, can itself have a conscience, even less a Christian conscience based on Christian love. Nevertheless, it is interesting that so many leading business people consider that the company which they manage has, as it were, a mind, an ethos and a conscience of its own. Perhaps it is more accurate to say that a company can have 'values', as brought out in the discussions in Chapter XII, but even those values depend from time to time on the direction and, therefore, the ethics of the controlling Board.

The next question was somewhat more searching.

Q.8 Would you, in general, put ethical considerations ahead of shareholder interests if there was an apparent conflict?

This question obviously caused a lot of heart-searching and prompted a number of supplementary comments, as mentioned below. A high proportion of respondents, viz. 60%, indicated that they would put ethical considerations ahead of shareholder interests if there was a conflict. Some respondents considered that long-term the interests of the company and the shareholders should coincide, but there may be short-term conflict. Quite a number considered that it was a question of degree and there were a number of qualified answers such as 'some of the time' and 'if serious' and in other cases, the answer was to 'look for common ground' and 'circumstances would dictate'. What stands out is the overwhelming importance attached to the maintenance of ethical values although, as suggested above, those values may at times be somewhat flexible. We come then to the question of competition.

Q.9 Is it acceptable, in your view, for a committed Christian to engage in competitive business at the expense of others?

Bearing in mind that all the respondents were engaged in business of one kind or another, it was not surprising that 92% considered it acceptable for a 'committed Christian' to engage in competitive business – the operative words being 'at the expense of others'. Some considered that it was inevitable for competition to be at the expense of others; some quoted good Biblical authority, particularly the parable of the talents. There seemed to be a general view that, in matters, for example, of pricing policy, competition could inevitably be at the expense of others. The answer seems to turn on what is legal and what is fair.

The tenth question turned on the issue of wealth creation and Christian stewardship, viz.

Q.10 Is it acceptable, in your view, for a committed Christian to seek to generate wealth other than as a matter of Christian stewardship?

This question presented no great problem to most respondents, of whom 89% voted 'Yes', although this would be contrary to the view of many theologians who would regard the creation of wealth, for its own sake, as unacceptable and for whom the management of one's personal resources should be a matter of Christian stewardship. A number of respondents pointed out very reasonably that the generating of wealth is something in which society, in general, can share.

Q.11 In general, are you aware of any undue conflict between Christian ethics and modern business practice?

It seems that 28% of respondents consider that there is 'undue conflict', 'in general', between Christian ethics and modern business practice. Some respondents took refuge behind the words 'in general' and obviously some would not necessarily have a wide knowledge of standards in other businesses. However, it is perhaps a little surprising that, in a survey in which 80% considered that their own business decisions had their root in their Christian faith or in basic Christian teaching, there should be as many as 28% who claim to be aware of conflict between Christian ethics and modern business practice (presumably in the business of others).

Q.12 Does this conflict induce any personal stress or strain?

Some 16%, not an insignificant figure, replied in the affirmative. Our respondents appear to have fairly clear-cut views on this subject, judging by the fact that hardly any sought to qualify their answers. One respondent indicated that 'compassion' was the principal area of difficulty, 'but experience shows that giving in to compassion at the expense of good judgement is a mistake for everyone concerned'.

The next question was susceptible of a multiple answer.

Q.13 Would you best describe moral standards in business life as based on:

(i) Christian principles
(ii) fairness

(iii) **reasonableness**
(iv) **the greater good**
(v) **the rule** of law

Respondents could of course choose one or more of these basic principles and a few of the respondents voted for all five. In the result, however, only 32% thought that category (iv) 'the greater good' was the moral standard on which business life was based and only 34% cast their vote in favour of (i) 'Christian principles' as a source of today's moral standards in business. Moving up the scale, 39% considered item (ii) 'fairness' as a principal source of business standards, whereas item (v) 'the rule of law' received a substantial 48% vote. Of special interest is the fact that item (iii) 'reasonableness' received the highest vote of 58%. 'Reasonableness' is difficult to define. It may owe something to the virtues of tolerance and reasonableness sometimes attributed to the British. It has a good parenthood in the law where, over many years, tests of reasonableness have had to be applied in the Courts. Perhaps in a business sense it is no more than a spirit of 'live and let live'.

Thus, we come to the last question.

Q.14 On the whole, do you consider there is an acceptable standard of ethics, whether Christian or not, in the business life of the United Kingdom?

The survey was rounded off with a fairly emphatic 73% 'Yes' to this last question.

In the concluding answers, most respondents let their 'Yes' be yes and their 'No' no, but there were those who considered that the standard of ethics was 'only just' acceptable and two respondents added the rider 'compared with many countries', and among the 'No' respondents there was one who said: 'And it is getting worse'.

Insofar as any firm conclusion can be drawn from such diverse answers to some very searching questions in some very sensitive areas, we can say with some confidence that:
a) there is a significant awareness of ethical values among the leading business people in this country;
b) a high proportion of those business leaders claim to be committed Christians;
c) as high a proportion as 80% of responses acknowledge that their business decisions were guided by, or had their root in, Christian faith and teaching; but
d) only a modest proportion of those responding claimed to be regular churchgoers, yet 28% report an 'undue conflict'; and

e) more of the respondents considered that moral standards in business were based more on 'reasonableness' than 'Christian principles'.

It seems appropriate to end with the words of the Bishop of Oxford in our discussions in Chapter XII:

> *It is Christianity which has shaped and moulded our society ... I see nothing wrong myself in a kind of common language of morality which can be owned by all people. For Christians, there will be a difference in that they will not simply see it in moral terms, but they will see morality, as it were, being under-girded and impelled and inspired by their Christian beliefs. There will be a religious motivation. So Christians will not just talk about what is right, but talk about trying to do God's will.*

PART III

The Hope

CHAPTER XIV

Some Practicalities and Proposals

... a Company to be called the Duke of Plaza-Toro
Limited is in course of formation to work for me.
(W.S. Gilbert)[1]

In the preceding investigation of the principal developments in ethical attitudes to business over the centuries, we moved from the well-documented Old Testament references to wealth creation, through the very limited New Testament teachings on the subject, to the spread and eventual urbanization of the Early Church, the power of Rome and then the comparative indifference to economic matters on the part of the people and the Church throughout the Middle Ages. During those years business was conducted principally by individuals (rather than institutions) with their neighbours for their own sustenance. There then followed three fundamental and fairly rapid changes in the economic scene – the Industrial Revolution with the concept of mass employment (see Chapter VIII), the gradual disappearance of the owner-manager (Chapter IX) and the introduction of capitalism (Chapter X) with its concomitant development of company law.

The principle of limited liability was first enacted in 1855 and consolidated in the Companies Act of 1862. Here again, we are indebted to W.S. Gilbert.

Mr Goldbury	*And soon or late I always call*
	For Stock Exchange quotation –
	No scheme's too great and none too small
	For Companification.
Chorus	*All hail, astonishing Fact!*
	All hail, invention new –
	The Joint Stock Companies Act
	Of Parliament Sixty-Two![2]

Overall, there have been approximately sixteen Companies Acts from 1862 onward and it has been said that:

---

1 W.S. Gilbert, *The Gondoliers*, Act 1.
2 W.S. Gilbert, *Utopia (Limited)*, Act 1.

161

company law in Britain and in the USA is in many essential respects the same as when it was first enacted over a century ago.[3]

The frequency of these enactments illustrates the need at times for radical change and at other times for fine tuning in company law. It will be argued here that the rigid adherence to the limited company concept has had dramatic consequences for business ethics in virtually the whole of the present century.

Sir Arthur Bryant, writing of the years 1840-1940, said:

> The consequences of the Companies Act, 1862 were perhaps greater than any single measure in English parliamentary history. *They completed the divorce between the Christian conscience and the economic practice of everyday life.* They paganised the commercial community.[4]

And again:

> A limited liability company has no conscience. A priesthood of figures cannot consider claims of morality and justice that conflict with its mathematical formulas; it must live by its own rules. Man, who once tried to model his life on the divine, came to take his order from the lender of money and the chartered accountant acting in their purely professional capacity. It is not the profit motive which is to blame. Free men have at all times sought profit from their labour. It is its enthronement to the exclusion of other motives far more important.[5]

It is, we think, widely accepted that a limited company cannot have a conscience – even less can it have a Christian conscience. This has been borne out, to a degree, in our interviews with Church and business leaders, but less so in the responses to the survey among business executives. The whole point, well recognized among lawyers following the 100-year-old case of A. Salomon & Co. Limited v Salomon,[6] is that a company is a separate, legal person. Thus, if, for example, two people form a limited company they create a third person – there are two natural persons and one 'legal' person.

So it is that whilst shareholders, whether two or two thousand or twenty thousand, come and go, the legal person, the company, remains until liquidation, or at least cessation of trading. The effect of this is twofold: first, the company itself, in whose name the business is conducted, is obviously incapable of any human sentiments, whether ethical or not, and second, the shareholders are clearly quite incapable (in all but the smallest of companies) of arriving at any unanimity of view in relation to the conduct of the company. Indeed, the situation is worse than that bearing in mind that a very high proportion

---

3 Goyder, *The Just Enterprise*, p. 4.
4 Sir Arthur Bryant, *English Saga 1840-1940*, Collins, 1940.
5 Ibid.
6 A.C.22, (1895-99).

(approximately 70%) of all shares in companies quoted on the London Stock Exchange are themselves owned by institutions, usually as incapable of a common ethical policy as the companies in which they are invested.

Thus, *de facto*, it is not feasible for a company to be driven by conscience, nor is it possible within the legal framework of the Companies Acts. A company exists for the purposes set out in its Memorandum and Articles of Association and since 1862 company law has required the directors of a company only to have regard to the interests of the shareholders, although in the consolidating Act of 1985 directors of a company are required to have regard to 'the interests of the employees in general'.[7] It is not without significance that this is a duty owed by the directors to the *company* and not to the employees as such.

It is not surprising that George Goyder wrote:

> It is absurd that a law designed for family business a century ago should continue to apply without substantial change to the whole of industry today regardless of the size and purpose of the company.[8]

To the extent that the 'interests of the employees' may be taken into account, worthy enough in itself, the workforce is better placed than the consumers for whom there is no such provision. As long ago as 1942 William Temple wrote:

> The reason why goods are produced is that men may satisfy their needs by consuming those goods. Production, by its own natural law, exists for consumption. If then a system comes into being in which production is regulated more by the profit obtainable for the producer than by the need of the consumer, that system is defying the Natural Law or Natural Order.[9]

George Goyder agreed:

> Although the company serves the consumer and depends upon his custom, company law does not require the directors to exercise any particular care for the interests of its customers. Such protection as exists has been achieved by legislation in specific areas such as product liability. In this, the company differs from the mediaeval guild where quality and control and craftsmanship were prime objects of the 'corporation' itself. The essential function of craft corporations ... was to assume responsibility for the practice of their trades in matters such as workmanship, quality and fair dealing.[10]

It may be thought that this immunity from any kind of ethical constraints applies only to the larger companies with worldwide businesses and a vast number of employees. Admittedly, ethical

---

7 Companies Act, 1985, s.309.
8 Goyder, *The Just Enterprise*, p. 20.
9 William Temple, *Christianity and Social Order*, London, Penguin, 1942, p. 57.
10 Goyder, *The Just Enterprise*, p. 17.

standards are easier to maintain where the ownership and management of a company is closely related as in most smaller enterprises. It must be remembered, however, that approximately one hundred companies account for one-half or so of the total manufacturing industry in this country and they, in turn, control or influence thousands of other smaller concerns which depend on them for business. Thus, a large motor manufacturer, for example, may affect the trade of thousands of dealers, suppliers and sub-contractors.

In which way, therefore, may ethical standards be raised allowing for the dead hand of the Companies Acts within the existing legal environment?

There are two particular developments which may be achieved, with perhaps varying degrees of success, within the current legal framework. The first is the development of stakeholder values variously known as stakeholder capitalism, stakeholder democracy or, in political terms, a stakeholder Britain. In 1995, a Report entitled *Tomorrow's Company* was published by the Royal Society for the Arts, having been sponsored by such leading companies as Cadbury Schweppes, Guinness, Midland Electricity, Unipart and NatWest Bank. The Report asserted that:

> Those companies which will sustain competitive success in the future are those which focus less exclusively on shareholders and financial measure of performance and instead, include all their stakeholder relationships ... in the way they think and talk about their purpose and performance.

This type of stakeholder philosophy was labelled 'the inclusive approach' seeking to stress the importance of partnership with and between employees, customers, suppliers, investors and the community. In recent years, the concept of stakeholder capitalism in Japan and Germany was held up as an example to the rest of the world, principally because of their highly successful economies. In Germany there was the concept of lifetime employment for 'core' workers and in Japan, salaried employees had in any case traditionally been guaranteed jobs for life. The image, however, was somewhat dented by the decline in the economic health of both countries and the increase in unemployment. In the case of Japan, the first people to bear the brunt of unemployment were women, part-timers and prospective recruits.

There are those who consider that the stakeholder concept suffered a blow from the recently published Report of the Hampel Committee (chaired by Sir Ronnie Hampel, Chairman of Imperial Chemical Industries) on the subject of corporate governance. Much of the Report does not concern us here, but overall it tended to place the emphasis on the accountability to shareholders compared with other 'stakeholders' such as employees, customers and local communities. The interim Hampel Report stated:

The importance of corporate governance lies in its contribution both to business prosperity and to accountability. In the UK the latter has preoccupied much public debate over the past few years to the detriment of the former. We would wish to see the balance corrected.

The second, more important, development in recent times in terms of social responsibility and business ethics has been the introduction of mission statements. We have referred in Chapter XI to the growing tendency in this country and America to issue 'codes of conduct' to their employees and in this country, nearly 150 leading companies have introduced such codes of business standards. The illustrative code published by the Institute of Business Ethics covers such matters as relations with customers, relations with shareholders and other investors, relations with employees, relations with suppliers, relations with the government and local community, relations with competitors and issues relating to international business, mergers and takeovers and certain ethical issues concerning directors and managers. In recent times, among a large number of companies it has become the practice to issue 'mission statements', sometimes called 'expressions of corporate philosophy' or 'expressions of general business principles' and these statements, usually issued to the public at large, serve as umbrellas for the more detailed ethical codes for each company's employees. A limited number of current mission statements are included in the Appendix to this work. Richard Higginson,[11] Director of the Ridley Hall Foundation, in his book *Transforming Leadership* refers to the repeated appearance of the word 'integrity' in a large number of mission statements, including those of Cadbury Schweppes, NatWest Bank, Ford Motor Company, British Petroleum, London Buses, Shell, Hewlett-Packard, United Biscuits and British Aerospace. Professor Higginson explores some of the biblical origins of the word 'integrity' and refers to its meaning in the ultimate sense of 'God and human beings acting together in harmony with the human qualities of faithfulness and peace responding to the divine attributes of love and righteousness'.[12] A little further on, however, the writer refers to the fact that

> most corporate cultures settle for something less than the fine ideals they proclaim in public. Mission statements can have the feel of empty shells or hollow promises where there is a major gulf between what the organisation says and what it does.[13]

According to a Survey conducted by the Industrial Society in 1996, there was a gap between theory and practice in relation to ethics and

11 Richard Higginson, *Transforming Leadership: a Christian Approach to Management*, London, SPCK, 1996.
12 Ibid, p. 59.
13 Ibid, p. 62.

the ethical management of people. More than 50% of those questioned said that ethical standards had become more of a priority over the past three years, but 40% said they had never consulted their employees on ethics.[14]

Whilst the stakeholder concept and the increasing issue of mission statements will be welcomed by the Christian observer, not least because they present windows of opportunity, the main drive should be directed, we believe, at the stultifying effect of the successive Companies Acts.

'What has gone wrong with company law?' asks George Goyder and continues:

> Principally that it fails to state what the purpose of a company is. It gives to the directors, as agents for the shareholders, *de facto* control of the company's policy and to the other interests, such as the workers, no corresponding rights.[15]

> The challenge we face is to discover a philosophy of company law which is socially and morally acceptable and at the same time encourages efficiency. We need to apply the principle of trusteeship which is an expression of the Natural Law.[16]

No Act of Parliament can saddle corporate entities with consciences, nor lay down particular codes of ethics. Nevertheless, it should not be beyond the wit of parliamentary draftsmen to compose a statute which requires incorporated companies to issue mission statements (rather than the existing system of barren and somewhat meaningless 'objects' clauses) and to require the boards of directors of such companies to have regard to the interests of employees, consumers, competitors, the environment and national and local government with provision for discussion with such parties, as may be appropriate, and with such tests of 'reasonableness' as, if necessary, the Courts would have to interpret.

We may conclude these thoughts with the words of George Goyder in another publication, *The Future of Private Enterprise*:

> Industry in the twentieth century can no longer be regarded as a private arrangement for enriching shareholders. It has become a joint enterprise in which workers, management, consumers, the locality, government and trade union officials all play a part. If the system which we know by the name of private enterprise is to continue, some way must be found to embrace the many interests which go to make up industry in a common purpose... The alternative is to create a structure in industry which recognises each of the parties as having definite rights and provides for those rights in the legal constitution of the single company... Since it is the legal structure of the

---

14 *Managing Best Practice No. 26*, Industrial Society, 1996.
15 Goyder, *The Just Enterprise*, p. 5.
16 Ibid, p. 6.

company which determines its formal responsibilities to the parties to industry, we must examine the legal structure of the limited liability company and see to what extent it is capable of adaptation, to make possible full co-operation between the parties to industry on a basis of justice.[17]

There, surely, is plentiful food for thought for the campaigning Christian.

Whatever the prospects of company law reform, ought we not to look again at some of the alternative structures within which business can be conducted? We have referred to some of these in Chapter X, viz. building societies, mutual life offices, friendly societies, credit unions and co-operative societies with their respective potted histories. We may add the various forms of trust vehicles, e.g. unit trusts and pension funds. It is not without significance that all these various organizations operate on either a non-profit-making or a profit-sharing basis not, normally, having any shareholders as such. Many of these organizations had Christian, or at least ethical, origins – they were created for human need rather than for human greed and for the most part they have been managed with integrity and sensitivity.

Accordingly, it seems somewhat sad that the movement in recent years has been away from mutuality towards incorporation and stock market listing and a self-inflicted change of character.

The reasons for demutualization were not difficult to understand. There was, for example, the facility which incorporation offered for raising more equity capital in the market and, indeed, for obtaining long-term loan finance. There was the attraction of substantial bonuses for the members of mutual societies, a greater freedom to acquire and dispose of shares in the new enterprise and generally to share in the financial success of the business by way of dividends. We can safely say that over the years nobody 'invested' in a building society in the hope of profit. They were looking for a safe repository for their liquid funds at a competitive rate of interest with, depending on the housing climate, the added hope of obtaining a mortgage should the need arise. Although technically a building society belonged to its depositing members, there was no way in which those members could receive a share of the assets except on liquidation or, in more recent times, acquisition and conversion. It is all the more remarkable, therefore, that during those pre-demutualization years building society deposits reached a level of 55% of all personal savings in this country. Mutual life offices also enjoyed considerable success, although with them the profits of the enterprise were shared with the insured members with no predatory shareholders waiting in the wings – and yet neither

17 George Goyder, *The Future of Private Enterprise*, Oxford, Blackwell, 1951, p. 1.

building societies nor mutual life offices owed anything to the
Companies Acts!

There are two other forms of saving in the United Kingdom, which
are also quite outside the framework of the Companies Acts. They are
unit trusts and pension funds. The trust concept had its origin in
England in the beginning of the fifteenth century and is comparatively
unknown on the Continent and in other countries which do not share
the Anglo-Saxon legal heritage. Although trust law cannot claim a
particularly Christian origin, it is a matter of interest that it grew out of
the equity jurisdiction of the Court of Chancery where the law was
administered according to conscience and fairness. The concept is
simple enough – 'A' may hold property or goods for the benefit of, i.e.
in trust for, 'B', whether by Will or other trust instrument or by way of
an implied trust. 'A' is the legal owner: 'B' is the beneficiary.

Trust funds were set up in Victorian England to offer a spread of
investment to the members, but this foundered on the old company law
rule that a business association could not have more than twenty
members. In 1931, the first trust with members holding units in a
portfolio was set up by Municipal and General Securities Company
Limited (now the M & G Group) and this was followed by a number
of trusts set up in the 1930s. It was not, however, until after the War
that the unit trust movement gathered momentum. The movement
enjoyed enormous success with the minimum of statutory supervision
and virtually no cases in the Courts. At the end of September 1997,
there were nine million units held by investors in the United Kingdom
with a total value of £163 billion.[18] The significance of unit trusts for
our present purpose is that the unit-holders share exclusively in the
profits of the enterprise *pro rata* to their individual investments and
subject only to a published management charge and other modest
expenses.

Another phenomenon peculiar to Anglo-Saxon systems of law is the
trust concept of pension funds. Occupational pension funds in this
country, in total, exceed in value the comparable funds of all the other
EC countries collectively. At the time of writing, the value is
approximately £560 billion. The pension funds are of course quite
separate from the employer companies and indeed, would normally
survive after the time when a company ceased for any reason to trade.
The trust funds are held by trustees, who may be private individuals or
a trust corporation or a small trust company set up by the employer.
Professional trustees may be paid a fee for managing the funds, but
there are no circumstances in which the trustees may share in any
profits. The funds belong entirely to the fund members past, present

18 *Financial Statistics*, Government Statistical Service, November 1997.

SOME PRACTICALITIES AND PROPOSALS 169

and future. In 1993, the Goode Committee undertook a detailed provision of pension funds in the United Kingdom and chose not to disturb the trust concept under which the funds operate. A large number of recommendations on other aspects were subsequently incorporated in the Pensions Act, 1995.

So it is that a total of approximately £700 billion is held in trust form in unit trusts and pension funds which, together with the surviving building societies and mutual life offices, accounts for a very high proportion of total personal liquid assets in this country – all beyond the suffocating reach of the Companies Acts.

It must be acknowledged that mutual societies, unit trusts and pension funds act almost exclusively in the field of savings and investment and do not generally engage in trading activities, although there has been some relaxation on that subject in recent years.

However, for the enterprising Christian bent on pursuing a virtuous business career, there are few structures better suited to his or her ideals than the co-operative concept or the various forms of common ownership.

In an Appendix to this work, we include a note on the history of the co-operative movement extracted from a lecture given by Mr Roger Sawtell, former Chairman of the Industrial Common Ownership Movement and a leading figure in the revival of the co-operative movement.

It is over twenty years since the late George Goyder, whose work we have mentioned above and in Chapter IX, observed that our preoccupation with economic problems is something relatively new.

Economics have certainly always mattered, but our age differs from former ages in being predominantly the age of economic man, rather than of military or religious or aesthetic man, or even political man.[19]

He continued:

Since the last war, a new form of capitalism has emerged, consisting of nation wide or international companies with little or no family control or sense of local responsibility and in that time something like a quarter of all British public companies were being subjected to takeover bids ... A man may devote the best years of his life to working for a firm and be thrown out through no fault of his own, but solely for reasons of financial policy.

And George Goyder concluded:

... there comes at last the realisation that the true end of man is not economic at all, but moral and social and spiritual, and that it is to be found in the course of everyday life lived in fellowship through the kind of economic organisation that best expresses the notion of mutual aid.

19 George Goyder, the 1976 Ernest Bader Common Ownership Lecture.

The co-ordinating body for co-operative organizations at the present day is Industrial Common Ownership Movement Limited (ICOM). They, in turn, are linked with the many co-operative enterprises which exist throughout the world. The salient features of a modern co-operative are:

- Co-operatives are locally owned, creating and retaining profits and jobs within their communities.
- They are democratically controlled, putting into practice the principles of social justice and equal opportunity.
- Co-operatives operate in the competitive market and combine commercial and social objectives.
- They are not controlled by remote shareholders.

At the present time, co-operatives may be classified in various ways, viz. worker co-operatives, community co-operatives, marketing co-operatives, care co-operatives, and food, housing and consumer co-operatives. Information on these and all forms of co-operative enterprise is obtainable from ICOM at their Head Office in Leeds. In the case of worker co-operatives, in particular, ICOM claim that:

- They enable people to take control over their means of earning a living, i.e. the business is run primarily for the benefit of the workforce rather than for investors.
- Worker co-operatives provide greater job security as they are owned and controlled by the employees.
- They can organize their businesses to suit their members in such matters as working hours and child care provision.
- Because the employees own the business, they usually take great pride in their work.

To some extent, Britain is behind other countries in the development, or perhaps we should say, redevelopment of co-operative structures. There are apparently approaching 800 million paid-up members of co-operatives throughout the world co-operative movement but, as Lord Thomas pointed out in our discussions referred to in Chapter XII, we are concerned here not so much with co-operative structures as with co-operative strategy and philosophy. For example, The Co-operative Bank, which we think we may say has led the field in modern co-operative thinking, seeks to observe five basic conditions, or questions, in its business strategy:

1. Does our understanding of the business include a systems perspective and does this perspective incorporate all necessary ecological considerations?
2. Do we fully appreciate the manner in which the business is dependent on a number of different partners?
3. Does information flow freely from each partner?

4. Do we, in the first instance, pursue co-operation at every opportunity?
5. If co-operation cannot develop, do we pursue self-interest in a selfish manner?

The emphasis throughout is on 'partnership', not in the narrow legal sense of people trading together as an unincorporated association, but as an overall strategy embracing shareholders, staff, suppliers, customers, the local community and past and future generations. It is noteworthy that 90% of the respondents to a Co-operative Bank survey in May 1997 agreed that 'commercial organizations have a purpose beyond profit' and that the Bank 'had a responsibility to all its partners and not just shareholders'.

The very word 'partnership' calls to mind the John Lewis Partnership, one of the largest retailers in Britain and arguably the most successful example of common ownership. The concept had been developed by John Spedan Lewis in the Peter Jones department store during the First World War and extended to the Oxford Street business on his father's death in 1928. It was, in essence, a profit-sharing arrangement by which Spedan Lewis transferred first his dividend rights and subsequently the voting rights in his shares to the Partnership, i.e. to the employees. Today, the business is represented in over 150 establishments in Britain and has approximately 36,000 'Partners'. Under the Partnership constitution, all the profits, after all expenses, including the cost of servicing the capital, have been paid, belong to the employees, present and future. In other words, as described in the Partnership's literature, 'instead of the standard practice of capital hiring labour, labour hired capital and kept for itself the profits generated by the business.' The distribution of profits is in addition to normal salaries at market rates, but is not necessarily distributed in cash. Before the bonuses are paid, substantial sums are applied in subsidizing the amenities and social activities of the partners. In the words of John Spedan Lewis: 'The supreme purpose of the John Lewis Partnership is simply the happiness of its members.' As related in Chapter XII, we had the privilege of a discussion with Mr Temple, Chief Registrar of the Partnership, who has a very special, senior responsibility for the smooth operation of the Partnership arrangements.

We have referred in Chapter X to those other outstanding examples of common ownership, building societies, mutual life offices and friendly societies. It is truly remarkable how they grew from their modest, local, usually Christian ventures in self-help and became, as we have said, among the major repositories of people's savings in the United Kingdom. In recent years, the windfall payments were a great encouragement to their members to agree to some form of demutualization, but there are many well-informed people who have expressed their regret at the passing of these leviathans of the savings world. It is improbable that we shall see their like again, although no doubt a few large societies and many of the smaller, more local societies will continue in their mutual way. Both the Building Societies Association and the Consumers Association are lobbying the Government to introduce a moratorium on building society conversions, although at the moment this seems unlikely.

On the other hand, there is some indication that the Government would favour something of a resurgence among mutual groups such as building societies and friendly societies. Mr Frank Field, the former Minister for Welfare Reform had conversations with mutual groups about the possibility of playing a leading role in welfare provision such as pensions, long-term care, unemployment benefits and help for the sick and disabled. He said that, because the mutual groups were 'non-profit-making and not answerable to City shareholders and were accountable chiefly to their members, they embodied the principles of self-help that the government was keen to promulgate'.[20]

In the meantime, an interesting stimulus has been made available to one small building society. The Roman Catholic Church has agreed that a volunteer team of representatives in the Westminster Diocese may act on behalf of the Catholic Building Society to offer mortgages to those in the lower income groups.

Yet another development of the mutual concept is the encouragement now given to small businesses to set up mutual societies, similar to credit unions (see page 88) to guarantee bank loans to their members. Under the scheme, companies operating in the same locality may create such a mutual society and deposit cash with the society in interest-bearing accounts. The scheme is the brainchild of the Co-operative Bank, with whom the deposited cash would be placed and the Bank will make loans to the mutual society members at preferential interest rates with the backing of the mutual society's guarantee.

Another outstanding example in our own time of ethical partnership is the Scott Bader Commonwealth, a chemical resins company founded by Ernest Bader, a Swiss émigré and transferred by him in 1951 to a charitable trust for the benefit of his employees and charity. The Commonwealth is now a £100 million-a-year, international company (although the overseas employees are not beneficiaries of the Trust). The Life President of the Commonwealth is Godric Bader, son of the founder, who recognizes that the business has lost something of its links with the past. On the other hand, the management team is apparently

---

20 Mr Frank Field speaking at an Insurance Seminar in London (*The Times*, 25 September 1997).

committed to basic principles of the Commonwealth which, by the terms of the Trust Deed, is protected from merger or acquisition over the heads of the employees (or 'members' as they are called). The organization still seeks to adhere to the principles of the True Social Order drawn up by Quakers after the First World War and stating that the ownership of land and capital 'should be so regulated as best to minister to the need and development of man'.[21]

In the meantime, large corporations and company law reign supreme and are assuming ever-greater international influence. If we may quote Joe Rogaly, writing in the *Financial Times* in November 1997:

> *Corporations matter more than ever. They are heading for dominance over the affairs of most advanced countries – or, as the headline says:*
> *'Forget governments – companies rule, O.K.'*

---

21 Richard Wolffe in the *Financial Times*, 20 September 1997.

CHAPTER XV

The Kingdom and the World

*Hope is exercised without benefit of sight; hope
might be termed the 'future tense of faith'.*[1]

Hope is the Christian's lifeblood. It is not born out of despair. It is not merely cheerful optimism. It is based on faith and that faith, as described by Bonhoeffer, is 'something whole involving the whole of one's life. Jesus called men, not to a new religion, but to life.'[2]

In Old Testament writings, hope lies in the expectation of a brighter future. ('The hope of virtuous men is all joy,'[3] and 'I will hope continually.'[4]) But there is also a sense of a judgement to come.

> For it is with Yahweh that mercy is to be found, and a generous redemption;
> it is he who redeems Israel from all their sins.[5]

For the Christian, however, hope also lies in the coming of the Kingdom of God and the return of Jesus (see Matthew 24, *The Eschatological Discourse*).

In St John's Gospel there are only two references to the Kingdom of God, viz. 'I tell you most solemnly unless a man is born from above he cannot see the Kingdom of God.'[6] and 'Jesus replied: "Mine is not a kingdom of this world ... " '[7] On the other hand, there are more than a hundred references to the Kingdom in the Synoptic gospels, including the many parables used by Jesus to describe the Kingdom, e.g. the parable of the sower, the wheat and the tares, the mustard seed, the yeast in the bread, the hidden treasure, the pearl of great value and the dragnet of fish.

Thus, the pilgrim Christian is left to reconcile three different, albeit complementary, approaches to the Kingdom, viz. 'Repent, for the Kingdom of Heaven is close at hand,'[8] 'The Kingdom of God is within you,'[9] and 'Mine is not a kingdom of this world ... '[10]

---

1 D.W. Gill, *Christian Ethics and Pastoral Theology*, Leicester, Inter-Varsity Press, 1995, p. 456.
2 Dietrich Bonhoeffer, *Letters and Papers from Prison*, 30 April 1944.
3 *Proverbs* 10:28.
4 *Psalm* 71:14.
5 *Psalm* 130.
6 *John* 3:3.
7 *John* 18:36.
8 *Matthew* 3:2.
9 *Luke* 17:21.
10 *John* 18:36.

It was no doubt inevitable that in our discussions with Church and business leaders, differing opinions should be attached to the meaning of the Kingdom of God or the Kingdom of Heaven. For example, from Dr Jenkins:

> It does seem to me that one of the very powerful notions in the Bible and in the Christian faith is this business of eschatology, namely that you are on your way, you never get there, but the point is you are responding to God opening up the next step.

From Bishop Graham:

> It has been established by the constant resurrection of Christ and the rest is in the out-working of that.

From the Bishop of Oxford:

> The Kingdom of God should literally mean God's rule rather than the place where God rules ... God's Kingdom exists in Christ crucified and risen and Christ's Kingdom exists in an anticipatory sense where Christ is acknowledged and obeyed by Christians ... It has a dimension of the past, the present and the future (see also page 111).

From Sir Leslie Fielding:

> The Kingdom of God is here and now ... It is in receiving the Gospel, acknowledging the mastership of Christ and trying to follow him ... We are encouraged to think not only in terms of the self's salvation, but the redemption of mankind and the gathering of people together.

From Bishop Bowlby:

> The Kingdom of God is very much to do with life here, although it may be, like the iceberg, that what we experience here is part of something much bigger ... In the end, a community of people who are living in the world in a way which God wants them to and becoming the people that God wants them to be, based on certain values which we derive in the end essentially from Christ's teaching ... The Kingdom would be about people treating each other justly.

From Bishop Montefiore:

> The Kingdom, the fully established Kingdom of God, is something we cannot even imagine. It belongs to eternity, but it does not mean that we have not got a foretaste of it here on earth ... We should work towards it, although we have to realise that it is the Kingdom of God and, therefore, we cannot, by our own energy, bring it about. We can only help it to come.

And from Sir Richard O'Brien:

> ... all we have at the moment is this world ... We must think in terms of people living this life even though we have hopes and objectives about the life to come.

Whatever the differences and difficulties of interpretation, the overriding hope for all Christians is the same, i.e. to live 'holy and saintly lives while you wait and long for the Day of God to come ... '[11] and we can say with St John: 'Surely everyone who entertains this hope must purify himself, must try to be as pure as Christ.'[12] Most journeying Christians will no doubt seek to observe the words of St Paul:

> ... to fill their minds with everything that is true, everything that is good and pure, everything that we love and honour, and everything that can be thought virtuous or worthy of praise.[13]

Which way should a Christian turn? How can he or she survive *in* the world without being *of* the world? He or she may be torn between 'you must not love this passing world or anything that is in the world'[14] and 'make a point of living quietly, attending to your own business and earning your living ... '[15] and does a Christian have to distinguish between Troeltsch: 'Trade was suspect because it meant taking from one to give to another and enriching oneself at the expense of others ... '[16] or Dr Johnson: 'Man is never so innocently occupied as when he is getting money.'[17]

What course should a Christian pursue? Clearly, a younger person seeking a career may consider ordination, medicine, law, social work, teaching or perhaps farming, none of which, at their best, need strain the Christian ethic too greatly. Similarly, he or she may engage in politics or the retail trades (if there is no objection to particular products), the construction industry, mining and other healthy exploitation of the world's resources.

The probability is that a Christian will become a small cog in a very large machine. We have already referred to the transition from the concept of owner-manager in business to that of the large corporation. In the previous chapter we considered the impact of company law on the ethos of business in this country and in America, and the inadequacy of the Companies Acts as we know them in this country. Unless and until that system is changed, it is arguable that employees, however senior, are slaves to an amorphous and somewhat faceless group of shareholders where the success or otherwise of the enterprise is judged by the so-called 'bottom line' and where, at times, most servants of that company may be able to do little to control or influence the destiny of the business.

11 2 *Peter* 3:11-12.
12 1 *John* 3:3.
13 *Philippians* 4:8-9.
14 1 *John* 2:15.
15 1 *Thessalonians* 4:11.
16 Troeltsch, *The Social Teaching of the Christian Churches*, p. 127.
17 Boswell, *The Life of Samuel Johnson*.

Even more significant is the development in our own day and age of the multi-national company. At least in domestic or national business life it is possible to encourage, monitor, control and even impose ethical standards, as discussed in Chapter XI. It is exceedingly difficult and, to some extent, impossible to influence ethical conduct in international companies operating in the global economy. Inevitably, differing standards apply throughout the world, whether it be in terms of human exploitation, arms dealings, suppression of competition, environmental issues, despotic governments and corruption. (On the brighter side, however, even as we write these words, leading international banks are seeking to set up a new system of global self-regulation to cut through the maze and disparity of national banking regulations. A Washington-based 'think-tank' is seeking to set up a standing committee to arrive at universally agreed standards for evaluating risk management proceedings and internal controls of global financial institutions.)

A Christian then has a difficult choice. If he or she is to 'seek first the Kingdom of God and His righteousness',[18] is he or she to keep this to himself or herself and is he or she likely to find the Kingdom in the major business enterprises of our day? If he or she is to 'go ... into all the world and preach the Gospel',[19] is the Christian left with a limited choice of career?

A more fundamental issue and one which is a continuing theme in this work is whether or not a practising Christian can reconcile himself or herself to the profit motive of business life. Does he or she say with Troeltsch, drawing on Thomas Aquinas:

> It is an actual duty, both to oneself and to one's relations, to gain sufficient measure of property to ensure the maintenance of the family according to the standards of one's class ... [20]

and

> the capitalist is always a steward of the gifts of God whose duty it is to increase his capital and to utilise it for the good of society as a whole and retaining for himself only that amount which is necessary to provide for his own needs.[21]

Or, does he or she agree with Luther:

> It is against all law, both natural and divine, to wish to rise in the world, to break through existing institutions on one's free initiative, to agitate and destroy Society by individual efforts, to improve one's manner of life or to improve one's social position.[22]

---

18 *Matthew* 6:33.
19 *Mark* 16:15 .
20 Troeltsch, *The Social Teaching of the Christian Churches*, p. 319.
21 Ibid, p. 647.
22 Ibid, p. 554.

There are those of course who find it possible, if not always easy, to reconcile Christian virtues with the business role of today. Richard Harries, Bishop of Oxford 'discerns Christian potential in the social device of the free market, in private property, in innovation, in the business firm, in profit and even in the trans-national corporation'.[23] Michael Novak quotes Montesquieu:

> Commerce cures destructive prejudices. It polishes and softens barbaric morals. It makes men less provincial and more humane. The spirit of commerce unites nations. Commerce obliges nations to be pacific from principle.[24]

Novak quotes from Adam Smith on the subject of the 'invisible hand':

> an individual intends only his own gain and he is in this, as in many other cases, led by an invisible hand to promote an end which was not part of his intention. Nor is it always the worse for the society that it was not part of it. By pursuing his own interests he frequently promotes that of the society more effectively than when he really intends to promote it.[25]

Novak's *The Spirit of Democratic Capitalism* is discussed at some length in Chapter X. On the theology of democratic capitalism, he writes:

> Writers of the Biblical era did not envisage questions of political economy such as those we face today. It is a mistake ... to try to bind the cogency of scripture to one system merely. The Word of God is transcendent. It judges each and every system and finds each gravely wanting. There is a great gap between the Word of God and systems of economic, political, social and cultural thought in modern societies.[26]

A Christian, therefore, has some hard decisions to take. He or she may prefer to stand aside from the world, either because of Biblical injunctions or because he or she has a subjective view of business as being exploitative, unethical and self-seeking. Is this not a form of monasticism? Dietrich Bonhoeffer tells us that Martin Luther, on become a monk, 'had renounced the world in order to live the Christian life ... the call to the cloister demanded of Luther the complete surrender of his life',[27] but disillusionment followed as we have discussed in Chapter V and thus, we repeat Bonhoeffer's words:

> Luther's return from the cloister to the world was the worst blow the world had suffered since the days of early Christianity. The renunciation he made when he became a monk was child's play compared with that which he had

---

23 The Rt. Rev. Richard Harries, Bishop of Oxford, *Is There a Gospel for the Rich?*, London, Mowbray, 1992, p. 72.
24 Novak, *The Spirit of Democratic Capitalism* (see Chapter X).
25 Quoted from Smith, *An Enquiry into the Nature and Causes of the Wealth of Nations*, p. 423.
26 Novak, *The Spirit of Democratic Capitalism*, p. 335.
27 Bonhoeffer, *The Cost of Discipleship*.

to make when he returned to the world. ... the only way to follow Jesus was by living in the world. ... the conflict between the life of the Christian and the life of the world was thus thrown into the sharpest possible relief. It was a hand-to-hand conflict between the Christian and the world.[28]

One central truth may emerge from all this – that the Christian who chooses to be isolated from the world, whether in a monastic sense or in affinity groups, mystical sects of their own creation or even the Christian Church itself at varying times and places, denies to his own day and generation the benefits of his God-given talents, the reforming zeal of the true disciple and his own contribution to the Messianic hope. Reinhold Niebuhr reminds us that man cannot fulfil his life within himself

> but only in responsible and mutual relations with his fellows ... the order of a community is, on the other hand, a boon to the individual as well as to the community. The individual cannot be a true self in isolation.[29]

As we have said above, the Church itself is not always immune to this isolationism. It can become comfortable and introspective and needs to be reminded from time to time of Bonhoeffer's dictum that 'the Church is the Church only when it exists for others.'[30]

Johann Baptiste Metz, in his stringent attack on 'bourgeois' religion, tells us that:

> hope has to pay a very high price for becoming detached from expectations, expectations which of their very nature may be disappointed. Hope becomes a power without expectation and hope without expectation is, in its essence, hope without joy. This, I think, is the root of the joylessness of what passes for joy in bourgeois Christianity.[31]

If a Christian thus chooses to live in the real world, but cannot reconcile himself or herself to the profit motive, the creation of wealth, the exploitation of the world's resources and the widening of the gap between rich and poor, where should he or she turn to give maximum effect to his or her Christian impulses? Ought he or she to choose to preach, to proselytize and to heal? Are these the marks of true discipleship? Is there a distinction between the saints and the rest of us? Is it the case that 'many are called but few are chosen'?[32]

Indeed, if all Christians are saints and if they have been successful in their mission to the less saintly, who is going to conduct the nation's business, fill the supermarket shelves, convert wool and cotton into clothing, aggregates into roads and housing, herbs and chemicals into

---

28 Ibid.
29 Reinhold Niebuhr, 'The Children of Light and the Children of Darkness', Lecture, 1944.
30 Bonhoeffer, *Letters and Papers from Prison.*
31 Johann Baptiste Metz, The Emergent Church, London, SCM Press, 1981.
32 *Matthew* 20:16.

medicines? Who would provide the value added, the human endeavour which converts the world's resources into the stuff of human needs?

Perhaps a better distinction is that of Reinhold Niebuhr between the Children of Light and the Children of Darkness. The Children of Light are those who seek to bring self-interest under the discipline of a more universal law and in harmony with a more universal good; the Children of Darkness are evil because they know no law beyond the self. Niebuhr tells us that Adam Smith clearly belonged to the Children of Light, 'but the Children of Darkness were able to make good use of his creed.'

> His dogma, which was intended to guarantee the economic freedom of the individual, became the ideology of vast corporate structures of a later period of capitalism used by them and still used, to prevent a proper political control of their power – an international capitalism which recognised neither moral scruples nor political restraints in expanding its power over the world.[33]

Where then does all this lead us? Are there any golden rules to guide our Christian pilgrim in his or her progress through a worldly jungle? As a pilgrim, he or she may not encounter Giant Despair, foul fiend, chained lions, Mr Talkative or the Slough of Despond, but will almost certainly come across Mr Greedy, Mr Corrupt, Lord Fat Cat, Mr and Mrs Ambition, Mr Bottom-Line, Mr Tax Evasion and Mr All-Powerful.

If Christian hope is to be maintained and encouraged, a Christian may have to have recourse to some basic guidelines. For example:

1. The Christian goal must always be to work towards the Kingdom of God – Christian hope may vary in its concept and in degree, but always it will have its roots in the love of God made known to us in the life and death of Jesus Christ.

2. The Christian should evaluate his or her talents and inclinations in terms of his or her particular skills and knowledge and his or her background, experience and determination. That analysis, like many a business plan or strategy, will require constant review and perhaps updating so that individual talents and resources may be put to better use.

3. The Christian should seek financial gain primarily for the sustenance of self and dependants, not merely in terms of living standards or self-betterment, but in order to achieve overall a better use of God's gifts, whether of one's own or in the surrounding world.

---

33 Niebuhr, *The Children of Light and the Children of Darkness.*

4. The Christian must come to a view regarding profit-making in business life, particularly its motivation, its worthiness, its integrity and, most of all, its overall contribution to the well-being of society.

5. He or she should eschew all that is corrupt, divisive, self-seeking, dishonest or in any way destructive of Christian hope.

6. He or she may well seek to engage only in those activities which are 'true, noble, good, pure, virtuous and worthy of praise'.[34]

7. Throughout it all, and most important of all, the Christian will regard his or her earnings, business profits and wealth creation as a matter of Christian stewardship *so that the world may be a better place.*

It may not be Augustine's City of God, but we can ask the same questions and accept the same answer:

What shall we do? ... What will be there? ... What business shall we have? ... What activity? ... This will be our activity, the praise of God.[35]

---

34 *Philippians* 4:8-9.
35 *Expositions on the Psalms.*

Postscript

Perhaps it is inevitable that in a study of this nature there will be a number of loose ends, but it would be agreeable if we could tie some of them together in a meaningful conclusion. To some extent, that has been done in the closing paragraphs of Chapter XII and Chapter XIII and there seems little purpose in seeking to restate those particular conclusions.

For the most part, the questions posed in the Introduction have been answered although not always with complete unanimity. Yes, business is primarily concerned with making a gain or a profit. Yes, there are reciprocal losers. Yes, motivation in business can be compatible with Christian love. Yes, the Christian businessman has a very special role in the world and no, the Church has not always fulfilled its role in the support of business people. Yes, the ultimate test is that of personal attitudes and priorities and for the Christian, the stewardship of wealth should be the primary concern both in its creation and its use.

We sought to approach this whole subject with an open mind lest the discussions, the survey or, indeed, the study of the various sources should become unduly coloured or weighted in one direction or another as a result of our own preconceived notions. Here then are some overall impressions.

First, we found ourselves agreeing with Hauerwas (see page 3) that 'the kind of alternative the Church provides will differ from society to society ... from culture to culture ...' Second, it has been borne in upon us that the world of today is vastly different from that of the early Christians and, whilst acknowledging that basic Christian truths are immutable, indeed sacrosanct, we recognize that the world is not just an enlarged Galilee – it is a very different world. Third, there is almost universal agreement among Christian-minded people that Christians should seek to play a full part in that world and not seek some modern form of isolationism.

Next, we encountered a clear thread of Christian origin woven through the pattern of present-day business life. This, as we have seen, wore different labels such as reasonableness, fairness and the greater good.

As for church-going, it was no great surprise that the pattern of church attendance among business people was not significantly different from that which is known to exist throughout the adult population at large.

Then, among business and Church leaders, there is clearly great concern about undue obsession with money and with the practice of 'money making money'. There is very considerable concern about the increasing inequalities in the world, both domestically and internationally, and time and again strong feelings came through to us on the subject of oppressed minorities, exploitation to the point of slavery, arms dealing and, not least, the environment.

There is obvious anxiety about the power of very large corporations and the comparative remoteness of shareholders. The business world has moved from the days of the owner-manager, who in the early days of this century could be philanthropic with his own money, through to the stage of executive control of large corporations with, here and there, some 'fat cats'.

There was remarkable agreement that Company Law in its present form was an anachronism and that new structures would have to be devised which took into account the interests of the employees, consumers, suppliers and the environment.

Perhaps most encouraging was the general view that, even if a corporation could not strictly speaking have a conscience, it could have *values*. Hence, the increasing importance attached to mission statements, some of which, by way of examples, we include in an Appendix to this work. Such statements are a public indication of the growing concern about business integrity, something which has come through to us very clearly in our own discussions and researches, not least in some very significant contemporary writing referred to in these pages.

There was a certain nostalgia about the passing of mutuality from business life and, to our pleasure and surprise, there is a widespread hope that we may yet see a resurgence of common ownership in its various forms, hence the extract from Roger Sawtell's speech contained in the Appendix. As mentioned above, there is certainly a disenchantment with Company Law and, as we go to print, we welcome the announcement by HM Government that there is to be a comprehensive review of the Companies Acts.

Any renaissance of mutuality can probably come only from small beginnings. In any case, common ownership is not necessarily a Christian concept. Nevertheless, the sharing of business decisions, the sharing of responsibility to the outside world and the sharing of business profits is much nearer to the communitarianism of the early Church and makes for a common bond of purpose and probity among the members.

Lastly, we have been helped by the views expressed here by Church and laity alike on the subject of the Kingdom of Heaven – the eschatological hope of the Christian. We began with perhaps an undue emphasis on the gulf between the Christian and 'the world', and we have touched on the teaching of St Thomas Aquinas, St Augustine, Luther and Calvin and the 'dualism' of the Christian life – the world of the Kingdom and the world in which we live. However, we have come to realize that there is no absolute dualism and we recall again the words of the Bishop of Oxford:

> We live literally with our feet in two worlds – our feet in this continuing world and, therefore, with all the necessity upon us, moral obligation upon us, of maintaining the fabric of this world so long as it lasts and at the same time pressure of the eschatological, i.e. of last things, when everything will be new.

We began this study with the words of Christ very much in our mind, viz.: 'Go ye into all the world and preach the Gospel.'[36] These important words were apparently spoken only to the eleven disciples and thus we have touched on the meaning of discipleship in our discussions in Chapter XII. Was it not an injunction to all Christians rather than a chosen few – and, if for example, one is called to preach the Gospel, is it not a contradiction of one's calling and a waste of one's talents to indulge in business for the sake of earthly profits? In our discussions and researches, no-one has made a particular point of these words of Christ, but perhaps we should transfer the emphasis to the opening words: 'Go ye into all the *world* ...'

---

36 *Mark* 16:15.

Is Wealth Creation the Answer?

Extracts from the Report of the Archbishop of Canterbury's Commission on Urban Priority Areas – *Faith in the City*

If the national standard of living is to grow, the process of wealth creation must be supported wholeheartedly. The pursuit of efficiency in industry is to follow the Biblical insistence on the proper stewardship of resources – providing, that is, such a pursuit does not become a short-sighted and selfish exploitation of human and material resources, and that, as we have stressed, it is accompanied by the fair distribution of the wealth created. To affirm the importance of wealth creation – as we do – is not enough. Economic policy should be as concerned with the distribution of income and wealth as with its creation. What seems to be lacking at present is an adequate appreciation of the importance of the distributive consequences – for cities and regions, and for groups of people – of national economic policies.

The responsibilities and burdens placed upon management in promoting economic growth are obviously heavy, and must be appreciated and recognised as such. Business management in today's complex world is a challenging calling for many Christians. Management must, however, respond to changes in the economic scene. Given the increasing competitive pressures in international markets, the requirements for firms to modernise to stay in competition is likely to result in different – and perhaps fewer – jobs in the future. Present trends suggest that these jobs are more likely to be concentrated in the so-called 'sunrise' areas such as the M4 corridor, which have modern factories (with room for expansion at low cost), a pleasant environment, good infrastructure and modern working practices, than in the older urban areas with few of these advantages.

It is unrealistic to assume that even the skilled and mobile residents of our cities can all 'get on their bikes' and move to the small towns and rural areas which are the focal points of economic growth to get a job – even if there were sufficient jobs (and housing) available for all. Certainly a middle-aged, redundant shipyard worker in Gateshead cannot be expected to compete with a young school leaver in the South-East for a new service sector job.

Although, therefore, continued growth in the economy should be pursued, we cannot ignore the probability that increased competition in manufactures, particularly from our European competitors and the newly industrialized countries, will lead to greater pressures on the UK share of world markets, even if the world economy grows. If British industry is to remain productive and competitive in world markets without a substantial shift to protectionism, an increasing substitution of high technology capital for labour is virtually inevitable. In modern conditions wealth creation tends not to result in job creation.

Some may argue that the benefits of economic growth will somehow 'trickle down' to unemployed people in the Urban Priority Areas. We are not convinced by such arguments. We share the view of Business-in-the-Community that 'the principal way businesses can help is to stay in business and secure a healthy economic base ... But it is fanciful to think that the results will trickle down to deprived areas to make a significant and self-sustaining effect'. Although the size of the national economic cake may grow, there is no automatic mechanism in the market economy for distributing the net increase to those who are not employed.

No Alternative?

'Unemployment', said Archbishop William Temple in the 1930s, 'is the most hideous of our social evils.' The effects of unemployment in the 1980s have been all too clear to us on our visits to Britain's Urban Priority Areas. We have been confronted time and time again with the deep human misery – coupled in some cases with resentment, in others with apathy and hopelessness – that is its result. The absence of regular paid work has eroded self-respect. 'Give me back my dignity' was the heartfelt plea from one man – made redundant, and with no prospect of a job – at one of our public meetings in the North-West.

We must make it perfectly clear that we believe there is no instant, dogmatic or potent solution to the problem of unemployment. Certainly the Church of England cannot 'solve' the problem of unemployment. It possesses neither the mandate nor the competence to do so. Yet as it is in the position of being the national Church, it has a particular duty to act as the conscience of the nation. It must question all economic philosophies, not least those which, when put into practice, have contributed to the blighting of whole districts, which do not offer the hope of amelioration, and which perpetuate the human misery and despair to which we have referred. The situation requires the Church to question from its own particular standpoint the *morality* of these economic philosophies.

There is always a need, we believe, for an explicit debate about the moral basis for, and implications of, policy decisions taken on 'economic' grounds. Different value systems are implied in much economic analysis and policy, and it is vital for Christians to scrutinise them to see how they match up to their understanding of human relationships and to Christian moral concepts. This view was endorsed by the General Synod in November 1984 when it affirmed that 'the world of economics is not a closed world, and economic values are not self-justifying, but need to be set in the larger context of human values.' We believe that most economists would agree with this.

We must not fall into the trap of letting economics suffocate morality by taking decisions for us: economic determinism is an insidious philosophy. The role of economic science is to tell us the likely effects of choices we make on moral grounds.

Extracts from The Common Good and the Catholic Church's Social Teaching:

A Statement by the Catholic Bishops' Conference of England and Wales, 1996

Morality in the Market Place

The Catholic doctrine of the common good is incompatible with unlimited free-market, or laissez-faire capitalism, which insists that the distribution of wealth must occur entirely according to the dictates of market forces. This theory presupposes that the common good will take care of itself, being identified with the summation of vast numbers of individual consumer decisions in a fully competitive, and entirely free, market economy. Its central dogma (as expressed by Adam Smith, the founding father of capitalist theory, in his *The Wealth of Nations*, 1776) is the belief that in an entirely free economy, each citizen, through seeking his own gain, would be 'led by an invisible hand to promote an end which was not part of his intention', namely the prosperity of society. This does sometimes happen; but to say that it invariably must happen, as if by a God-given natural law, is a view which can amount to idolatry or a form of economic superstition. Smith himself did not appear to think the rule was invariable, for he also observed: 'By pursuing his own interest he *frequently* promotes that of society ...' (italics added).

The Catholic Church, in its social teaching, explicitly rejects belief in the automatic beneficence of market forces. It insists that the end result of market forces must be scrutinised and if necessary corrected in the name of natural law, social justice, human rights, and the common good. Left to themselves, market forces are just as likely to lead to evil results as to good ones. It is often overlooked that Adam Smith himself did not envisage markets operating in a value-free society, but assumed that individual consumer choices would be governed by moral considerations, not least the demands of justice.

The Church recognises that market forces, when properly regulated in the name of the common good, can be an efficient mechanism for matching resources to needs in a developed society. No other system has so far shown itself superior in encouraging wealth creation and hence in advancing the prosperity of the community, and enabling poverty and hardship to be more generously relieved. Centrally commanded economies, in contrast, have been seen to be inefficient, wasteful and unresponsive to human needs. Nor have they fostered a climate of personal liberty. In a market economy the existence of a wide variety of consumer choice means that individual decisions can be made according to individual wants and needs, thus respecting certain aspects of human freedom and following the principle of subsidiarity. Moreover the good functioning of the market requires ethical behaviour and the embodiment of certain ethical principles within a regulatory and legal framework. This reflects the corresponding principle of solidarity. There is no doubt, too, that competition can often harness creative energy and encourage product innovation and improvement.

The distinction has always to be kept in mind between a technical economic method and a total ideology or world view. Catholic Social Teaching has constantly been aware of the tendency of free market economic theory to claim more for itself than is warranted. In particular, an economic creed that insists the greater good of society is best served by each individual pursuing his or her own self-interest is likely to find itself encouraging individual selfishness, for the sake of the economy. Christian teaching that the service of others is of greater value than the service of self is sure to seem at odds with the ethos of a capitalist economy.

As a result of that ethos there is bound to be a general discouragement and devaluing of unselfish actions, and the cultivation of the cynical assumption that those engaged in unselfish actions do in fact have hidden selfish motives. This attitude is one of the causes of the general discredit in which politicians and other public servants are held. It has wide implications for the moral health of society generally. Those who advocate unlimited free-market capitalism and at the same time lament the decline in public and private morality, to which the encouragement of selfishness is a prime contributing factor, must ask themselves whether the messages they are sending are in fact mutually contradictory. People tend to need more encouragement to be unselfish than to be selfish, so it is not difficult to imagine which of these two messages will have most influence. A wealthy society, if it is a greedy society, is not a good society.

The search for profit must not be allowed to override all other moral considerations. For instance, the creation and stimulation of markets by advertising is in danger of producing a society where the satisfaction of real or artificial needs takes priority over all else. It leads to an ideology of consumerism. The individual is reduced to the status of an isolated economic agent, whose life has meaning only as a consumer.

Those most likely to suffer from over-reliance on competition to the detriment of the common good are the poor, vulnerable, powerless and defenceless. To promote the idea that the individual is primarily to be considered by society as a consumer – that is to say when an individual's greatest significance is as a possessor of wealth and purchaser of goods and services – is both contrary to the Gospel and to any rational idea of what a human being really is. It gravely disadvantages those who do not have wealth to spend. Unlimited free markets tend to produce what is in effect an 'option against the poor'.

The World of Work

Work is more than a way of making a living: it is a vocation, a participation in God's creative activity. Work increases the common good. The creation of wealth by productive action is blessed by God and praised by the Church, as both a right and a duty. When properly organised and respectful of the humanity of the worker, it is also a source of fulfilment and satisfaction. At best, workers should love the work they do. The treatment of workers must avoid systematically denying them that supreme measure of satisfaction. We would oppose an unduly negative view of work even from a Christian perspective, which would regard it purely as a burden of drudgery; or even worse, a curse consequent upon the Fall. On the contrary, even before the Fall human work was the primary means whereby humanity was to co-operate with and continue the work of the Creator, by responding to God's invitation to 'subdue the earth'.

The Church insists that an employed person is a full human being, not a commodity to be bought and sold according to market requirements. Recognition of the humanity of the employee should persuade managements to bring their workforce into creative partnership, and to regard employees as entitled to a fair share in any rewards as a result of increased profits. Profits should not be regarded as solely of interest to managers or shareholders, but as a source of a social dividend in which others have a right to benefit. The Church recognises that co-ownership and worker shareholding schemes can sometimes offer more human ways of running business and industry than the traditional sharp separation of employees from employers.

Ownership and Property

The ownership of wealth is a right the Church protects, and regards as an essential ingredient and safeguard of human freedom. Measures designed to increase the spread of ownership are desirable, subject to the common good. But the ownership is governed by a 'social mortgage', and past abuses of the ownership of wealth have led Catholic Social Teaching to accept significant restrictions on the rights of wealth owners.

The economy exists for the human person, not the other way round. Any economic enterprise has a range of 'stakeholders': shareholders, suppliers, managers, workers, consumers, the local community, even the natural environment. None of these interests should prevail to the extent that it excludes the interests of the others. A manager in one enterprise may be the consumer of the products of another; the neighbour of a third, the supplier of a fourth, a shareholder in a fifth; and may subsequently become a redundant ex-employee, the victim of the very policies that as a manager he or she may have helped to create.

APPENDIX III

The Co-operative Alternative

An Extract from a Lecture given in October 1994
by Roger Sawtell, Past Chairman of
The Industrial Common Ownership Movement

The social bonds of the village were loosened and the large scale urban employer no longer knew his employees, still less was he concerned for their security of employment or quality of life. He was providing wages; what more did they want? He had enough problems with his competitors snapping at his heels. But fair wages were much more difficult to establish in a company of 1,000 rather than a work group of 10, and redundancy was more serious in towns where families had shallow roots. Of course the Industrial Revolution brought material rewards undreamed of in 1750, but is also brought new forms of social misery and spiritual disaffection.

Some employers did try not to shuffle off their obligations. A prominent Sheffield steelmaker, John Brown, whose Atlas Works employed 3,000 men in 1864 built a fine church in one of the blackest areas of the town. Perhaps it was the only way he could think of to acknowledge God's presence in a bleak industrial valley. In the rural agricultural area, God's hand could be discerned every day in the crops and the weather and not many farmers are agnostics. But the steelworks with its unremitting hard labour and huge furnaces seemed more like hell and many steelworkers no longer went to their employer's church.

Most employers were content to shelter behind the 1862 Companies Act and to pay little attention to moral consequences of investment-led industrialisation. In such an activist society, this was bound to bring a reaction and it was the co-operative movement which emerged as an alternative to capital ownership and the joint stock company.

The co-operative movement as we know it is generally agreed to have started with the Rochdale Pioneers Society which was inaugurated on 15 August 1844. After years of trial and error it was the Pioneers, a group of weavers and craftsmen, who enunciated the principles that have since formed the basis of the movement. In 1848 a remarkable pressure group came together to pioneer 'the way to a new and better social order'. It was led by a social reforming barrister, J.M. Ludlow,

192

and included several prominent clergy, including F.D. Maurice who was Professor of Theology at King's College, London, and Charles Kingsley who wrote *The Water Babies*. They stood for 'a living community under Christ ... in which there is spiritual fellowship and practical co-operation'. To show that they were doers as well as talkers, they were instrumental in getting the first co-operative legislation on the statute book in 1852, the Industrial and Provident Societies Act. They were followed by a strong group of co-operators who met on Christmas Day, 1860 in Manchester to discuss amendments and this resulted in an even more significant Act in 1862, on which all contemporary building societies and co-operatives are based. These men were indeed idealists who knew how to get things done; their influence remains with us today. Nowadays, we make advisory reports and hope that governments will listen; at that time they formed a direct and formidable parliamentary lobby which was able to draft the Bills they were promoting, even on Christmas Day, and again on Good Friday, 1863. How many of us now would turn up to a meeting on Christmas Day, even if we thought the results might last for over 100 years?

So while businesses based on the Companies Act were eroding the concept of justice between employers and employees, the Industrial and Provident Societies Acts were simultaneously promoting these concepts by the simple device of making shoppers into shopkeepers and employees into employers, by means of co-operative societies.

The principles of co-operation are those of free men joining together for mutual aid and concern for the disadvantaged, principles which can be traced back to the Gospel teaching of Jesus Christ. The fundamental co-operative principle of 'one person one vote' was already established in parliamentary democracy but miles away from the Companies Act, in which votes are proportional to shares held. The company director's job, now enshrined in law, was to maximise the return to his shareholders, of whom he was usually one. This dazzling thought of unlimited capital gains which share investors saw before them was very different from the sober co-operator's principle of limited return on capital employed. Investment-led joint stock companies were formed unashamedly to make the rich richer; in doing so, sometimes the poor became richer also, but on many occasions the poor just got poorer.

The two opposing business structures grew together. Although the co-operative movement flourished it was outstripped by investment-led businesses incorporated under the Companies Acts. These latter have become the norm and have produced the material comforts and complex mode of living in which we find ourselves today. Most people equate the word 'co-operative' with the high street shops which also grew rapidly after the 1862 Act and are theoretically owned and controlled by us, the customers. Perhaps they now have a slightly old-fashioned image as they fight for survival against the encroachment of the supermarket chains. Certainly they have lost most of their pioneering concern for education and social reform, but it is worth a thought that the middle-aged co-op with the brown lino is still among the largest retailers in the UK.

Co-operatives can merge with each other or they can go into liquidation, but they cannot be taken over by predatory investment-led asset strippers, nor can they be subjected to a management buyout – a tribute to those early legislators who saw the co-op business as a vehicle for fair trading and social advancement and not a vehicle to be bought and sold like a second-hand car.

The Co-op Museum in Toad Lane, Rochdale, showing the restoration on the original site of the world's first Co-op shop set up in 1844. (Photograph courtesy of Lancashire Life Magazine.)

APPENDIX IV

Some Mission Statements

Mission Statement of
Imperial Chemical Industries Plc

We know what we want to achieve over the next decade and are transforming ICI to make it happen. We intend to be the world leader in the chemical industry in creating value for customers and shareholders – and to achieve it through the following means:

- Market-driven innovation in products and services

- Winning in quality growth markets worldwide

- Inspiring and rewarding talented people

- Exemplary performance in safety and health

- Responsible care for the environment

- The relentless pursuit of operational excellence

Extracts from the
Mission Statement of
The Halifax Plc

VALUES
What are the things we expect of ourselves?

- Demonstrating commitment and integrity – *being determined to see things through, without compromising our standards of honesty and fairness.*
- Being passionate about quality and efficiency – *doing things well, first time, with minimum fuss or bureaucracy.*
- Meeting or exceeding our customers' expectations of us – *delighting them with our products, policies and service.*
- Valuing and respecting each other – *operating as a team and sharing the challenges ahead.*
- Being justly proud of our personal contribution – *a job well done is something to be proud of.*

THE MISSION CRITICALS
The six things in which the Halifax must excel to achieve the Mission.

- **Customers:** understanding them, attracting them, keeping them, impressing them and building the relationship.
- **Channels:** all parts of the Group working in harmony to serve the customer and make profit.
- **Contribution:** giving staff what they need to realise their full potential for the Halifax.
- **Costs:** not simply bringing costs down, but understanding them, and making them work harder.
- **Computers:** building the right IT systems to support our service ambitions.
- **Control:** managing profit margins and controlling risk.

Statement of Ethical Policy
of The Co-operative Bank

Following extensive consultation with our customers, with regard to how their money should and should not be invested, the bank's position is that:

It will not invest in or supply financial services to any regime or organisation which oppresses the human spirit, takes away the rights of individuals or manufactures any instrument of torture.

It will not finance or in any way facilitate the manufacture or sale of weapons to any country which has an oppressive regime.

It will actively seek and support the business or organisations which promote the concept of 'Fair Trade', i.e. trade which regards the welfare and interest of local communities around the world.

It will encourage business customers to take a pro-active stance on the environmental impact of their own activities, and will invest in companies and organisations that avoid repeated damage of the environment.

It will actively seek out individuals, commercial enterprises and non-commercial organisations which have a complementary ethical stance.

It will welcome suppliers whose activities are compatible with its Ethical Policy.

It will not speculate against the pound using either its own money or that of its customers. It believes it is inappropriate for a British clearing bank to speculate against the British currency and the British economy using deposits provided by their British customers and at the expense of the British tax payer.

It will try to ensure its financial services are not exploited for the purposes of money laundering, drug trafficking or tax evasion by the continued application and development of its successful internal monitoring and control procedures.

It will not provide financial services to tobacco product manufacturers.

It will not invest in any business involved in animal experimentation for cosmetic purposes.

It will not support any person or company using exploitative factory farming methods.

It will not engage in business with any farm or other organisation engaged in the production of animal fur.

It will not support any organisation involved in blood sports, which involve the use of animals or birds to catch, fight or kill each other, for example fox hunting and hare coursing.

In addition, there may be occasions when the Bank makes decisions on specific business, involving ethical issues not included in this policy.

We will regularly re-appraise customers' views on these and other issues and develop our ethical stance accordingly.

Introduction to
Mission Statement of
United Biscuits Plc

Democratic capitalism by its nature couples opportunity and accountability and it provides the freedom to compete in the marketplace. It also provides the discipline which requires business to meet the expectations of the society of which it is a constituent part; in other words, business is subject not only to the law, but also to the tolerance of the public.

A company is more than a legal entity engaged in the production and sale of goods and services for profit. It is also the embodiment of the principles and beliefs of the men and women who give it substance; it is characterised by guiding principles which define its view of itself and describe the values it embraces. Such values have, for our company, existed implicitly for very many years – United Biscuits is what it is and as good as it is because a great many individuals over a long period of time have contributed their own best efforts to preserving and enhancing the values that cause it to endure.

In the last two decades United Biscuits has grown from a relatively small 'family' grouping of biscuit manufacturers to an international diversified food group operating in the world league. From its beginnings our company has had a reputation for high standards, not only of people and of product but also of business conduct. To hold firmly to guiding beliefs within an intimate 'family' working environment is one thing; it is quite another to do so in a business with tens of thousands of employees world-wide.

We believe in and obey both the letter and the spirit of the law, but the law is the minimum and no set of rules can provide all the answers or cover all questionable situations. While it is the responsibility of top management to keep a company honest and honourable, perpetuating ethical values is not a function only of the chief executive or a handful of senior managers. Every employee is expected to take on the responsibility of always behaving ethically whatever the circumstances. Beliefs and values must always come before policies, practices and goals; the latter must be altered if they violate fundamental beliefs.

To endure, a company must serve well all those who have an interest in it. United Biscuits wants to have solid lasting relationships with its shareholders, employees and franchisees, with customers and suppliers, with the communities where we live and work and with governments and the public at large. It is our policy always to deal with all our constituencies fairly, responsibly and with integrity.

Bibliography

St Thomas Aquinas, *Summa Theologica*.

T.S. Ashton, *The Industrial Revolution*, Oxford, 1957.

Salo Wittmayer Baron, *A Social and Religious History of the Jews*, New York, Columbia University Press, 1937.

C.H. Bellman, *Cornish Cockney*, London, 1947.

Dietrich Bonhoeffer, *Letters and Papers from Prison*, 30 April 1944.

Dietrich Bonhoeffer, *The Cost of Discipleship*, 1937.

Sir Gordon Borrie, *Law and Morality in the Marketplace: Ethical Conflicts in Finance*, Blackwell, 1994.

Asa Briggs, *A Social History of England*, Weidenfeld & Nicholson, 1983.

Business in the Community, Annual Report, 1995.

The Button Collection, Business Biographies, Cambridge, Robinson College.

Andrew Buxton, Lecture – *Business Ethics: Getting on the Right Track*, The Chartered Institute of Bankers, January 1997.

Robert Byron, *The Byzantine Achievement*, 1929.

Chadwick (trans.), *Origen Contra Celsum*, Cambridge University Press, 1965.

S.G. Checkland, *Cultural Factors and British Business Men 1815-1914*.

Christian Aid, *The Global Supermarket*, 1996.

Christian Aid, *Change at the Check-Out*, 1977.

Codes of Business Ethics, The Institute of Business Ethics, London, 1996.

D.C. Coleman, *Courtaulds*, Oxford, 1969.

Michael D. Coogan, *Oxford Companion to the Bible*, Oxford University Press, 1993.

Alistair Cooke, *America*, New York, Alfred A. Knopf, Inc., 1974.

Joe Cribb (ed.), *Money*, British Museum Publications Limited, 1986.

Daniel Defoe, *A Tour through the Whole Island of Great Britain 1724-26*.

The Economist – 'Stakeholder Capitalism', 10 February 1996.

The Economist – 'The Uncommon Good', 19 August 1995.

David L. Edwards, *Christian England*, London, William Collins, 1983 and Fount Paperbacks, 1989.

Eusebius, HE6.43.

Faith in the City, Church House Publishing, 1985.

The *Financial Times*, 1996 and 1997.

The *Financial Times* and Price Waterhouse – 'Europe's Most Respected Companies', September 1996.

John Finnis, *Natural Law and Natural Rights*, Oxford, Clarendon Press, 1980.

F.J. Foakes-Jackson, *History of the Christian Church*, George Allen & Unwin.

Margaret Forster, *Rich Desserts and Captain's Thin: a Family and their Times*, Chatto, 1997.

Ludwig Friedlander, 1901 Leipzig: Hirzel.

Friendly Societies Act, 1793.

A.G. Gardiner, *The Life of George Cadbury*, London, Cassell, 1925.

John D. Gay, *The Geography of Religion of England*, London, 1971.

George Goyder, *The Just Enterprise*, 1989.

George Goyder, *The Future of Private Enterprise*, Oxford, Blackwell, 1951.

Lord Griffiths, *Morality and the Marketplace*, Hodder & Stoughton, 1982.

Hakluyt, *Principal Navigations, Voyages and Discoveries of the English Nation*.

Stuart G. Hall, *Doctrine and Practice in the Early Church*, SPCK, 1991.

Stuart Hampshire, Epilogue in the *Socialist Idea*, New York, Basic Books, 1974.

The Rt. Rev. Richard Harries, Bishop of Oxford, *Is there a Gospel for the Rich?*

The Rt. Rev. Richard Harries, Bishop of Oxford and Lord Laing of Dunphail, *Business Values*, Oxford, 1996.

Stanley Hauerwas, *A Community of Character*, Notre Dame, University of Notre Dame Press, 1981.

D. Hay, *Economics Today: a Christian Critique*, Grand Rapids, 1986.

Richard Higginson, *Transforming Leadership: a Christian Approach to Management*, SPCK, 1996.

Ronald F. Hock, *Paul's Tent-making and the Problems of his Social Class*, Journal of Biblical Literature, 1978.

Industrial Society, *Managing Best Practice* no: 26, 1996.

Lisa Jardine, *Worldly Goods: A New History of the Renaissance*, Macmillan, 1996.

David J. Jeremy, *Capitalists and Christians: Business Leaders and the Churches in Britain 1900-1960*, Oxford University Press, 1990.

David J. Jeremy and C. Shaw (ed.), *Dictionary of Business Biography*, London, 1984-86.

Dr Richard Jolly, *The United Nations Human Development Programme's Report*, 1996.

P. Joyce, *Work, Society and Politics*, Brighton, 1980.

L. Jung, *The Rabbis and the Ethics of Business*, New York, 1964.

Leszek Kolakowski, *Main Currents of Marxism*, Oxford, Clarendon Press, 1978.

Hans Küng, *On Being a Christian*, Collins, 1977.

John Lawson, *The Biblical Theology of St Irenaeus*, Epworth Press, 1948.

Ramsay MacMullen, *Roman Social Relations*, Yale University Press, 1974.

Father Francis McHugh, Paper – Conference of the Institute of Business Ethics, London, 1988.

Dr Hugh McLeod, *Religion and the People of Western Europe 1789-1970*.

Henry May, *The Enlightenment in America*, New York, 1976.

Wayne A. Meeks, *The First Urban Christians*, Yale University Press, 1983.

Johann Baptiste Metz, *The Emergent Church* (trans. Peter Mann), London, SCM Press, 1981.

Juergen Moltmann, *The Experiment of Hope*, SCM Press, 1975.

Juergen Moltmann, *Theology of Hope*, 1964.

The Rt. Rev. Dr Hugh Montefiore, 'Is Interest Immoral?' – *Banking World*, December 1984.

H. Richard Niebuhr, *Christ and Culture*, New York, Harper & Row, 1951.

Reinhold Niebuhr, *An Interpretation of Christian Ethics*, 1936.

Reinhold Niebuhr, Lecture – *The Children of Light and the Children of Darkness*, 1944.

Edward R. Norman, *Christian Businessmen: Church and Society in England 1770-1970*, Oxford, Clarendon Press, 1976.

Michael Novak, *The Spirit of Democratic Capitalism*, New York, Madison Books, 1991.

Desmond O'Grady, *The Victory of the Cross*, Harper Collins, 1991.

Pope John Paul II, *Centesimus Annus*.

Pope Pius XI, *Quadragesimo Anno*.

The Ridley Hall Foundation, *Faith in Business*, 1997.

Richard Roberts, *Religion and the Transformation of Capitalism*, Routledge, 1995.

A.L. Rowse, *William Shakespeare*, London, 1963.

John Ruskin, *The Crown of Wild Olives*, 1866.

John Ruskin, *Unto This Last*, 1860.

Dr Jonathan Sacks, *The Politics of Hope*, Jonathan Cape, 1997.

Dr Jonathan Sacks, *The Warburton Lecture*, Lincoln's Inn, 16 June 1993.

St Justin, *Apologia*, AD 150.

J.J. Scarisbrick, *The Reformation and the English People*, Oxford, 1984.

The Rt. Rev. Dr Peter Selby, Bishop of Worcester, *Grace and Mortgage: the Language of Faith and the Debt of the World*, Darton Longman & Todd, 1997.

W.J. Sheils, and D.Wood, *The Church and Wealth*, Oxford, 1987.

Samuel Smiles, *Self-Help*, 1859.

Adam Smith, *An Enquiry into the Nature and Causes of the Wealth of Nations*, 1776.

The Social Affairs Unit Research Report, 1996.

Josiah Stamp, *Motive and Method in a Christian Order*, 1936.

The Stationery Office, *Eliminating World Poverty: a Challenge for the Twenty-First Century*, White Paper on International Development, 1997.

The *Sunday Times* – 'Sweatshops put Heat on Bosses', 28 July 1996.

R.H. Tawney, *Religion and the Rise of Capitalism*, Penguin, 1939.

William Temple, *Christianity and Social Order*, 1942.

Tertullian, *Apologeticus*, 50.

Tertullian, *Apologia XLII*.

Terry Thomas, 'The Co-operative Bank', *The Times*, 14 September 1996.

G.M. Trevelyan, *English Social History*, London & New York, Longmans Green & Co., 1942.

Ernst Troeltsch, *The Social Teaching of the Christian Churches*, 1909.

Michael Wakelin, *J. Arthur Rank: the Man behind the Gong*, Lion Books, 1996.

J.W.C. Wand, *Anglicanism in History and Today*, London, 1961.

Max Weber, *The Protestant Ethic and the Spirit of Capitalism*.

John Wesley, *On the Use of Money*.

S. Yeo, *Religion and Voluntary Organisations in Crisis*, 1976.

Index